Counselling Children

SAGE has been part of the global academic community since 1965, supporting high quality research and learning that transforms society and our understanding of individuals, groups and cultures. SAGE is the independent, innovative, natural home for authors, editors and societies who share our commitment and passion for the social sciences.

Find out more at: **www.sagepublications.com**

Counselling Children

A Practical Introduction

Fourth Edition

**Kathryn Geldard, David Geldard
and Rebecca Yin Foo**

Los Angeles | London | New Delhi
Singapore | Washington DC

Los Angeles | London | New Delhi
Singapore | Washington DC

SAGE Publications Ltd
1 Oliver's Yard
55 City Road
London EC1Y 1SP

SAGE Publications Inc.
2455 Teller Road
Thousand Oaks, California 91320

SAGE Publications India Pvt Ltd
B 1/I 1 Mohan Cooperative Industrial Area
Mathura Road
New Delhi 110 044

SAGE Publications Asia-Pacific Pte Ltd
3 Church Street
#10-04 Samsung Hub
Singapore 049483

Editor: Susannah Trefgarne
Assistant editor: Kate Wharton
Production editor: Rachel Burrows
Copyeditor: Clare Weaver
Proofreader: Fabienne Pedroletti Gray
Marketing manager: Tamara Navaratnam
Cover design: Lisa Harper
Typeset by: C&M Digitals (P) Ltd, Chennai, India
Printed and bound by TJ International Ltd,
Padstow, Cornwall

Library of Congress Control Number: 2012949475

British Library Cataloguing in Publication data

A catalogue record for this book is available from
the British Library

MIX
Paper from
responsible sources
FSC FSC® C013056
www.fsc.org

ISBN 978-1-4462-5653-4
ISBN 978-1-4462-5654-1 (pbk)

Contents

About the Authors

Dr Kathryn Geldard is adjunct senior lecturer in counselling in the faculty of Arts and Business at the University of the Sunshine Coast (USC), Australia. Her academic career includes program leadership of the Counselling program at USC as well as development of the postgraduate Master of Counselling degrees. Her research interests include adolescent peer counselling, and counsellor training, assessment and effectiveness. Additionally, Kathryn conducted research with Australian Aboriginal adolescents with regard to developing a culturally sensitive peer support programme in a regional community. She is the author of a number of textbooks founded on her extensive clinical counselling background with children, young people and their families and has several years' experience in supervising and training counsellors.

David Geldard has extensive experience in working as a counselling psychologist with troubled children and their families. He has worked in mental health and community health settings, and also in private practice. Together with his wife Kathryn he has been heavily involved in training counsellors, social workers and psychologists, in ways to use media and activity when counselling children. Additionally he has shown a keen interest in training workers in the use of experiential counselling methods and in family therapy. He and his wife Kathryn are the authors of several counselling texts published internationally and translated into several languages.

Rebecca Yin Foo is an educational and developmental psychologist who is experienced in providing psychological support for children with developmental disabilities and their families at the Cerebral Palsy League. Her work has led her to take a high level of practical and academic interest in ways of working with children to promote optimal positive outcomes. She currently works in private practice in Brisbane, Australia. Prior to obtaining her honours degree in Psychology and Masters degree in Educational and Developmental Psychology she completed a Bachelor of Medical Engineering. She has published a number of journal articles and presented conference papers nationally and internationally in relation to her studies in both Engineering and Psychology.

Introduction to the Fourth Edition

It is with excitement that I write this introduction to the fourth edition of *Counselling Children*. I first met Kathryn in my Honours year of Psychology. In my Honours thesis we explored a technique Kathryn and David have used in their practice: the metaphorical fruit tree. It was wonderful to see how the artistic metaphor allowed children to more fully explore their concept of self. During my Masters studies we had the opportunity to build on this research, developing a program based on the concept of the metaphorical fruit tree. Our program met with much engagement from the participants in our study and confirmed my feelings that creative approaches are an essential component when counselling children. When I received the invitation from Kathryn and David to join them in updating *Counselling Children* for its fourth edition it was a great honour for me to accept!

A number of changes have been made to this edition of *Counselling Children*, with the aim of making the book more useful to readers. Two new chapters (3 and 20) have been included. One of these chapters (Chapter 3) is about ethics when counselling children, an area of great importance when working with children. To be of most use to the reader, rather than providing solutions this chapter discusses the ethical considerations Kathryn, David and I have encountered in practice and offers readers the opportunity to reflect on their own ethical practice. Chapter 20 provides an overview of the current research into using media and activity in counselling; an important consideration as you want to make sure the strategies you are using have been shown to be effective! Where appropriate, research has been linked to strategies throughout the book, particularly when referring to the various play therapy techniques covered in Part 4. It is hoped this overview of the current research will provide you with confidence when using the range of media and activities covered in *Counselling Children*.

Another feature, which it is hoped will be of use to readers, is the addition of a number of case studies which can be found at the end of selected chapters just before the Key Points. These particularly feature at the end of each of the chapters (22 to 30) on media and activity which can be used in counselling. Each case study has been linked to an area in which the play therapy technique has been shown to be useful. At times the case study has also been linked with a certain phase of the Sequentially Planned Integrative Counselling for Children model (the SPICC model) as described in Chapter 8. It is hoped that these case studies are helpful in providing examples for using the media and activities and also the opportunity for readers to explore which techniques are appropriate across different settings and at different stages of the SPICC model.

The practical focus of *Counselling Children* has been maintained in this edition. It is hoped that this will support those who counsel children in developing and extending their practice. To support this practical focus, an interactive style has also been maintained. It is hoped this style will encourage you, the reader, to think about your own practice while reading and how the concepts introduced could contribute to your practice. In saying this, I believe counselling is influenced by each counsellor's individual qualities and attributes, therefore I also see the importance of the reader being able to accept those ideas which do, and reject those ideas that don't, fit with their own approach to counselling.

Kathryn, David, and I sincerely hope that this edition of *Counselling Children* will be a helpful addition to your counselling library and support the development of your practice!

Rebecca Yin Foo

Part 1

Counselling Children

1

Goals for Counselling Children

It is probably obvious, even to people who have never been involved in counselling children, that we cannot counsel children in the same way that we counsel adults. We counsel adults by sitting down with them and inviting them to talk with us. If we were to try to use the same strategy with children, many of them would say nothing except to answer direct questions. Those children who were able to talk with us would be unlikely to tell us anything of importance. Additionally, they would probably become bored with the conversation after a short while, or would withdraw into silence. Even if they did talk to us, they would probably deflect away from important issues.

If, as counsellors, we are to engage children so that they will talk freely about painful issues, then consideration of other strategies in conjunction with verbal counselling skills is important. For example, we might involve the child in play, or in the use of media such as miniature animals, clay or various forms of art. Alternatively, we might involve the child in storytelling, or take them on an imaginary journey. As a consequence of combining the use of verbal counselling skills with the use of media or some other strategy, we are able to create an opportunity for the child to join with us in a therapeutically useful counselling process. We, as counsellors, provide the child with the environment in which to undergo therapeutic change.

Because we cannot use verbal counselling skills alone, and because we are promoting the possibility of a therapeutic outcome, we will in this book frequently refer to child-*therapy*. Clearly, therapeutic change is the outcome we hope to achieve by using counselling in conjunction with media.

Before becoming a counsellor for children it is important to have an understanding of the nature and purpose of counselling children. This includes being clear about our goals and to have clear ideas about how these goals can be achieved. As we will discover, the achievement of goals is not only dependent on the media used and on the style of working, but is critically dependent on the child–counsellor relationship. We will therefore consider goals for counselling children in this section and then move on to consider the child–counsellor relationship in Chapter 2.

Before you read on, we would like to invite you to stop, if you would like to, and do some thinking of your own. What do you think the most important goals should be, when counselling children?

We would like to ask you another question that has some ethical implications. Should the specific goals for an individual session or a series of sessions be set by the counsellor, or by the child's parents or guardians, or by the child? What do you think?

We think that the answers to the above questions are quite complex, and have identified four different levels at which goals can be set:

- Level 1 goals – fundamental goals
- Level 2 goals – the parents' goals
- Level 3 goals – goals formulated by the counsellor
- Level 4 goals – the child's goals.

All of these goals are important and have to be kept in focus during the therapeutic process. However, at various times during the process some goals need to have preference over others. How this is achieved is the responsibility of the counsellor. We will now discuss our ideas with regard to each of the four levels of goals.

Level 1 goals – fundamental goals

These goals are globally applicable to all children in therapy. They include the following:

- To enable the child to deal with painful emotional issues.
- To enable the child to achieve some level of congruence with regard to thoughts, emotions and behaviours.
- To enable the child to feel good about themselves.
- To enable the child to accept their limitations and strengths and to feel OK about them.
- To enable the child to change behaviours which have negative consequences.
- To enable the child to function comfortably and adaptively within the external environment (for example, at home and at school).
- To maximize the opportunity for the child to pursue developmental milestones.

Level 2 goals – the parents' goals

These are set by the parents when they bring their child for therapy. They are related to the parents' own agenda and are usually based on the child's current behaviours. For example, if a child is smearing faeces on walls the parents' goal is likely to be to extinguish this behaviour.

Level 3 goals – goals formulated by the counsellor

These goals are formulated by the counsellor as a consequence of hypotheses which the counsellor may have about why the child is behaving in a particular way. Take the example of the child who is smearing faeces. The counsellor may have a hypothesis that the smearing is a consequence of the child's emotional issues. Hence the counsellor may have the goal of addressing and resolving the child's emotional issues.

Clearly, when formulating hypotheses about the possible causation of child behaviour, counsellors will draw on information from their own casework experience, from their theoretical understanding of child psychology and behaviour, and from their knowledge of current research and the relevant literature.

Level 4 goals – the child's goals

These goals emerge during the therapy session and are effectively the child's own goals, although the child will usually be unable to verbalize them as such. They are based on material which the child brings to the session. Sometimes these goals will match the counsellor's goals and sometimes they will not. For example, a counsellor may enter a session having a *level 3* goal that the child needs to be empowered. It may emerge during the session that the child wants to talk about a painful loss and is not ready to be empowered. In this situation the counsellor can respond to the child's needs by attending to the *level 4* goal and allowing the grieving process to occur.

If a counsellor goes into a particular session with a specific agenda, there may be times when sticking to this agenda will be effective and appropriate. However, generally there is danger in holding rigidly to a predetermined agenda because the child's own needs might then be overlooked rather than addressed. For the child's real needs to emerge and be adequately dealt with therapeutically, the counsellor must stay with the child's own process. The alternative would be for us, as counsellors, to structure sessions which would meet our own needs rather than those of the children who come to us for help. This is clearly unacceptable, and it follows that generally *level 4* goals must take precedence.

Here is another illustration of what we mean when we talk about a child's goals or agenda being the most important. If we are working with a child who has come from a violent family, we may very strongly believe that an important goal for therapy (a *level 3* goal) is to explore strategies to help the child discover ways of staying safe. This would certainly be important, and in the long term would be a useful and essential goal. However, the child may be more interested in exploring the fears they have with regard to their mother's safety (a *level 4* goal). Our belief is that unless the issues which are uppermost for the child are addressed first, then the likelihood of counselling having a successful outcome will be diminished.

It is important to view each child's experience as unique, so we need to be careful in setting *level 3* goals. Our assumptions about what a child needs in therapy might be wrong. Therefore, we continually review our goals during the course of counselling and are open to amending them wherever necessary. Developing the skills required to discover the child's real needs takes practice and experience.

If therapy sessions are properly conducted, the child's goals will naturally emerge. If these goals are recognized by the counsellor, rather than submerged below other goals set by the counsellor or parents, then they can be formally incorporated into the process through consultation with the parents. In our view, wherever possible these *level 4* goals, involving the child's own agenda, should take precedence.

Thus we strongly suggest that, in general, the specific goals for a counselling session, or series of sessions, need to be determined by giving precedence to the child's *level 4* goals, while attending to the parents' *level 2* goals and the counsellor's *level 3* goals. Our experience is that when we follow this process, the fundamental *level 1* goals will automatically be achieved. Whenever possible, it is important for the goal-setting process to be interactive and consultative, with the full participatory involvement of the child, the parents or family, and the counsellor.

In setting goals we are implying that the child is our primary client, yet it is the parents who pay our bill! Although this may seem to raise an ethical dilemma, we find that by using the process we have proposed, the parents' goals are also achieved.

In considering what counselling children involves, we have looked at goals first. As stated before, another important aspect of counselling children is the child–counsellor relationship, which we will discuss in the next chapter.

CASE STUDY

You have just received a referral for a new client. The referral has been made for 12-year-old Mike by his mother, June. The information provided by June in the referral indicates that she is concerned about Mike's change in behaviour over the last six months. June feels that Mike is becoming more 'oppositional' and, at times, verbally and physically aggressive. She hopes that this behaviour can be improved if Mike sees a counsellor. She also noted that the family has moved interstate this year for her husband, John's, work which has also meant longer working days for John. June also shared in the referral that Mike saw the School Counsellor off and on following intense bullying, including physical aggression, at his previous school. Mike hasn't reported any incidents of bullying to his parents at his new school; therefore June feels this is no longer an issue for Mike. How might you approach goal-setting with this family? How would you introduce the process of goal-setting to the child/family? What would you say? How might you approach conflict between the parents'/child's/counsellor's goals?

KEY POINTS

- Using media or activity in conjunction with counselling skills supports children to talk about sensitive issues.
- As counsellors there are four different types of goals for us to keep in mind:

  ○ fundamental goals
  ○ parental goals
  ○ goals we formulate as a counsellor
  ○ the child's goals.

- Fundamental goals are usually best achieved by giving precedence to the child's goals while attending to parent and counsellor goals.

2

The Child–Counsellor Relationship

It has long been recognized, going right back to the 1950s, that the relationship between an adult client and a counsellor is a critical factor in therapeutic outcomes. Original research on the adult client–counsellor relationship was done by Carl Rogers many years ago. He believed that the important ingredients in such a relationship were congruence, empathy and unconditional positive regard. Since then other workers have described what they have believed to be desirable attributes of the counselling relationship, and have generally agreed that the relationship is of major importance in influencing positive outcomes from therapy.

In the same way that in adult therapy the relationship with the counsellor is of major influence, it is generally agreed that in child therapy the child–counsellor relationship is significantly important in influencing the effectiveness of therapy. There have been a number of attempts to define the important attributes of this relationship (Virginia Axline, 1947; Anna Freud, 1928; Melanie Klein, 1932). Unfortunately, there are major differences of opinion about what type of relationship is desirable for therapy to be maximally effective. We don't intend to discuss the differing schools of thought in depth because this is a *practical* guide to counselling children rather than a book about the theory of child therapy. However, we have included a brief overview of the historical background and contemporary ideas about counselling children in Chapter 5.

In this chapter we would like to share with you our own ideas about what we believe is important in the child–counsellor relationship. We suggest that you might like to compare our ideas with other schools of thought and then decide for yourself what you consider to be appropriate.

We agree with other workers in child therapy that the child–counsellor relationship is crucial to the process of therapeutic change. Further, we claim that this relationship is the single most important factor in achieving successful therapeutic outcomes.

One factor that the child–counsellor relationship is dependent on is the personal attributes which the counsellor brings into the relationship. These will be discussed in Chapter 4. Here we will consider what we believe to be appropriate and necessary attributes of the child–counsellor relationship. These attributes inevitably impact on the parent–counsellor relationship, on which we will also comment. Additionally, we will consider the effect of *transference* on the child–counsellor relationship.

Attributes of the child–counsellor relationship (and the influence of these attributes on the parent–counsellor relationship)

To be optimally effective, we believe that the child–counsellor relationship must be all of the following:

- a connecting link between the child's world and the counsellor
- exclusive
- safe
- authentic
- confidential (subject to limits)
- non-intrusive
- purposeful.

We will now discuss the attributes listed above in more detail.

The child–counsellor relationship as a connecting link between the child's world and the counsellor

The relationship is primarily about connecting with the child and staying with the child's perceptions. The child may see the environment in which they live quite differently from the way in which their parents see this environment. The counsellor's job is to join with the child and to work from within the child's framework. Approaching the child–counsellor relationship with judgement, affirmation or condemnation, invites the child to move away from their own perceptions and towards those of the counsellor. Instead, it is important for the child to stay with their own values, beliefs and attitudes rather than to be influenced by the counsellor's values, beliefs and attitudes.

The child–counsellor relationship provides a link between the child's world and the counsellor, enabling the counsellor to observe with clarity the experience of the child. This observation will inevitably be partially distorted by the counsellor's own experiences, and some projection of these onto the child is unavoidable. However, the counsellor's aim is to minimize the influence of their own experience, so that their connection with the child's experience of the world is as complete as is possible.

The child–counsellor relationship as an exclusive relationship

As counsellors it is important for us to establish and maintain good rapport with the child so that trust is developed. This development of trust can be supported if the child experiences a strong flavour of exclusivity, that is, a unique relationship with the counsellor which is not compromised by the unwanted intrusion of others, such as parents or siblings.

The child will have a personal perception of themselves, which will not be the same as the parents' perception. For the therapeutic relationship to be effective it is important for the child to feel accepted by the counsellor for the way in which that child perceives themselves. It won't be helpful if the child thinks that the counsellor's views of them have been influenced by the parents or by significant others. This can be avoided if the child–counsellor relationship is exclusive.

Keeping the relationship exclusive means not allowing others to intrude or to be included without the child's permission. Consequently, preparation of the child and parents for therapy requires specific attention because there is clearly an ethical issue involved. The parents have care and control of the child, yet in therapy we are proposing that the counsellor builds an exclusive relationship with the child. How do you think the parents will feel about that?

The situation may be aggravated in cases where parents are using public health services or the services of large non-government agencies. Some parents may feel disempowered and overwhelmed by the system, even though individual workers may try to create a personal consumer-oriented service. Such parents may be worried by the suggestion that they will not be fully included in the counselling process.

This ethical issue can only be addressed satisfactorily if the counsellor is clear with parents about the nature of the therapeutic relationship and gains their acceptance of what is required. Therapy is generally a new experience for the child and the parents. We find that parents are likely to have a satisfactory level of comfort and to have confidence in the process if they are fully informed about the need for the counsellor to maintain an exclusive relationship with the child.

It is helpful to warn parents that at times their child may not wish to disclose information arising from a therapy session. It is reasonable to expect that parents may feel anxious and believe that they might be left without information which they should rightfully know. Parents need to have reassurance that in time they will be given all the information that is important for them. They need to understand that children often have great difficulty sharing important and private information and that such sharing needs to be done when the child is ready and feels safe about sharing.

Sometimes, particularly at important points in the therapeutic process, a child may develop behaviours which are more difficult for the parents to manage than the presenting behaviours apparent at the commencement of therapy. It is helpful to warn parents that there may be a period of improvement soon after treatment begins which is often followed by a setback. Passing general information to the parents, such as that mentioned in this and the previous paragraph, does not compromise the exclusivity of the relationship. However, to pass on specific details of a therapy session without the child's agreement would certainly compromise exclusivity.

As the child's confidence in the counsellor increases and the counsellor's understanding of the child's issues becomes broader, the trust that the child experiences becomes stronger. This trust is reinforced by the knowledge that fears, anxieties and negative thoughts towards parents, events and situations will not be disclosed to the child's parents or family members without the child's agreement. We believe that a child has a right to privacy, subject to certain limitations, but do understand that it is sometimes difficult for parents to accept this.

Clearly, it's highly desirable to enlist the support and encouragement of parents so that the child feels free to talk openly with the counsellor. We have found that if we are open with parents about the nature of the child–counsellor relationship, parents will most often be very supportive of our work with their children.

We try to build a trusting relationship with the parents in the child's presence. Thus the exclusivity of the child–counsellor relationship is maintained, the child is fully aware of the parents' acceptance of that relationship, and is given permission and encouraged by the parents to join with us.

Naturally, there are times when parents have a right and a need to know information which is disclosed to the counsellor in counselling sessions with a child. The issues of exclusivity and confidentiality are clearly complex ones and will be discussed more fully in Chapters 3 and 9.

The child–counsellor relationship as a safe relationship

Creating a permissive environment in which the child feels free to act out and to gain mastery over their feelings in safety is another important task of the counsellor. The child should feel safe to make disclosures with the confidence that doing so will not have repercussions or consequences which may be emotionally harmful or damaging. The issue of confidentiality is involved here and will be addressed later in this section and again in Chapters 3 and 9.

For the child to feel safe, structure is required. Structure gives the child a sense of security and predictability during therapy sessions. It also allows the counsellor to remind the child that indulging in repetitive non-purposeful activity will reduce the amount of time for constructive work. Structure includes setting behavioural limits and the giving of information about the expected length of each session. Additionally, the child needs to be prepared for the termination of each session.

With regard to limit setting, we believe that limits should be imposed to protect the child, the counsellor and property from damage. Early in the joining process we make it clear to the child that there are three basic rules:

1 The child is not permitted to injure themselves.
2 The child is not permitted to hurt the counsellor.
3 The child is not permitted to damage property.

We then make it clear that there are consequences for breaking the rules. If the rules are contravened, then the therapy session ends but without recrimination. However, the counsellor does make it clear to the child that the session has to end because the rules have been broken. At the same time, the child is made to feel welcome to come back another time and a new appointment is made.

By using only the three rules, we avoid having to control the child and having to behave like a parent during a session. Also, a uniquely therapeutic relationship is created where the child has permission to be themselves with little restraint.

Although some external controls are set, this does not mean that counsellors should expect that all sessions will be free of acting-out behaviour. Intermittent periods of testing behaviour are a normal part of the child therapy process.

Safety needs must also be considered when choosing materials for play therapy sessions. Equipment or toys which can be easily broken may be a source of anxiety for many children. Most children don't want to be held responsible for inadvertently damaging property.

The child–counsellor relationship as an authentic relationship

An authentic relationship is a genuine and honest relationship where the interaction is one between two real people. This means that at all times the whole relationship is consistent with the real person who is the counsellor, and the child as the child genuinely is. It cannot be superficial, or a relationship where the counsellor pretends to be someone they are not. The authentic relationship allows the child an opportunity to give up the pretence of being someone they are not, and to allow the inner self to be exposed. This leads to a deep level of trust and understanding.

Authenticity in the relationship means allowing natural, spontaneous interplay between the counsellor and the child to occur, without inhibition or censorship and without unnecessary anxiety. By being authentic, the relationship between the child and the counsellor will at times be serious because of the gravity of the issues being discussed and the intensity of the emotions involved. However, the authentic relationship will not always be serious; it will also allow the child and counsellor to spontaneously engage in playful and enjoyable interaction. Most importantly, in the authentic relationship the emerging issues of the child are not suppressed, avoided or violated.

The child–counsellor relationship as a confidential relationship

When working with children the counsellor tries to create an environment where the child feels safe enough to share very private thoughts and emotional feelings. In order for the child to feel safe, a level of confidentiality is required. It is important to discuss confidentiality, and its limits, with the child early in the relationship-building process.

Firstly, we need to consider problems which might arise from confidentiality, so that we can recognize appropriate limits.

Inevitably, there will be times when the child will share information with the counsellor which the counsellor believes needs to be shared with others: for example, if a child discloses sexual or physical abuse. However, to disclose this information inconsiderately, or without giving consideration to the impact of disclosure on the child, might lead the child into believing that they have been betrayed. Clearly, there is a dilemma for the counsellor here.

Take a few moments, if you will, to think about how you could satisfy the child's need for confidentiality and at the same time prepare the child for the possibility that important information might be shared with others.

Here is our approach to the confidentiality problem. Right at the start of the therapeutic process, we tell the child that what they say to us will be private and that information will generally only be disclosed to parents or other people with the child's permission. However, we warn the child that there may be times when it is important for information to be passed on. We explain that in such instances we will discuss with the child how and when the information is to be shared with others. We do this so that the child does not become disempowered but has control over the way in which disclosures are shared with other people.

When we need to pass information on to parents or other people, we remind the child that we had previously said that there might be information which needed to be passed on. We tell the child that this is the case and then ask the child what it will be like for them when the information is passed on. We then explore both positive and negative consequences of the proposed disclosure so that the child is fully aware of what outcomes there might be. We deal with the child's anxieties about sharing the information. We also give the child some level of control of the timing and conditions surrounding the disclosure. We will ask the child questions such as the following:

- Would you like to tell your parents yourself, or would like me to tell your parents?
- Would you like me to be present while you tell your parents, or would you like to tell your parents on your own?
- Would you prefer me to tell your parents with you present, or would you prefer me to tell your parents without you being present?
- Would you like this to happen today, or at another time?

It is usually best if a child will tell their parents or others themselves, but the child needs to have some level of control over how and when the information is shared.

When working with children from families who have ongoing contact with statutory or government service agencies, it is sensible to ascertain from those agencies what they expect from the child and the family. Finding out what these expectations are can sometimes avert a child's removal from the family, or in other cases may facilitate the child's reintegration into the family. With such knowledge the counsellor may be able to tell the child about agency expectations and thus be in a position to warn the child that at times information may need to be passed on to the relevant agency.

We believe that it is important for us, as counsellors, to take steps to minimize the impact of a child's disclosures, particularly about abuse or mistreatment. Children often regret having made such disclosures, because the outcomes may be painful for them. Certainly, the counsellor needs to be sensitive to the child's predicament with regard to the disclosure of sensitive information.

Although we have been discussing confidentiality issues related to the disclosure of abuse of a child, confidentiality also relates to the disclosure of a child's intrapersonal issues to the family, particularly to parents. However, we have found that children will usually agree to the sharing of such information with others if they think that positive changes may occur as a consequence. We are, of course, careful to explore with children the possibility of negative aspects of disclosures.

In all cases, unless we consider that it is essential to make a disclosure to others, we will, after full discussion with the child, accept the child's decision to share or not to share information. However, we do make it clear to the child that they are free to share any information from or about the counselling session with their parents or with anyone else if that is what they would like to do.

The child–counsellor relationship as a non-intrusive relationship

When working with children the counsellor is encouraged to join with the child in a way which is comfortable for the child. Some counsellors believe that questioning the child and enquiring about the child's family and background during the joining process is a useful way of getting to know the child and the child's world. Although we agree that this approach can be valuable, it needs to be used with care or it will be intrusive.

There is a danger in asking too many questions, because the child may fear being asked to disclose information which is private and/or too scary to share. If this happens the child will feel intruded upon and will withdraw into silence or will engage in distracting behaviour. Similarly it can be risky to use information about the child which the counsellor may already have obtained from parents, care-givers or other agencies. When the child discovers that important information has been given to the counsellor without their own consent or knowledge, they may feel threatened, exposed, vulnerable and uncertain about how much more information the counsellor may have. There is effectively an erosion of the child's ego boundaries and the child is likely to feel disempowered. To intrude on the child's world in this way is likely to contribute to anxiety about coming for counselling and about being in the child–counsellor relationship.

The child–counsellor relationship as a purposeful relationship

Children enter into the therapeutic process more willingly and confidently if they know exactly why they are coming to see a counsellor. They need time to prepare themselves for counselling, and will usually do so if given suitable notice and if told why they are being brought to see a counsellor. Because of anxiety, parents sometimes wait until the last moment before letting their children know that they are going to see a counsellor and before telling them what to expect. Unfortunately, some parents give their children no information whatsoever, but just arrive at the counsellor's door with their children feeling puzzled, uncertain and anxious about what might happen!

It can be risky to assume that parents have given their child a truthful and clear explanation about their concerns and reasons for coming to see a counsellor. Some parents are very careful to explain to their children, in ways that are helpful and positive, the reasons they are going to see a counsellor. However, other parents are not so skilled and say to their children things like, 'You will be seeing a doctor who will help you solve your problems', or 'I am taking you to see a woman who will make you behave'. Both of these approaches will certainly raise barriers for the counsellor to overcome. It is important for the counsellor to know precisely what information the child has received about coming to counselling and to clarify, affirm or correct perceptions about what will happen. Doing so in the presence of both the parent and the child helps to circumvent misunderstandings or avoidable differences between expectations.

If the child clearly understands the reasons for coming to see a counsellor, then the child–counsellor relationship has the potential to be purposeful. Many counselling sessions involve play because play is an effective way to produce change in children. It is the counsellor's task to ensure that play or any other activity is facilitated in a purposeful way, rather than being aimless. However, this does not mean that the play will necessarily be directed: it may well be free play, completely devised and controlled by the child. What is important is that the counsellor seeks to facilitate or engage the child in a process which will be therapeutically useful.

We recognize that undirected play can be therapeutic for some children. However, we believe that in most cases allowing a child to play endlessly over time, without appropriate counsellor interventions to promote some purposeful expression, is not useful. In our view, a skilled counsellor is one who takes advantage of opportunities which occur through play to intervene in a purposeful way.

We have discussed seven attributes which we believe are necessary in the child–counsellor relationship. You may have some additional or different ideas. Even so, we hope that our suggestions will be a starting point for your own exploration of the qualities which are required in the therapeutic relationship.

At this point we also need to consider the effect of *transference*, which is inevitable in the child–counsellor relationship. It is important for the counsellor to understand the nature of transference, to recognize it when it occurs and to know how to respond to it.

Transference

'Transference' is a term which comes from psychoanalytic theory. In child therapy, transference occurs when the child behaves toward the counsellor as though the counsellor were the child's mother, the child's father or another significant adult in the child's life. The behaviour occurs because the child projects their beliefs about a significant person on to the counsellor, believing that the counsellor is like that person. Transference can result in the child perceiving the counsellor either positively as a nurturing parent (positive transference) or negatively as a critical parent (negative transference).

Naturally, it is quite possible for the counsellor to inadvertently fall into playing the role in which the child sees them and to respond as if they were a parent. If this happens we say that counter-transference is occurring. Counter-transference is likely to occur when the child triggers off the counsellor's own unresolved issues or fantasies from their past.

It is inevitable that transference and counter-transference will occur at times in the child–counsellor relationship, but provided this is recognized and dealt with appropriately, then it is not a problem. It certainly would be a problem if transference or counter-transference was not dealt with. Therapy would be compromised if the child continued to treat the counsellor as a parent and the counsellor continued to behave as a parent. For a fuller understanding of the nature of transference and counter-transference see Bauer and Kobos (1995).

Children will often transfer feelings or fantasies which they would like to direct at a parent on to a counsellor. The counsellor may then inadvertently and unconsciously respond with counter-transference. For example, if a child has been rejected by a parent, that child may not feel able to face the painful truth and may instead project on to the counsellor the negative characteristics which belong to the parent, and may believe that it is the counsellor who is rejecting them (as transference occurs). Consequently, the child's attitude to the counsellor may be negative and the counsellor may unthinkingly respond as a rejecting parent (as counter-transference occurs).

When we, as counsellors, suspect that transference is occurring, we need to try to be as objective as possible. To achieve this objectivity we may need to discuss the case in question with our supervisor so that we can deal with our own issues, projections and unconscious desires in connection with the child–counsellor relationship. Once we have owned our counter-transference we can then deal with it and with the transference problem by bringing this into the child's awareness, as described in Chapter 14.

For an appropriate child–counsellor relationship to be created and maintained, it is important for the counsellor to bring certain personal qualities or attributes into the relationship and to engage in some specific behaviours. We will consider these attributes and behaviours in Chapter 4. However, first we would like to explore in more detail the ethical considerations which may arise when counselling children, some of which we have already touched on, for example, setting goals and confidentiality.

KEY POINTS

- The child–counsellor relationship:

    - is the single most important factor in achieving positive therapeutic outcomes;
    - provides a connecting link between the child's world and the counsellor;
    - needs to be exclusive, safe, authentic, confidential (subject to limits), non-intrusive, and purposeful.

- Transference is said to occur when the child behaves towards the counsellor as though the counsellor were their mother or another significant adult.
- Counter-transference occurs when the counsellor responds to the child's transference by unconsciously fulfilling the role in which the child sees them.
- It is important for counsellors to own counter-transference when it occurs so that it can be dealt with appropriately.
- Transference can be addressed by bringing it into the child's awareness.

3

Ethical Considerations when Counselling Children

Counselling children presents unique ethical considerations. Such considerations often don't have a clear solution: shades of grey can be more frequent than black and white! Indeed, similar ethical considerations may require different approaches depending on the unique characteristics of the child, family and situation. The codes, frameworks and guidelines provided by the British Psychological Society (BPS, 2002, 2009), British Association for Counselling and Psychotherapy (BACP, 2010), British Association of Play Therapists (BAPT, 2008), Australian Psychological Society (APS, 2007, 2009), and Queensland Counsellors Association (QCA, 2009) are essential starting points. Speaking with a supervisor can also be a helpful source of guidance. There are also a number of ethical decision-making models that may help when thinking through an ethical issue (e.g., Miner, 2006; Pope and Vasquez, 2007). In this chapter we aim to discuss some of the ethical considerations we have experienced when counselling children. Rather than providing solutions, we hope that this discussion will instead be an additional source of guidance and reflection during your own practice.

Setting up the counselling relationship

Our approach to counselling is based on the Sequentially Planned Integrative Counselling for Children model (the SPICC model), which we will introduce in more detail in Chapter 8. There are five phases in the SPICC model and we will discuss the ethical considerations which arise in each of these phases. The first phase in the SPICC model is that of relationship-building. This initial phase is focused on developing a positive child–counsellor relationship in which the child feels comfortable, safe, valued, respected, and free to share their story. In setting up this supportive environment, a number of ethical considerations arise.

Informed consent

As highlighted in Chapter 1, it is generally the parent/s who bring the child for counselling, rather than the child seeking this relationship for themselves. Hence, while obtaining informed consent from the parent/s is important, it is equally important to obtain the informed consent of the child. Indeed, both the BPS and APS stress the importance of providing children with the opportunity to understand the counselling service being offered (BPS, 2009) and to provide their consent 'as far as practically possible' (APS, 2007). Furthermore, including the child in the process of informed consent is a way in which to give them a voice in the process of counselling; encouraging feelings of being valued and respected. We would like to invite you to take a moment to brainstorm some factors which might impact on the process of informed consent. One factor we would like to draw your attention to in particular is the developmental level of the child: does the child have the cognitive and emotional ability to understand the nature of, and make a decision about, the counselling relationship (Lawrence and Robinson Kurpius, 2000)?

During the process of obtaining consent, another situation which may arise is when one party gives their consent but the other does not. This can raise a number of possibilities to consider! What if the child does not provide their consent but the parents are keen for their child to receive counselling? How would you proceed if the child seeks counselling, for example within a school environment, but doesn't want their parents to know? What factors might impact on your decision? It is difficult to provide a definite answer for many of these questions as each child, family, and situation is unique and must be considered in context (Hall and Lin, 1995). However, it is important to keep in mind that the child is most likely to benefit from counselling when they enter the child–counsellor relationship voluntarily, that is, with their informed consent (Bond, 1992).

Confidentiality

It is important to be very clear about confidentiality and its limits when commencing a new counselling relationship (Mitchell et al., 2002). In particular, when working with children it is important to consider what, and how, information is shared with parents and associated parties. Additionally, it is important to keep in mind our duty to warn and reflect on how this might be accomplished while maintaining a supportive child–counsellor relationship. Our duty to warn covers risk of harm to the client or others (Mitchell et al., 2002). Many associations provide guidelines for reporting risk of harm, particularly when this concerns child abuse and neglect (e.g., APS, 2009; BPS, 2007). It is worthwhile to familiarize yourself with these guidelines along with your local legislative requirements or any organizational guidelines which apply to your counselling context. A further discussion on confidentiality regarding sharing information with parent/s is covered in Chapters 2 and 9.

Another aspect of confidentiality is the documentation of the counselling process. It is important to consider who has access to this documentation, how the documentation is protected, and how to respond to requests for documentation. It is important to ensure that any confidential client information is securely stored, including both hard and electronic copies, and accessible only to the counsellor. When a request for information is received, speaking with the child and/or parents is always a good starting point. If the request comes in the form of a subpoena or court order you may also want to seek the advice of a supervisor or lawyer. A good general rule to follow is to 'disclose only that information which is necessary to achieve the purpose of the disclosure, and then only to people required to have that information' (APS, 2007: 16). It is also important to consider what information is included in the client's file. Information should be comprehensive and factual; free of judgemental and emotive language.

Including family members

Children come within a family! Therefore, it is important to consider the child within the context of their family and to be aware of the possible ethical considerations which may arise. As highlighted earlier, it is generally the parent/s who initiate the child–counsellor relationship with certain goals in mind. However, the child may also bring their own goals to the counselling relationship. This raises the question: who is your client? In particular, whose goals are to be followed? As highlighted in Chapter 1, it is important from the outset to be clear about the goals of the counselling relationship and to frequently reflect on these goals as the child–counsellor relationship develops. This process can become more challenging when there are different goals or opinions about the counselling process from different family members. How might you approach a situation where the parents have different views about what the counselling should focus on? Or if one parent does not want their child to enter a counselling relationship at all? In some situations, for example if parents are separated or divorced, one parent may not want the other to be informed about the child accessing counselling or receive limited information. On the other hand, the child may express a wish that their parent/s not be informed about certain information. How would you approach such a situation? Do the parent/s in question have a right to be informed? The APS provides some helpful guidelines around provision of counselling when a child's parents are separated or divorced (APS, 2009), with a focus on keeping clear communication open with the child and involved parent/s.

Another consideration when working with children and their families is whether or not the presenting issue is such that counselling within the context of family therapy may be more suitable. For more information about counselling children within the context of family therapy please refer to Chapter 9.

Connecting with associated parties

Sometimes it is important to consult, work with, or gather information from associated parties in the child's life such as schools, doctors, and other professionals. How might you continue to maintain the child's sense of trust and safety with the child–counsellor relationship while making connections with associated parties? What if the child or parent/s insist that the associated parties not be contacted? Again, speaking with the child and/or parent/s first is a good starting point. Discussing the potential pros and cons of connecting with associated parties and what (and how) information is to be shared may help to find a solution the child and parents are comfortable with. This discussion may then form the foundation for obtaining the required verbal and written consent from the child and parent/s to connect with an associated party.

Maintaining the counselling relationship

Once a child–counsellor relationship has been developed, the next step is maintenance of this relationship in such a way as to support increased awareness and change. The maintenance of the relationship corresponds to Phases 2 to 5 of the SPICC model (Chapter 8) during which the child increases their awareness (Gestalt Therapy), changes their view of self (Narrative Therapy), challenges any self-destructive beliefs (Cognitive Behaviour Therapy, CBT) and rehearses and experiments with new behaviours (Behaviour Therapy).

Boundaries and power in the child–counsellor relationship

It is the responsibility of the counsellor to maintain appropriate boundaries within the child–counsellor relationship. From the outset of the counselling process it is important that the child and parents understand the nature and limits of the child–counsellor relationship. Setting up boundaries about your role as a counsellor includes: time (for example, session length and availability outside the session); place (where the sessions take place); self-disclosure (how much disclosure is appropriate); behaviour during the session; and appropriate touch (Gutheil and Gabbard, 1993). Maintaining clear boundaries defines the child-counsellor relationship as a professional one. While it is important for the child to feel safe and supported, the relationship remains different to a personal adult relationship.

Another consideration which falls under boundary maintenance is that of power imbalance in the client–counsellor relationship, which can be magnified when working with children. Power imbalances will always be present, however it is very important to reflect on and guard against the consequences of power imbalances. How can you identify when a power imbalance is impacting on the child–counsellor relationship? One sign, which may indicate the impact of a power imbalance, is dependency developing within the child–counsellor relationship. The counsellor may also notice themselves becoming more directive rather than allowing the relationship to be child-led. Feelings, such as protectiveness for the client or frustration that the client isn't 'fitting into' your plan, may also be indicators of a power imbalance starting to impact on the child–counsellor relationship. Such factors can lead to the child feeling disempowered within the relationship. This disempowerment can then lead to decreased effectiveness within the counselling relationship. Children may respond to power imbalances by either withdrawing or attempting to comply with what they feel is expected of them (Bond, 1992). As such, it is important to guard against the consequences of power imbalances to ensure the child doesn't feel disempowered and to maintain the effectiveness of the counselling relationship. Indeed, the BACP guidelines highlight the importance of respecting and encouraging the autonomy of the client (BACP, 2010). How might you guard against setting up dependency and disempowerment within the child–counsellor relationship? In what ways could you encourage the autonomy of your client within the child–counsellor relationship? We believe that ongoing self-reflection is a good starting point, along with appropriate supervision. Ensuring a safe and supportive environment for the child to share within and taking your lead from the child where possible can also help to limit the consequences of power imbalances.

The counsellor's role and responsibilities

Being a counsellor brings with it a variety of roles and responsibilities. Maintaining these roles and responsibilities requires frequent self-reflection, which can be further supported within a supervision relationship. Here we will focus on two areas that fall within the counsellor's roles and responsibilities: the counsellor's values and professional competence.

Values

We all have a unique set of values, which guide our thinking, decisions, and actions. These values also have an impact on our practice as counsellors. As such, it is important to understand our values and how they may influence the ethical decisions we make regarding the child–counsellor relationship. We would like to invite you to take a moment now to reflect on your own values. What values are core to yourself? In what way may your values impact on your counselling approach? How might your values impact on a specific child–counsellor relationship? How might your values clash with a child and/or family? How will this clash impact on your counselling relationship? In our own practice we find that being proactive and self-reflective is one of the best ways to ensure our values are not impacting on the child–counsellor relationship. As this relationship is dynamic and changeable, it is important that this process of self-reflection occurs repeatedly throughout the counselling process.

Values are generally influenced by our cultural context. As such, it is also important to consider how culture has impacted on your values and to be aware and sensitive to the cultural values of your clients (Leebert, 2006). While this may mean researching a particular culture, it is important to also keep in mind that culture is ever changing and may mean different things to different people (Chantler, 2005). We would like to invite you to take some time to reflect on your cultural identification. What values are attached to this identification? In what ways might these values impact on the child–counsellor relationship? For more information about working across cultures, Yan and Wong (2005) have provided a good overview of self-awareness within a cultural framework. Ivey and colleagues (2001) also explore the impact of cultural issues in counselling.

Professional competence

As highlighted in the BACP guidelines, an important duty of counsellors is to maintain and develop their professional competence (BACP, 2010). This includes being aware of the limits of your competence, working within these limits, and identifying factors which restrict your competence. It is also important to regularly reflect on your professional competence within the context of the child–counsellor relationship. Some questions you might ask yourself are: Do your experience and skills meet the needs of the child? Is the child–counsellor relationship beneficial for the child? Is there evidence of change? To support your self-reflection it is helpful to include frequent evaluations of outcomes and incorporate the child's and parents' feedback. Do the child and their parent/s report benefits of the counselling relationship? Do they see change? If the child–counsellor relationship does not appear to be beneficial for the child, or you feel your experience and skills are not meeting the needs of the child, you may need to seek supervision and/or training or consider other referral options in order for the child's needs to be met.

Another aspect of professional competence is that of self-care: it is difficult to provide a supportive counselling relationship when you require support yourself! Again, being self-reflective about your capacity to provide support is important; as is being able to identify when you may be close to burning out. What factors might you look for as early signs of burn out? Koocher and Keith-Spiegel (2008: 91) suggest a number of warning signs including: 'uncharacteristic angry outbursts, apathy, chronic frustration, a sense of depersonalisation, depression, emotional and physical exhaustion, hostility, feelings of malice or aversion toward patients, reduced productivity or lowered effectiveness at work'. We have found that the best solution for burn out is being proactive! We recommend putting into place self-care strategies in order to decrease the probability of reaching the point of burn out in the first place. What self-care strategies could you put in place? Some common self-care strategies include exercise, music, taking a bath, reading or spending time with friends and/or family. You may also find it helpful to talk with a supervisor when you first notice the signs of burn out.

Bringing the counselling relationship to a close

Once the child reaches a resolution and has achieved adaptive functioning, it is time to begin the process of bringing the child–counsellor relationship to a close. This includes preparing the child for the end of the child–counsellor relationship and supporting the child to achieve a sense of closure. It can also be helpful to provide opportunities for the child (and parent/s) to express how they found the counselling experience. These opportunities also allow for the child and parent/s to evaluate the outcomes of the child–counsellor relationship. In the event that the relationship has to be ended due to other considerations (child–counsellor relationship is not beneficial or outside counsellor's professional competence) it is the counsellor's responsibility to also source an appropriate referral for the child. When seeking such a referral, the counsellor may consider whether the referral is appropriate for the child's needs and likely to be beneficial and whether the service referred to is able to accept the referral. Disclosure of information should also be discussed with the child and parent/s during the referral process, including what information is to be provided to the new counsellor (BACP, 2010). For those interested in reading further, Lendrum (2004) has reflected on a number of potentially challenging aspects of bringing the counselling relationship to a close.

In this chapter we explored the ethical considerations which may arise during the counselling relationship. In the next chapter we will explore another factor which impacts on the child-counsellor relationship: the attributes and behaviours of a child-counsellor.

CASE STUDY

You have just received a new referral for nine-year-old Sally. The referral was made by Sally's father, Fred, who is concerned about her behaviour when she returns from her mother's house. During your initial meeting with Fred he remains elusive about Sally's mother, only stating that they have been separated for some time. Fred isn't comfortable disclosing information about the custody of Sally and has specifically asked that her mother not be contacted. However, he did share that Sally spends every second week at her mother's. He has not provided any contact details for Sally's mother. How would you proceed? Would you attempt to make contact with Sally's mother? What legal aspects might you need to consider? How might custody arrangements impact on your decision? How would Sally's response to the proposed counselling impact on your decision?

KEY POINTS

- Ethical considerations when counselling children are often complex, without a clear answer. Seeking advice from the relevant ethical codes and guidelines, along with a supervisor, is a good starting point.
- When commencing a new counselling relationship, informed consent, confidentiality, including family members, and connecting with associated parties are important ethical considerations.
- During the maintenance of the child–counsellor relationship, ethical considerations include maintaining boundaries, power imbalances, and your roles and responsibilities as a counsellor including the impact of your values and professional competence on your practice.
- It is also important to bring the child–counsellor relationship to close in an ethical manner, including the child (and parent/s) in the process and, where needed, seeking an appropriate referral.

4

Attributes of a Counsellor for Children

We know that each counsellor will bring into the therapeutic relationship their own unique personality. No two counsellors are going to be alike. Your individual personality will influence what you bring to the therapeutic relationship, and you can use your own strengths and personal attributes to enhance your work. Having said this, there are some basic attributes and behaviours which are desirable in the counsellor if an appropriate child–counsellor relationship is to be achieved. There are also some roles which the counsellor will play.

We invite you to think about the child–counsellor relationship and to consider the question: 'In what ways would it be useful for a counsellor to relate to a child in a similar way to one of the following?'

- a parent
- a teacher
- an aunt or uncle
- a peer
- a blank sheet.

What do you think?

None of the above would fit for us. In fact, when we find ourselves behaving in any of the roles listed above, we know that it is time for us to visit our supervisor. Our belief is that there are a number of important attributes which are desirable for a counsellor.

Desirable attributes for a child-counsellor

An effective counsellor is:

1 Congruent.
2 In touch with their own inner child.
3 Accepting.
4 Emotionally detached.

Being congruent

The child needs to perceive their relationship with the counsellor as trustworthy and the counselling environment as safe. For this to happen it is important for the counsellor to be personally integrated, grounded, genuine, consistent and stable, so that trust can be developed and maintained. Children are very good at recognizing people who are not congruent and who are trying to play a role which is not consistent with the rest of their personalities.

Being in touch with our own inner child

The adult world is very different from a child's world. However, as adults we have not lost our child: it is still a part of our personality. This inner child is available to us if we learn how to access it. Accessing our inner child doesn't mean being childish or regressing to childhood, it means getting in touch with that part of ourselves which fits comfortably with a child's world.

If we are able to get in touch with our own inner child and to enter the child's world, then we are more likely to be able to join with the child successfully, to understand the child's feelings and perceptions, and to provide opportunities for the child to experience them fully. By helping the child to experience current feelings, we minimize the possibility of these feelings being stored and repressed to become the foundation of some future emotional disturbance and neurosis.

Children usually want to avoid strong unpleasant emotions. For them, as for ourselves as adults, getting in touch with feelings which haven't been accessed before may be very frightening. Consequently there will be a natural tendency for our child clients to push such feelings down, to repress them, and unfortunately to lock them in. It can be a huge leap for some children to learn that negative feelings can reduce in intensity and change in quality once they are verbalized, shared and fully experienced. Similarly, as counsellors, if we can get in touch with our own inner child and the pain of unresolved issues from our own childhood, then we will be better able to understand the difficulties and the release that comes from confronting those issues. If we are more open and more in touch with our own feelings, then the children we work with will come into a different relationship with us. They will be freer to be more open with us.

As counsellors we become models for the children we work with, so it is essential that we change those things in ourselves which we might want to change in the children we work with. To do this it is helpful to regularly work through our own personal issues in supervision with a competent therapist. We believe that it would be irresponsible for us to engage in counselling children without regular supervision where we can discuss case issues and personal issues of our own. It is inevitable that our own issues will be triggered off by the counselling work we do with children. If we fail to deal with these issues, they will interfere with our ability to help our clients.

Accepting

Right from childhood, all of us learn to respond to the verbal and non-verbal behaviour of others. When we are in the company of others we modify our behaviour to suit other people. We control our behaviours, we censor what we say, and we generally only reveal the more socially acceptable parts of ourselves. If we fail to comply with expected norms we are punished by the disapproval, criticism or withdrawal of others.

If we want to encourage children to explore the private, and maybe the darker or shadow side of themselves, then as counsellors responding in the most accepting way we can give our child clients permission to be who they are, without restraint. In being accepting we do not show approval or disapproval. To do either of these things would have an effect on the child's behaviour. What we do is to accept, in the most non-judgemental way possible, whatever it is the child is saying or doing. We even avoid, as far as possible, making statements such as 'That's OK', because by doing so we give the child information about what we like and what we don't like. If we do that, the child's behaviour will change and we will never see and be able to understand the whole child. In being accepting, we don't put our expectations on to the child, we do not withdraw or come closer in response to changes in behaviour, and we are not overwhelmed by the child's behaviour.

Naturally, it will take a child a while to trust that we will continue to be accepting. We will admit to you that being accepting, particularly with a child who is acting out, is not easy. Remember, though, the three rules mentioned earlier (see Chapter 2). When the rules are invoked, and as a consequence a therapy session ends, there still needs to be an uncritical acceptance of the child's decision to behave in the way that they did. It is essential to be non-judgemental at such a time, because the child is testing the limits which provide security in the therapeutic situation and needs to know that it is expected that they will come back another time.

As a counsellor for children, can you put aside your parent role to accept a child in the way we have described? We believe that such acceptance is one of the most important attributes of a counsellor.

Emotionally detached

In order to be accepting in the way just described, an essential attribute for a counsellor to have is a level of emotional detachment. This is often difficult for the new counsellor.

Unfortunately, there are problems for children who are clients of counsellors who are too close, warm and friendly. The child may be controlled by the relationship, because the child will not want to risk losing such a relationship by behaving in ways which might attract disapproval. Further, transference issues will be hard, if not impossible, for the counsellor to manage appropriately.

Most often, children who are being counselled deal with extraordinarily painful issues. If a counsellor becomes emotionally involved, then the counsellor is likely to become distressed by those issues in a way which is apparent to the child. The child will then experience additional pain at seeing the counsellor in pain, may believe that the counsellor is being overwhelmed by what is being shared, and will be likely to withdraw from discussing further painful material. Children find it hard to cope with a crying counsellor! They have enough trouble coping with their own pain.

While it is important for the counsellor to avoid displaying emotional distress, it is also important to try to avoid showing other strong emotional responses in connection with the child's issues. For example, it is generally not useful for a counsellor to verbally or non-verbally give a child affirmation in connection with the child's issues or desires. To do so sets the child up to say and do things which will please the counsellor rather than encouraging the child to be authentic. Instead of giving either sympathy or affirmation, we would suggest the counsellor validate the child's experience. Nevertheless, it is both appropriate and necessary for a counsellor to affirm any sensible decisions a child may make. As counsellors, a valuable skill is the ability to discriminate between those things which need to be affirmed, and those things which should be accepted without affirmation, as belonging to the child.

Although a counsellor needs to have a level of emotional detachment, this does not mean that the counsellor needs be limp, lifeless and remote. On the contrary, the child does needs to feel comfortable with the counsellor, so it is a question of balance. The counsellor aims to be present for the child as a calm and stable facilitator who is able to participate when necessary and always to listen, accept and understand the child.

We have considered four major attributes, which we believe are important for a child-counsellor. You may have others which you can add to our list. Clearly, the therapeutic relationship is multi-faceted. Counsellors are adaptable and bring into play the various qualities which are needed at differing stages in the therapeutic process and at different points within a counselling session.

KEY POINTS

- Important attributes for a counsellor to have are being:
  - congruent – being genuinely who they are, rather than playing a role;
  - in touch with their own inner child – enabling them to join with the child successfully;
  - accepting – so that the child feels free to disclose who they are without feeling restrained by trying to live up to the counsellor's expectations;
  - a calm and stable facilitator who does not unnecessarily interrupt, constrain, or influence the child's natural expression of behaviour.

Part 2

Practice Frameworks

5

Historical Background and Contemporary Ideas about Counselling Children

This chapter gives only an overview of the background and recent ideas about counselling children. A solid foundation for counsellors who wish to work with children is a good understanding of the psychological theories which underpin their counselling work. We believe that it is important for counsellors to be familiar with all of the major theories and select ways of working developed from those theories which appeal to them personally and which they believe will be helpful for particular clients. We have fully referenced this section to enable you, the reader, to do further reading if you wish. Publications by the referenced authors are listed in the bibliography.

In moving from early history to the current time we will consider six overlapping periods during which significant ideas relevant to counselling children were developed:

1880 to 1940: The early pioneers developed underlying concepts.

1920 to 1975: Various theories of child development were proposed.

1940 to 1980: A number of humanistic/existentialist therapeutic approaches were developed.

1950 onwards: Development of Behaviour Therapy.

1960 onwards: Development of Cognitive Behaviour Therapy (CBT).

1980 onwards: More recent ideas for counselling children were proposed.

We will consider each of these periods in turn. In this discussion we will sometimes be referring to theoretical concepts and approaches which were initially developed for adults. Although there are major differences between the practical ways in which we counsel children and ways in which we counsel adults, many therapists of different orientations agree that the same underlying principles of psychotherapy apply to children and to adults (Reisman and Ribordy, 1993).

1880 to 1940 – the early pioneers developed underlying concepts

Included among the early pioneers were Sigmund Freud, Anna Freud, Melanie Klein, Donald Winnicott, Carl Jung, Margaret Lowenfeld and Alfred Adler.

Sigmund Freud

The first of the early pioneers was clearly Sigmund Freud, who developed his psycho-analytic model over a period from 1880 to the 1930s (Thompson and Rudolph, 1983). Much of psychoanalytic psychotherapy with children derives from Freud's discovery of unconscious processes and also of defence mechanisms employed by emotionally disturbed people in order to protect themselves from distressing and/or unbearable experiences with which they cannot cope (Dale, 1990). Additionally, Freud introduced conceptual ideas about the formation of personality. These included the concepts of the id, the ego and the superego. He also placed great emphasis on psychosexual development.

Some of Freud's ideas are directly useful when counselling children today. It is also important to understand them because some later theorists drew on his ideas but modified them. We consider the following aspects of Freud's theories to be the most relevant for counsellors who work with children today:

- Id, ego and superego
- Unconscious processes
- Defence mechanisms
- Resistance and free association
- Transference.

Id, ego and superego

Expressed simply, the id is the energizing part of us that strives to get our basic needs and drives met. The id is innate, uncontrolled and unconscious. The superego contains the qualities of conscience: it is a mixture of ideas which have been imposed by significant others, and ideas which are based on ideals. The ego is the part of the personality which seeks to strike a balance between the needs of the id and the conscience of the superego.

It is important for the contemporary counsellor who is working with children to recognize that when any stress occurs which causes anxiety or inner conflict, the child's id and superego are put into opposition. The id will strive to get instinctive and primary needs met, which may lead to unacceptable behaviours. By contrast the superego, which is said to be totally learned, imposes moral restrictions on these behaviours (Ivey et al., 2001). It is the ego's job to balance this struggle so that the id, ego and superego work together cooperatively. The counsellor's job is to help the child to gain in ego-strength so that this balance can be achieved.

Unconscious processes

According to Freud, anxiety occurs as a result of unconscious processes. These may arise as a result of the fear of memories, which may be conscious or unconscious.

Other unconscious processes occur as a consequence of conflict between the id and superego. For example, the id may drive the child to satisfy sexual impulses which the superego views as taboo. If this is happening at an unconscious level, then the child may become distressed because the ego is unable to resolve the situation.

Defence mechanisms

Defence mechanisms are unconscious. They protect a child from anxiety by helping them to avoid facing the consequences of unresolved differences between the id and superego. Defence mechanisms identified by Freud and described by Thompson and Rudolph (1983) include:

- repression
- projection
- reaction formation
- rationalization
- denial
- intellectualization
- withdrawal
- regression
- acting out
- compensation
- undoing
- fantasy.

It is useful for counsellors who work with children to become familiar with the definitions of all of the defence mechanisms because they are used by children as a way of dealing with their pain and anxiety (Thompson and Rudolph, 1983). Although defence mechanisms occur in normal human behaviour, Freud saw them as obstructing the ability of people to deal with the resolution of unconscious issues. Similarly, we can also attempt to recognize the ways in which these mechanisms block children from dealing directly with their issues.

Resistance and free association

Free association occurs normally in the progression of our thoughts from one topic or idea to another. However, this natural flow of thoughts and ideas becomes blocked as a consequence of the interference of defence mechanisms or resistance. Psychoanalysts see resistance as preventing the client from remembering painful experiences and preventing the client from talking about subjects which provoke anxiety. The psychoanalyst encourages the client to talk freely, looks for continuity of thoughts and feelings, identifies themes and then interprets the client's statements. This enables the client's free association to continue so that they can continue to talk about important material. It is the analyst's job to notice when blocks to free association occur as a consequence of resistance or defence mechanisms, and to interpret these for the client. Through this process the client is enabled to discover and understand why they think and feel the way they do, and to make sense of their current behaviours.

Psychoanalysts place considerable emphasis on encouraging the client to talk freely by listening, and then interpreting for the client. You, the reader, may wish to train and work psychoanalytically, and if you do we believe that you will be able to make use of many of the ideas in Part 4 for helping children to talk freely. Although we find Freud's basic theories very useful, in particular with regard to defence mechanisms, resistance and transference, we do not use a psychoanalytic approach ourselves. Instead, we use an integrated approach which incorporates theoretical principles and practical ideas from a number of therapeutic approaches (see Chapter 8). Even so, we think that it is important for us to include discussion of the major theoretical contributions to counselling children so that you may choose those ideas which best suit your style of working.

If you are working psychodynamically, it is important to recognize that there is a difference between working with adults and working with children with regard to free association. Free association in children may be observed not only through verbal behaviour but also through non-directive free play, particularly imaginative pretend play (see Chapter 29). Just as an analyst working with an adult will interpret themes and recurring concepts for the adult, the counsellor working with a child can interpret recurring themes and concepts observed during the child's play, storytelling or work with art.

Transference

Transference and counter-transference were important concepts of Freud's. These were described in Chapter 2 and will be discussed further in Chapter 14. Other early pioneers of importance are:

- Anna Freud
- Melanie Klein
- Donald Winnicott
- Carl Jung
- Margaret Lowenfeld
- Alfred Adler.

We will now briefly examine the contribution made by each of these.

Anna Freud

Whereas Sigmund Freud generally worked with adults, his daughter, Anna Freud, developed a method of working psychoanalytically with children by observing their play. She looked for the unconscious motivation behind imaginative play and drawings and paintings, and interpreted the content of the child's play to the child when the relationship with the child was established (Cattanach, 2003). Waiting until the relationship with the child was established was essential in Anna Freud's view. She took great pains to establish in the child a strong attachment to herself and to bring the child into a relationship of real dependence on herself. She believed that the child would only believe the 'loved person' and would only accomplish something to please that person. She believed that this affectionate attachment or positive transference with the therapist was a prerequisite to all work which was to be done with the child (Yorke, 1982).

Anna Freud also placed importance on what she called negative transference. In children negative transference occurs when the child sees the therapist as a competitor to the mother. For more information on Anna Freud's theoretical perspectives and practical methods see Yorke (1982).

Melanie Klein

Melanie Klein worked with children in a totally non-directive way, using play as a substitute for the verbal free association methods used by Sigmund Freud. She developed Freud's object relations theory (Klein, 1932). Freud believed that as children we attach to 'objects', such as our mother, and that growth and development involves separating from these objects. During the process of separation we attach to other objects, which are known as transitional objects. For example, when a child plays with a toy or a person, that toy or person becomes a transitional object because the child displaces their feelings from the mother on to the object.

Whereas Anna Freud believed that it was essential for a relationship to develop between the child and herself before using interpretations, Klein emphasized the immediate use of interpretation without waiting for the development of this rapport (Cattanach, 2003). She emphasized the object relations theory and the significance of transitional objects. Toys and other objects in the therapy room, and the therapist herself, were seen as transitional objects. Additionally, Klein sometimes recognized harmless explanations for a child's behaviour rather than always attributing symbolic meaning to that behaviour.

Understanding both Anna Freud's and Klein's perspectives is important for contemporary counsellors of children, particularly with regard to the nature of the counselling relationship, and the theoretical concepts of positive and negative transference. Clearly, your personal view of Freud's and Klein's differing theoretical perspectives will influence the way in which you use the counselling relationship in your work. Anna Freud's ideas can be useful in child psychotherapy which is open ended and not time limited. However, her perspective is not relevant to short-term or time-limited psychotherapy in which a long-term dependent relationship with the child is impossible. In such a situation Klein's ideas might be more suitable.

Donald Winnicott

Another important pioneer was Donald Winnicott. His account of the treatment of a young child in *The Piggle* (Ramzy, 1978) gives a description of the treatment as it develops and a theoretical understanding of what is happening. *The Piggle* illustrates Winnicott's contribution to psychoanalytic theory. Winnicott believed that a child grows and develops through the use of transitional objects and also through the experience of the transitional space between the mother and child (Cattanach, 2003).

Transitional space is the space in which the mother plays with the child in the process of helping the child to separate from her to establish a separate identity.

According to Winnicott, therapy with the child parallels the transitional space. This is consistent with our view that with some children the counselling session and the relationship with the therapist is sufficient in itself to enable the child to work through unconscious issues.

Carl Jung

Carl Jung's work was not specifically targeted at children, although he did recognize the importance of childhood experiences in the process of children establishing their sense of identity. We believe that the most important contribution of Jung's work is his development of Freud's idea of the unconscious. Jung (1933) suggested that there existed a collective unconscious which came from the primal motivations of human beings. In this collective unconscious, Jung believed, there are symbols which are common for all human beings. In his work he used symbolic representation, which is particularly relevant in counselling children when using the sand tray, clay and art (see Part 4).

Margaret Lowenfeld

Although Jung placed great emphasis on symbolic representation, he worked psycho-therapeutically through the use of verbal communication with the client. In 1925, Margaret Lowenfeld, who had been influenced by Jung's thinking, began working with children by using symbols in a sand tray to encourage non-verbal expression which was less influenced by rational thinking. She collected small objects, coloured sticks and shapes of paper, metal and clay, and kept them in what her young patients called her 'wonder box' (Ryce-Menuhin, 1992). Lowenfeld writes that this approach grew out of her attempts to find a way of helping children to talk without the use of language (Schaefer and O'Connor, 1983). Sand-tray work is a way of helping the child to tell their story with or without the use of words (see Chapter 23).

Alfred Adler

In the early 1900s, Alfred Adler was a member of a discussion group led by Sigmund Freud. This group later became the first psychoanalytic society. However, Adler broke away from that group in 1911 because he did not agree with Freud's psychosexual theories.

Adler (1964) believed that while people develop as individuals they also develop within a social structure: every individual is dependent upon other people. Adler focused on the interdependence of the person with the wider society. As a child develops they are influenced by other people, and behaviours develop in response to the way in which other people view the child. Adler's work has an important influence on counselling children, since it is clearly important to take account of a child's wider environment. If we view the child in a wider context, then the notion of consequences of behaviours arises. Reward and punishment are concepts rejected by Adler; instead he focused on natural and logical consequences. We ourselves favour this approach. In particular we make use of it when using worksheets and when working on social skills training (see Chapter 32).

Table 5.1 summarizes the work of the early pioneers.

TABLE 5.1 *The work of the early pioneers (1880–1940)*

Sigmund Freud	Developed psychoanalytic psychotherapy including the following concepts: unconscious processes, defence mechanisms, id, ego, superego, resistance, free association, transference, and psychosexual development.
Anna Freud	Sought an affectionate attachment with the child (positive transference). Interpreted child's non-directed free play after an affectionate attachment with the child had been established.
Melanie Klein	Started to interpret the child's behaviour early in the therapeutic relationship. Interpreted child's non-directed free play.
Donald Winnicott	Saw the therapeutic relationship with the child as a parallel to the transitional space in which the child is separating from the mother. Thought that the relationship with the therapist was sufficient in itself to produce therapeutic change.
Carl Jung	Introduced ideas about the symbolic representation of a collective unconscious.
Margaret Lowenfeld	Used symbols in a sand tray as a substitute for verbal communication.
Alfred Adler	Introduced the need to take account of the person's social context.

1920 to 1975 – various theories of child development were proposed

In order to understand the development of therapeutic work with children, we will now consider contributions to developmental psychology made by the following:

- Abraham Maslow
- Erik Erikson
- Jean Piaget
- Lawrence Kohlberg
- John Bowlby.

Abraham Maslow

Abraham Maslow (1954) aided our understanding of the needs of human beings by identifying a hierarchy of needs. This hierarchy was not specifically developed for children but is very relevant to them and includes the following levels:

1 Physiological needs – as the lowest level (the need for food, water, rest, air and warmth).
2 Need for safety.
3 Need for love and belonging.
4 Need for achievement of self-esteem.
5 Need for self-actualization – as the highest level (achievement of personal goals).

Maslow suggested that if lower-level needs aren't met, then the individual cannot direct their energies towards fulfilling higher-level needs. This has clear implications for counselling children because, if we accept Maslow's hierarchy, it is pointless trying to achieve higher-level needs without first addressing lower-level needs.

The hierarchy does not need to be viewed or used rigidly. It may be possible to work on some higher-level needs before lower-level needs have been *fully* met. Additionally, particular levels in the hierarchy may assume greater importance at different developmental stages for the child. Understanding the hierarchy does help a counsellor to recognize when specific needs of a child have not been met and should be addressed. For example, a child who has been physically abused will have a need to work on issues of safety before being able to address issues of self-esteem or self-actualization.

Erik Erikson

Erik Erikson believed that the individual has the potential to solve their own conflicts, and that competent functioning is achieved through the resolution of crises occurring throughout the individual's life at particular developmental stages. He emphasized the importance of the formation of an individual's personal identity; the personal identity being the way in which an individual sees themselves.

Specifically, Erikson divided an individual's life-span into eight stages, each of which is represented by a personal social crisis. He believed that dealing with each crisis gives the individual an opportunity to strengthen their ego and to become more adaptive so that life can be lived more successfully.

Erikson's work is relevant to issues relating to self-concept and to the counsellor's work in helping the child to gain ego-strength through the successful resolution of developmental crises. It is important for counsellors working with children to be familiar with, and understand, Erikson's eight stages (see Erikson, 1967) because these stages illustrate the inevitable crises which children will meet. Each stage contributes to the ongoing process of mastery and achievement, making their recognition in the counselling situation a significant consideration.

Jean Piaget and Lawrence Kohlberg

Jean Piaget and Lawrence Kohlberg both contributed to the concept of children acquiring particular behaviours and skills at various stages in their development. Piaget (1962, 1971) noticed that a child interacts with both human and nonhuman objects, and the relationships which the child has with these objects allow them to become progressively more adaptive in their behaviour. As the child becomes more adaptive, they develop higher levels of cognition and start to understand their environment in an increasingly complex way. Recognition of the child's development of cognition and acquisition of moral values is important for the counsellor when selecting activities such as games with rules (see Chapter 30).

Lawrence Kohlberg (1969) was interested in the relationship between Piaget's concepts of cognitive development and the acquisition of moral values. We invite you, as counsellors, to develop your understanding of the normal developmental sequence in which children come to understand moral concepts, because a child's decision-making processes will be based on their moral understanding and expectations of particular outcomes.

John Bowlby

Bowlby (1969, 1988) placed great emphasis on a child's attachment to their mother. He believed that the child's behaviours later in life would depend on the way in which they attached to their mother. He believed that children who securely attached to their mother were happy and well adjusted; where the attachment was less secure the child would be likely to become socially and emotionally maladjusted. He also believed that children who were securely attached to their mother would find it easier to separate and develop as individuals. Clearly, Bowlby's theories were culture specific and relate only to those cultures where primary attachment to the mother is socially promoted.

Ideas about attachment are relevant when counselling children who have poor attachment histories with their mothers and consequently are unable to form healthy relationships.

Table 5.2 provides a summary of the theories of child development.

TABLE 5.2   *Theories of child development (1920–75)*

Abraham Maslow	Introduced the idea of a hierarchy of needs.
Erik Erikson	Believed that the individual has the potential to solve their own problems. Postulated eight stages of development. Believed that ego-strength was gained through successful resolution of developmental crises.
Jean Piaget	Had a concept of children obtaining particular skills and behaviours at particular developmental stages and recognized stages of cognitive development.
Lawrence Kohlberg	Looked at the relationship between Piaget's concepts of cognitive development and the acquisition of moral concepts.
John Bowlby	Introduced theory of attachment whereby a child's emotional and behavioural development was seen to be related to the way in which a child was able to attach to its mother.

1940 to 1980 – a number of humanistic/existentialist therapeutic approaches were developed

A number of humanistic/existentialist approaches for counselling adults were developed from 1940 onwards (see Corsini and Wedding, 2004). As we saw before, styles of therapy used for adults can be adapted for use with children. Important contributors to humanistic/existentialist therapies include Carl Rogers, Frederick (Fritz) Perls, Richard Bandler and John Grinder. Additionally, Virginia Axline and Violet Oaklander have made important contributions to ways of working specifically with children.

We will now consider the individual contributions of:

- Carl Rogers
- Virginia Axline
- Frederick (Fritz) Perls
- Violet Oaklander
- Richard Bandler and John Grinder.

Carl Rogers

In 1942, Carl Rogers, who was the originator of Client-Centred Counselling, published his first book entitled *Counseling and Psychotherapy*, which at the time was controversial. Whereas in psychoanalysis the emphasis had been on the therapist's analysis and inter- pretation of the client's behaviour, Rogers (1955, 1965) believed that clients had the ability to find their own solutions in an environment where there was a warm and responsive counselling relationship. Thus he saw the counselling relationship itself as a catalyst for therapeutic change and believed that it was inappropriate for the counsellor to try to make interpretations on the client's behalf.

Rogers described desirable characteristics of the counselling relationship as congruence, empathy and unconditional positive regard, with the counsellor having a non-judgemental attitude to the client and the client's behaviour. Because Rogers believed that clients had the ability to find their own solutions, he was totally non- directive and used the technique of actively listening and reflecting back to the client what the client had said. Although Rogers's work was mainly with adults, we believe that his ideas are particularly useful when helping a child to tell their story, especially in the initial stages of therapy (see Chapters 12 and 13).

Virginia Axline

Virginia Axline's work with children in some ways paralleled Rogers's work with adults. She believed in a child's ability to solve their own problems in an environment where the relationship with the therapist was both secure and safe. She used Rogers's techniques of reflective listening based on the counselling principles of empathy, warmth, acceptance and genuineness (McMahon, 1992).

In *Play Therapy* (1947) Axline outlined eight principles for non-directive play therapy:

1 The therapist must develop a warm, friendly relationship with the child.
2 The therapist accepts the child exactly as they are.
3 The therapist establishes a feeling of permissiveness in the relationship.
4 The therapist is alert to recognizing the feelings that a child is expressing and reflects those back to them so that they gain insight.
5 The therapist maintains a deep respect for a child's ability to solve their own problems.
6 The therapist does not attempt to direct the child's conversation or actions in any manner.
7 The therapist does not attempt to hurry the therapy along.
8 The therapist establishes only those limitations that are necessary to anchor the therapy to the world of reality.

We find Axline's approach very useful in the early contact with the child and in the initial stages of therapy. However, later in the therapeutic process we usually become more directive.

Frederick (Fritz) Perls

Fritz Perls was the originator of Gestalt Therapy. Although he worked with adults, Gestalt Therapy can be a very valuable tool when working with children, as demonstrated by Violet Oaklander (1988). Perls initially trained as a psychoanalyst, but then challenged many of the assumptions of psychoanalysis, particularly those which placed heavy emphasis on the client's past (Clarkson, 1989). He believed that the focus should be on the client's current experience rather than the client's past and that the client should take responsibility for that current experience rather than blaming others or their past. Perls concentrated on raising the client's awareness of current bodily sensations, emotional feelings and related thoughts. By encouraging clients to become fully in contact with their current experience in the 'here and now', he believed that he could enable clients to work through 'unfinished business', sort out their emotional confusion, achieve what he called a Gestalt or 'Ah-ha' experience, and thus feel more integrated.

Perls used, but modified, some of Freud's concepts. For example, he redefined Freud's defence mechanisms as 'neuroses'.

Whereas the psychoanalysts dealt with resistance by interpreting the client's behaviour, Perls directly confronted resistance by raising the client's awareness of it, encouraging the client to explore the experience of resisting and to explore the resistance itself.

Perls used a number of counselling or therapeutic techniques which are especially useful when working with children:

- He gave the client immediate feedback about non-verbal behaviour as it was observed during the counselling process. This drew the client's attention either to feelings that were being suppressed or to resistance.
- He invited the client to get in touch with and describe bodily sensations and relate these to emotional feelings and thoughts.
- He encouraged clients to make 'I' statements and to take responsibility for their actions.
- He challenged and confronted what he saw as neurotic behaviour, for example deflection, introjection, projection and retroflection.
- He explored polarities of the self by bringing them into awareness so that neither polarity was excluded (for example, the love–hate polarity).
- He encouraged clients to role-play different parts of themselves and to create a dialogue between those parts.
- He encouraged clients to role-play themselves and a significant other and to create a dialogue between themselves and the significant other.
- He introduced the concept of 'topdog–underdog' and encouraged clients to role-play dialogue between these parts of self.
- He helped clients to explore dreams.

Violet Oaklander

Violet Oaklander (1988) has demonstrated a particular way to combine the use of Gestalt Therapy principles and practice with the use of media when working with children. She works therapeutically with children by encouraging them to use fantasy, and believes that usually the fantasy process will be the same as the life process in the child. She therefore works indirectly in bringing out what is hidden or avoided and relies on what is essentially a projective process.

Oaklander's book *Windows to our Children* consists of a number of excerpts from case studies and will be of interest to those readers who would like to use Gestalt Therapy and fantasy. Her working model specifies techniques such as:

- encouraging the child to dialogue between two parts of the child's picture;
- helping the child to take responsibility or own what they have said about the picture;
- watching for cues in the child's body posture, facial expressions, tone of voice, breathing and silences; and
- moving away from the child's activity with the media to work directly on the child's life situations and unfinished business as these arise from use of the media. Oaklander does this by directly asking the question, 'Does this fit with your life?'

We use Oaklander's approach sometimes when we use clay, the imaginary journey, storytelling and puppets (see Chapters 24, 26, 27 and 28). However, when we use Gestalt techniques, we usually work directly rather than through the use of fantasy.

Richard Bandler and John Grinder

Bandler (1985) and Grinder were the originators of Neuro-Linguistic Programming (NLP). Although NLP was not specifically developed for children, there are some important elements of NLP that are useful when counselling children. These include:

- recognition of the different ways in which children primarily experience the world;
- the concept of reframing.

Human beings can experience the world by using one or more of three modes:

1 Seeing
2 Hearing
3 Feeling (kinaesthetically).

As counsellors, it is useful for us to match the mode which the child is currently using or uses predominantly.

By using the NLP technique of reframing (Bandler and Grinder, 1982) we can help a child to view their situation differently so that they are able to feel better and respond more adaptively. Examples of the use of reframing are given in Chapter 15.

Comparison of humanistic/existential approaches

Table 5.3 summarizes major contributions to the humanistic/existential approaches between 1940 and 1980. These approaches continue to provide an important influence on counselling strategies for children today.

TABLE 5.3   *Major contributors to humanistic/existential counselling (1940–80)*

Carl Rogers	Introduced non-directive counselling and believed that the client could find their own solutions in an environment where there was a warm and responsive counselling relationship.
Virginia Axline	Believed in the child's ability to solve their own problems in an environment where the relationship with the therapist was safe and secure. Used non-directive play therapy.
Fritz Perls	Originator of Gestalt Therapy. Emphasized the current experience of bodily sensations, emotional feelings and thoughts. Gave the client feedback, challenged, confronted, used role plays and dialoguing.
Violet Oaklander	Combined Gestalt Therapy with the use of media and fantasy.
Richard Bandler and John Grinder	Originators of Neuro-Linguistic Programming (NLP). Recognized different modes in which people (and children) experience the world. Introduced the idea of reframing.

1950 onwards – development of Behaviour Therapy

Behaviour Therapy, or Behaviour Modification as it is often called, was developed from work done by Skinner (1953) and depends on operant or instrumental conditioning. In this type of conditioning a reinforcer is either used or withdrawn in order to promote or extinguish particular behaviours. For example, imagine that a parent wants a child to tidy their room on a regular basis. Every time the child cleans the room, the parent gives the child praise (a reinforcer). As a result of receiving the praise (the reinforcing stimulus) the child is more likely to continue tidying their room (tidying the room is the conditioned response to the reinforcing stimulus, the praise).

1960 onwards – development of Cognitive Behaviour Therapy (CBT)

Three important contributors to the development of Cognitive Behaviour Therapy were Beck (1963, 1976), Ellis (1962), and Glasser (1965, 2000).

Aaron T. Beck

Research by Aaron T. Beck on depressed patients suggested that his patients' emotional states were being heavily influenced by particular thoughts which were automatically occurring to them. Consequently, he developed an approach to therapy that would enable patients to change the way that they interpreted events in their lives and to challenge the core beliefs they held about their environment, themselves and others.

Underlying this form of therapy is the assumption that emotional problems result from dysfunctional thoughts. As a consequence, using this type of therapy, the therapist's role is to help the client to replace unhelpful thoughts by more helpful ones as proposed by Albert Ellis.

Albert Ellis

Albert Ellis originated what he called Rational Emotive Therapy, which is now generally referred to as Rational Emotive Behaviour Therapy (REBT). Originally developed for use with adults, REBT is equally useful with older children from the age of about eight years. If you are interested in this style of therapy we recommend reading *Brief Rational Emotive Behaviour Therapy* written by Dryden (1995).

Ellis believed in giving direct advice and indirect interpretation of a client's behaviour. His method involved confronting and challenging what he called *irrational beliefs* and persuading the client to replace these by what he believed were *rational beliefs*. The irrational beliefs were beliefs which tended to make the client feel bad about themselves or left them with negative or uncomfortable feelings. Additionally, they resulted in behaviours which would have negative consequences. Ellis believed that irrational beliefs had been learnt from significant others.

Ellis's ideas can be useful when counselling children, although we prefer to refer to *self-destructive beliefs* rather than irrational beliefs (see Chapter 15). Challenging self-destructive beliefs can be valuable when enhancing self-esteem, when engaged in social skills training and when educating children in protective behaviours (see Part 5). When working in these areas, previously held beliefs may need to be challenged so that appropriate problem solving and decision making can occur.

William Glasser

William Glasser (1965, 2000) was the originator of Reality Therapy (later sometimes called Control Theory or Choice Therapy), which has been used widely in school settings (as well as in detention centres and penal institutions for adults). Reality Therapy involves helping the client to take responsibility for the choices they make with regard to their behaviour, and to accept the reality of the logical and natural consequences of their behaviour. In Reality Therapy the client is encouraged to take responsibility for finding ways of getting their own needs met without infringing on the rights of others.

Reality Therapy is clearly useful at the point in the counselling process where children have gained insight into their own and others' behaviours and are looking for more adaptive ways of meeting their needs by behaving differently. Reality Therapy is also useful in social skills training.

Table 5.4 summarizes the work of important pioneers in the development of Behaviour Therapy and Cognitive Behaviour Therapy. These two therapeutic approaches are in common use today as they are considered to be time limited and cost effective. As will be explained in Chapter 8 we make use of these approaches in the later stages of our work in counselling children, although we do not see them as suitable for the earlier stages of the therapeutic process.

TABLE 5.4 *Major contributors to Behaviour Therapy and Cognitive Behaviour Therapy (1950 onwards)*

B. F. Skinner	Developed Behaviour Therapy (also known as Behaviour Modification), involving the use of operant or instrumental conditioning where a reinforcer is either used or withdrawn in order to promote or extinguish particular behaviours.
Aaron T. Beck	Recognized that thoughts influence emotions. Pioneered Cognitive Behaviour Therapy by developing an approach to therapy that enabled clients to change the way they interpreted events in their lives and to challenge their core beliefs.
Albert Ellis	Originator of Rational Emotive Behaviour Therapy. Challenged irrational beliefs and encouraged clients to replace them with more rational beliefs.
William Glasser	Originator of Reality Therapy. Encouraged clients to take responsibility for finding ways of getting their own needs met without infringing on the rights of others, and to accept the reality of the logical and natural consequences of behaviour.

1980 onwards – more recent ideas for counselling children were proposed

Perhaps the most significant more recent approach concerned with counselling children has been that of Richard Sloves and Karen Belinger-Peterlin, who introduced and developed time-limited play therapy (1986). Another important contribution to counselling is the narrative therapy approach developed by Michael White and David Epston (1990). Although narrative therapy was not specifically developed for use with children, it has been found to be of significant use when working with them.

Time-limited play therapy

A significant development in the 1980s was the introduction of ideas about brief therapy. From that time onwards and particularly in society today there is pressure on counsellors to be accountable by using cost-effective methods (Cade, 1993). De Shazer (1985) contributed to brief therapy by placing the emphasis on the process of finding solutions rather than focusing on the origins of the problem (see Walter and Peller, 1992; Zeig and Gilligan, 1990). At the same time there were other workers such as Davanloo, Malan, Mann, Goldmann, Sifneos, Strupp and Binder, with a psychodynamic background, who embraced the idea of brief therapy without relinquishing their psychodynamic orientation (Lazarus and Fay, 1990).

Time-limited play therapy (Sloves and Belinger-Peterlin, 1994) was developed as an approach for working with children, using ideas from brief therapy with a psychodynamic orientation.

The approach involves making a brief assessment of the child's issues. The therapist then selects a central theme and the therapeutic work is limited to this theme. The work with the child focuses on empowerment, adaptation and strengthening the ego. It focuses on the future rather than the past. However, the central theme will have been influenced by the child's past. Generally, individual work with the child is limited to 12 sessions. This form of therapy is both directive and interpretive.

Sloves and Belinger–Peterlin (in Schaefer and O'Connor, 1994) made it clear that time-limited play therapy is effective for some children and not useful for others. It is most effective for children with recent post-traumatic stress disorder, adjustment disorders, and for children who have lost a parent due to a chronic medical condition (Christ et al., 1991).

It is interesting to note that in a similar way, many years ago, Millman and Schaefer (1977) pointed out that traditional psychodynamic therapy had proved most effective for intelligent, moderately disturbed children, whereas more structured techniques had proven more cost effective with children who had situation-specific difficulties or traumatic reactions.

The literature suggests that there is not one preferred way of working which is appropriate for all children. Certainly, in our own work we have noticed that effective work with children depends on being flexible enough to select a method of working which is specifically suitable for a particular child and relevant for that child's issues. Such an approach was originally proposed by Millman and Schaefer (1977) and called a 'prescriptive approach'.

In their 1983 book, Schaefer and O'Connor describe the prescriptive approach. This emphasizes the therapist's responsibility for determining the most appropriate therapeutic technique for each particular child. The therapist is therefore expected to prescribe an approach that suits the child and is most relevant for the treatment of the presenting problem.

Even though we agree that therapists need to be flexible in working in a way that will suit the individual child and is relevant for treating the presenting problem, we ourselves do not use a prescriptive model. We generally use an integrative model that we have developed and describe in Chapter 8. This model makes use of ideas from a number of differing therapeutic approaches and can easily be varied to suit the needs of a particular child.

Narrative therapy

Narrative therapy makes strong use of language to help the child. Narrative therapy is based on the concept of storying. Stories are told about how the child's problem has influenced their life and retold by creating an alternative story in which the problem does not dominate the child's life.

Narrative therapy practice is primarily interested in separating the child's identity from the problem. This is based on the premise that the problem is the problem, as opposed to the child being seen as the problem. Externalization therefore is the foundation from which many narrative conversations are built. This requires a particular shift in the use of language. Often, externalizing conversations involve tracing the influence of the problem in the child's life over time and how the problem has disempowered the child by limiting their ability to see things in a different light. The counsellor helps the child to change by deconstructing old stories and reconstructing preferred stories about themselves and their life (Morgan, 2000; Parry and Doan, 1994; White and Epston, 1990). To help the child to develop a new story, the counsellor and child search for times when the problem has not influenced the child or the child's life and focuses on the different ways the child thought, felt and behaved. These exceptions to the problem story help the child create a new and preferred story. As a new and preferred story begins to emerge it is important to assist the child to hold on to, or stay connected to, the new story. One way of 'thickening' the alternative story involves finding witnesses who will act as an audience to the new story and can link their lives in some way to the new story. The audience may consist of people present or absent from the counselling session, real or imaginary, or from the child's past or present.

Fundamental differences in counselling styles

In our discussion of the historical background to counselling children we have only included reference to those people whose work, in our opinion, has significantly influenced the practice of counselling children. Many other people have extended either the ideas or the working methods of the people we have mentioned, or have introduced specific ideas related to the use of one particular medium; we have not mentioned these people because this is primarily a practical text and we want to provide only an overview of the theoretical background to counselling children.

The historical background provides the context into which recent ideas fit. Consequently, in considering recent ideas, we will summarize the historical background in two ways. Readers may wish to review Tables 5.1–5.4 to gain an overview of the historical background before considering Figure 5.1.

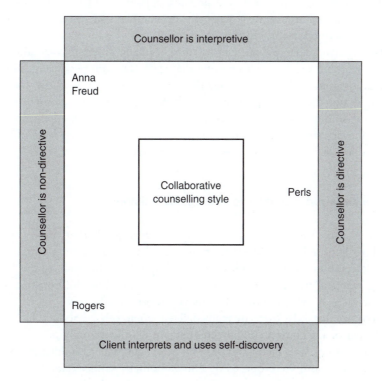

FIGURE 5.1 *Map of different counselling approaches*

Figure 5.1 provides a map which defines parameters within which counsellors work in being either directive or non-directive and interpretive or non-interpretive. The central part of the map relates to counsellors who do not take a strongly polarized position in relation to these variables but have a collaborative counselling style. Issues about being directive or non-directive and interpretive or non-interpretive have been, and are, contentious among counsellors who work with children. Some counsellors, in both the past and present, have taken very polarized positions with regard to these parameters. Counsellors who take a polarized position tend to use the approach of their choice within all of their counselling sessions.

We wonder whether you will agree with the positions which we have allocated in Figure 5.1 to the three counsellors we have shown on the map. We have placed Anna Freud in the top left-hand corner because she was non-directive and interpretive. We have placed Rogers in the bottom left-hand corner because he was non-directive and left the interpretation to the client. However, we found it difficult to place Perls. We placed him towards the right-hand side of the map because when he was working with clients he was very much in control of the process of the therapy, was directly confronting, and deliberately tried to frustrate the client. However, some Gestalt therapists would argue that it was the client's emerging experiences which controlled the direction of the process and would claim that Perls should therefore be further to the left. Similarly, there could be argument about where to place Perls on the vertical *interpretive* versus *self-discovery* continuum. It can be difficult to place some individuals in precise positions, but we think that the map is useful for bringing into focus differences in the theoretical positions and practical approaches of the therapists we have mentioned. You, the reader, may wish to see whether you can position the other counsellors described in this chapter on the map.

We believe that valuable work can be done in many different ways and that your individual working style needs to be one that appeals to you personally. Additionally, it is useful for us as counsellors to vary the ways in which we work to suit the individual child and the child's presenting problems. Consequently, sometimes we are directive and sometimes non-directive, and although generally we prefer the child to use self-discovery, sometimes we are interpretive. We believe that a level of flexibility is required in order to meet the needs of the individual child.

Is there a preferred approach to counselling children?

Having read this chapter you are probably wondering whether there is one 'best' approach to counselling children. Certainly, we have a preferred approach, which we will describe in Chapter 8. However, we hope that after reading this book and receiving practical training and supervision in counselling children that you will decide for yourself which approach suits you most comfortably.

We recognize that today there are many different points of view about which approach to use. We personally know a child psychotherapist who works only in a psychoanalytic way similar to that of Anna Freud, another who uses cognitive behavioural methods almost exclusively – such as those proposed by Ellis and others – and yet another who works predominantly in a Gestalt Therapy way but without Oaklander's emphasis on fantasy. Moreover, it seems to us that many of the ideas from the methods discussed in our review of the historical background to counselling children are still in use.

We ourselves have an integrative approach to our work as explained in Chapter 8. In that chapter we describe the model we have developed and use ourselves, called 'Sequentially Planned Integrative Counselling for Children' (the SPICC model). Using this model we incorporate those ideas which fit for us as proposed by the pioneers previously mentioned and from the developmental theorists. We make considerable use of the humanistic therapies, and strategies taken from Cognitive Behaviour Therapy and Behaviour Therapy, as well as strategies taken from some more recent approaches.

We would like to stress that we believe that, regardless of the approach used, the most important part of any counselling process with a child is to help the child to tell their story, as described in Chapter 13. Usually in order to help a child do this we need to make use of suitable media as explained in Part 4. While recognizing that each counsellor will work in their own individual way using their own preferred model, we hope that readers will find that they are able to adapt and make use of some of the methods we have described which will suit their work with individual children.

Although we place a high value on the importance of providing an opportunity for the child to tell their story in a safe environment where they can talk freely, we also believe that it is often useful to combine individual work with a child with family therapy or with counselling work involving the parents, as described in Chapter 9.

KEY POINTS

Early pioneers

- Important early contributors to psychotherapy theory and practice were Sigmund Freud, Carl Jung and Alfred Adler.
- Particular theoretical and practical approaches to counselling children were developed by early pioneers including Anna Freud, Melanie Klein, Donald Winnicott and Margaret Lowenfeld.
- Major child development theories were proposed by Abraham Maslow, Eric Erikson, Jean Piaget and Lawrence Kolberg, and John Bowlby.

Existential/humanistic counselling

- Major contributors to existentialist/humanistic counselling were Carl Rogers, originator of Client-Centred Counselling; Fritz Perls, originator of Gestalt Therapy; and Richard Bandler and John Grinder, originators of Neuro-Linguistic Programming (NLP). These approaches, although developed primarily for adults, can also be adapted for use with children.
- Important contributors to the practice of counselling children were Virginia Axline who believed in a child's ability to solve their own problems in an

(Continued)

(Continued)

environment where the relationship with the therapist was both secure and safe, and Violet Oaklander who combined the use of Gestalt Therapy principles and practice with the use of media when working with children.

Behaviour Therapy

- B.F. Skinner developed the idea of operant conditioning in which a reinforcer is used to promote or extinguish particular behaviours.

Cognitive Behaviour Therapy (CBT)

- Aaron Beck recognized that he could help people change their emotional state by making changes to their thinking.
- Albert Ellis developed Rational Emotive Behaviour Therapy (REBT), which involves challenging a client to replace irrational beliefs by more rational beliefs.
- William Glasser developed Reality Therapy in which the client has choice about their behaviour but needs to accept the reality of the consequences of that behaviour.

More recent approaches

- Richard Sloves and Karen Berlinger-Peterlin introduced time-limited play therapy, where the emphasis was on finding solutions rather than focusing on the origins of the problem.
- Michael White and David Epston were the originators of narrative therapy, which involves separating the problem from the client, and helping the client to deconstruct old unhelpful stories and reconstruct new preferred stories.

Styles of counselling

- Important fundamental differences in style relate to whether a counsellor is directive or non-directive, and interpretive or non-interpretive.
- The Sequentially Planned Integrative Counselling for Children model (the SPICC model, see Chapter 8) sequentially uses ideas from a variety of therapeutic approaches in a way that is designed to produce the most effective and long-lasting change.

6

The Process of Child Therapy

Our intention is that we, as counsellors, will engage our child clients in a therapeutic process by using counselling skills in conjunction with media and other strategies. When we talk about this therapeutic process we are really referring to a number of differing processes which are brought into play in order to support therapeutic change.

The flow chart in Figure 6.1 gives a simplified overview of the total process of child therapy. Each frame on the chart involves a specific process; for example, *Contracting with parent/s* is a process in itself.

Under the facilitation of a skilled counsellor, the processes described in each frame of Figure 6.1 will interact to form an integrated therapeutic process. Because each case is different, not all of the processes shown will be used for every child. Some may happen concurrently with others, and some may be repeated during the course of therapy. In this section we will describe the processes listed in Figure 6.1 in the sequence shown.

The initial assessment phase

The initial assessment phase is a time of preparation for therapy. During this phase, information is gathered about the child and the child's problems. This information enables the counsellor to hypothesize about what might be happening for the child. With a hypothesis in mind, suitable media can be selected to enable the counsellor to engage with the child and to commence working therapeutically. The initial assessment phase also includes meeting with and contracting with the parents.

Receiving referral information

In order for therapeutic work to be maximally useful and effective, the counsellor needs to have as much information as possible about the child, including the child's behaviour, emotional state, personality, the child's history, cultural background and the environment within which the child lives.

Initial information comes at the time of referral, from the referral source. Sometimes the person making the referral will be a parent, but at other times referrals may come from medical practitioners, schools, other professionals, statutory bodies and other

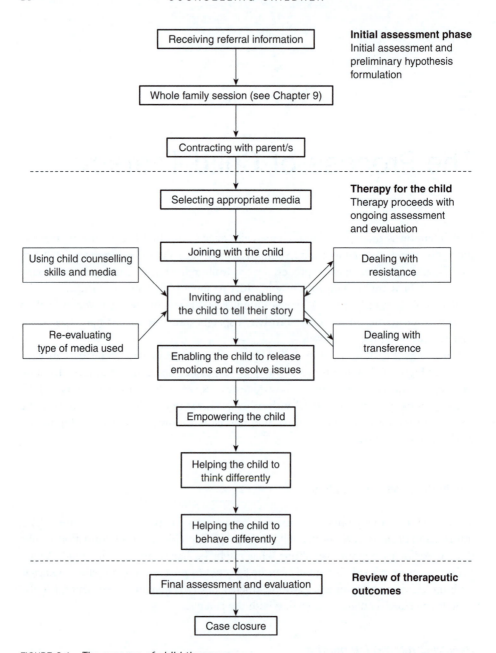

FIGURE 6.1   *The process of child therapy*

sources. Such information can be invaluable in helping the counsellor to understand the child.

It must be remembered that the information given by a referral source may be inaccurate and distorted because of the referrer's own agenda. However, such information is still useful because it is someone else's perception of what is happening. For example, we may have been told that a child was deliberately disobedient. Later, we may discover that the child has a high-order language problem and consequently has difficulty understanding instructions, but is not generally being deliberately disobedient. Although the first piece of information was factually incorrect, it would have helped us to understand what was happening in the child's life. It can therefore be valuable to collect several different opinions with regard to a child's behaviour and problems, but to remember that these are opinions which may not be factually correct.

In the initial assessment phase, wherever possible, we prefer to meet with the whole family as described in Chapter 9. By doing this we gain important information about the environment in which the child is living. Where it is not possible for the whole family to attend, we prefer to meet with the parent/s (or other care-givers) to get their picture of the situation and to contract with them with regard to therapy.

Contracting with parents (or care-givers)

Before beginning to work individually with the child, we find that it is generally useful to consult with the parents without the child being present. This enables the parents to talk freely and openly without being inhibited by the child. During this interview we record a detailed history, the parents' understanding of the problem and responses to the problem. We also contract with the parents with regard to the therapeutic process.

Parents of emotionally disturbed children are likely to be anxious and concerned about their children. They may also be worried about what may happen if their child is to enter into a counselling relationship with someone who is not personally known to them. It can be quite threatening for parents to know that their child will be talking to a stranger about personal and possibly family matters. Additionally, some parents feel inadequate in their parental role and may be worried about the possibility that the counsellor will blame them for their child's problems.

Because of the likelihood of parental anxiety, it is essential that parents be given the opportunity to talk to the counsellor, not only about the child but also about the counselling process and at some level about their own anxieties. During interviews with parents, it is important for the counsellor to be an empathic listener who is seen to value both the parents and the information they provide. Although we believe that it is appropriate for a counsellor to provide the opportunity for parents to talk about their anxieties in general terms, we prefer to try to avoid the situation where the child's counsellor becomes counsellor for the parents also. Although this is sometimes unavoidable, when the same counsellor acts as counsellor for both the child and the parents it may be difficult for the child to join with, and to trust, the counsellor. We will discuss this situation more fully in Chapter 9.

We think that it is important for parents to understand that it is preferable for the child–counsellor relationship to be exclusive. Therefore, we tell parents that for counselling to be effective their child will need to feel free to talk openly and confidentially with us. We also say that we realize that it may be uncomfortable for them not to be kept fully informed of what their child is telling us. However, we assure them that we will keep them informed with regard to the overall process. Further, we tell them that if information emerges which they, as parents, have a right to know, we will talk to the child about the necessity of sharing this with them.

When all of the available information has been gathered in the initial assessment phase, the counsellor is in a position to formulate a preliminary hypothesis with regard to the child's presenting issues. This hypothesis will be based not only on the information which has been received about the child from the referral sources and parents, but also on the counsellor's own understanding of child psychology and behaviour in the context of the relevant environmental climate. Thus, the hypothesis also takes account of racial, ethnic, cultural and religious differences in beliefs, attitudes, expectations and behaviours. Readers may wish to refer to *Theories of Counseling and Psychotherapy: a Multi-cultural Perspective* by Ivey et al. (2001) if they wish to explore the impact of cultural issues when counselling. We also touch on cultural issues in Chapter 3.

With a hypothesis in mind, therapy for the child can commence.

Therapy for the child

Selecting the appropriate media

Before meeting with the child, the first step for the counsellor is to make a decision on the most appropriate media to be used. This selection will be based on age, gender, personal characteristics and type of emotional problem. For details of the selection process see Chapter 21.

Joining with the child

Most children are brought to therapy sessions by their parents, and it is important to make the parents feel welcome and valued when they arrive. We believe that providing a friendly and hospitable environment is important, not only for joining with the child but also as part of the therapeutic process.

We usually offer parents a cup of tea or coffee and the children a cold drink when they arrive for an appointment. This is particularly appreciated by those children who come to consult with us after a busy day at school.

Children have their own unique and special personalities and needs. Some may be difficult to engage for a variety of reasons. They may have had their trust in adults betrayed, they may be hostile, they may have been frightened into silence, or they may act up and behave inappropriately. Very young children may lack the language to communicate effectively. Therefore, the process of joining is tailored to meet the individual requirements of each child. There are, however, some basic methods of joining which can be useful generally.

When the child arrives for the first time, we start to join with the child in the waiting room. However, we start this process by joining with the parents first. By doing this we allow the child to feel safe and comfortable and in the care and control of the parents. The child observes the way that we relate to the parents and is thus enabled to gain a level of trust and confidence in us. Additionally, the child will be encouraged by the parents and thus given permission to engage in a relationship with us. This process also allows the parents to experience the importance of their own role in the counselling process.

Asking the parents to clarify the reasons for bringing the child to counselling, in the child's presence, is an important part of the joining process. By doing this the child and the counsellor have the same information about the reason for the child coming to counselling, and both know that the other knows what the reason is. This minimizes the possibility of misunderstandings or misconceptions.

In the process of joining, we provide the child with choices and options about how the first therapy session should begin and proceed. Initially it might be useful to allow the child to explore the counselling environment and to let them know where their mother or father will be waiting. This approach is particularly useful if a child's anxiety levels are high.

Some children have difficulty in separating from their parents and engaging with a counsellor. When we encounter such a child, we invite the child and parents into the play therapy room. We then invite the child to explore this room while we talk with the parents or care-givers in the child's presence. During this process we intermittently engage the child in some of the conversation, or invite the child to tell us about things of interest in the room. Occasionally we may invite the child to play with their parents in the play room until they feel safe there.

With some children joining is easy. This is particularly so with children who do not have appropriate boundaries or are very needy. Such children may join without caution and may be inappropriately compliant. Taking note of the child's joining behaviour is useful for assessment purposes.

It is essential during the joining process to help the child to understand the nature of the child–counsellor relationship. Without this understanding the child would not know what to expect of the counsellor and would not know what the counsellor's expectations of the relationship were, and joining would be limited.

As children grow and develop they come into contact with, and are influenced by, many adults. Each of these adults has individual characteristics or attributes. Children notice these and learn from them. For example, school-teachers may be perceived by children as having authority: they direct children in carrying out tasks, and those tasks generally involve learning. Shopkeepers have a different type of authority, which is confined to behaviour in their shops. Aunts and uncles have authority which may not have clear boundaries, because while they don't have full responsibility for the management of the behaviours of their nieces and nephews, they may have some level of responsibility. Parents have overall authority across all areas of children's lives. Each child comes from a unique environment, and it is from their environment that the child learns the social rules for interacting with differing categories of people, such as the teacher, the shopkeeper, the aunt and uncle and, most importantly, the parent. The social rules which a child uses with any particular person will depend on the child's expectations of the relationship with that person. Hence it is essential for a child who is being counselled to have an understanding of the nature of the child–counsellor relationship, so that they know what the expectations are; otherwise they will not feel secure and comfortable in the relationship. To support this process we lay down guide-lines or ground rules at the beginning of the therapeutic relationship so that the child is clear about what is permissible and what is not. The rules we use were described in Chapter 2.

Explanation of the ground rules lets the child know what is not permissible during therapy. The child also needs to know that it *is* permissible for them to express them-selves in whatever way feels comfortable within the constraints of the rules, and that it is permissible to disclose and to talk about issues which are private and confidential.

The child's understanding of the relationship will develop further as the relation-ship is experienced. The child will learn by testing the relationship and accepting the consequences of their behaviour within the context of the relationship.

In summary, joining is primarily about creating a relationship which meets the child's needs in the therapeutic environment so that the child will feel comfortable enough to engage usefully in the therapeutic process. Once the child is observed to be feeling comfortable in the relationship, then they can be invited to tell their story.

Inviting the child to tell their story

Counselling skills using verbal communication alone will usually be quite useless with children, especially when children have poor communication skills, high levels of emotional distress and acute psychological disturbance. Often it will not even be possible for a counsellor to join with a child just by talking. However, effective joining followed by effective therapy is usually possible if the child is invited to tell their story through the use of play or suitable media.

Care needs to be taken in deciding what materials to make available for play and in selecting media. Two considerations when selecting the play environment and the media are the developmental age of the child and usefulness in enabling the child to tell their story. These are selected so that they provide the child with an opportunity to explore relevant emotional and psychological issues. For details about deciding what materials to make available for play, see Chapter 19, and for information about the selection of suitable media, see Chapter 21. After selection of media and play, the child can be invited to tell their story.

Inviting the child to tell their story, and enabling the child to tell that story, are the most central and effective components of any child psychotherapy process.

Through telling their story, the child has the opportunity to clarify and gain a cognitive understanding of events and issues. Additionally, they can ventilate painful feelings and gain mastery over anxieties and other emotional disturbances by active rather than passive means. The child becomes personally engaged and involved in the therapeutic experience with the consequence that intrapersonal psychological change is almost certain to occur.

It sounds very straightforward, doesn't it? We just invite the child to tell their story and therapy has begun. Unfortunately, in reality it is not always so simple and straightforward. Difficulties in the counselling process due to factors directly related to the nature of the child's problems can arise. If these are not carefully considered and confronted, then they may undermine the therapeutic process.

Disturbed children will often behave inconsistently and have difficulty in recognizing and/or communicating their feelings. Some have poor impulse control and a decreased attention span. Others exhibit pathological defence mechanisms. The therapeutic process may be blocked by one or more of these problems, and it will be difficult to engage the child in therapy. However, with appropriate use of child counselling skills, as described in Part 3, these blocks can usually be overcome.

When inviting the child to tell their story, the issue of trust is central. Without an adequate level of trust, the growth of the therapeutic relationship will be inhibited. Sometimes, because of the importance of this issue, we need to go very slowly at first. In initial sessions we might allow time for a young child to play freely, or we might engage an older child in a game to help the child to feel comfortable and safe in the environment. In other cases specific media may be used for this purpose.

Once a trusting relationship has been established in an environment which includes appropriate media, then the child can be invited to tell their story. In inviting the child, the counsellor doesn't attempt to hurry the therapeutic process but allows the child opportunities to express themselves and to explore feelings and issues which may be troubling for them. The counsellor doesn't interrogate, but instead invites the child to disclose what they wish.

There are some counsellor behaviours which are likely to inhibit a child. These include being restricted by time, or space, or by the media being used. The novice counsellor may be impatient and may want to move too quickly for the child. Sometimes, inexperienced counsellors who are starting to feel frustrated by initially slow progress fall into the trap of using questioning as a way of trying to move the process along. Unfortunately, unless questioning is used sparingly, the child may shut down communication for fear of intrusion by the counsellor into private and sensitive material.

Enabling the child to tell their story

We have already talked about the importance of trust, of creating a suitable environment, of the use of play and/or of media, in inviting the child to tell their story. However, in order to *enable* the child to tell their story we can additionally make use of appropriate child-counselling skills. For the therapeutic process to be effective, the counsellor creates and/or provides the following:

- a trusting relationship;
- appropriate media;
- facilities and opportunities for free and/or meaningful play; and
- the use of appropriate child-counselling skills.

By using appropriate child-counselling skills the counsellor enables the child to tell their story and accompanies the child as they go on a journey of exploration, revealing their story and in the process resolving issues. During this journey of exploration the counsellor will regularly re-evaluate the type of media used and make changes if appropriate. The counsellor may also need to deal with both *resistance* and *transference* (see Figure 6.1).

The issue of transference was initially discussed in Chapter 2. Discussion of approaches to use in dealing with transference and resistance are included in Chapter 14.

Resolution of issues

Sometimes a child will find that the telling of their story is in itself effective in reducing emotional pain and in leading to the spontaneous resolution of issues. Often, though, support from the counsellor is required to help the child to work through particular issues so that they are no longer troublesome. This may be done through play and/or through the use of counselling skills, and sometimes through educational input. When the issues are properly resolved the child will be enabled to relate to others more comfortably, to be freer of anxiety, and to live more adaptively in their social and emotional environment.

Empowerment of the child

Although in Figure 6.1 empowerment follows resolution of issues, it may have occurred spontaneously while the child told their story. Enabling the child to tell their story in an environment where the child is accepted and believed, with understanding and without judgement, is an important part of the empowerment process.

Empowerment involves gaining mastery over issues so that the child will no longer be excessively troubled by thoughts and memories which create anxiety and interfere with normal adaptive relationships. Consequently, the child will start to have a different view of self so that self-esteem and social relationships are enhanced. Thus the child is able to integrate with more comfort into their social and emotional world. The use of Narrative Therapy to promote empowerment is discussed in Chapter 8.

Helping the child to think and behave differently

As will be discussed in Chapter 17, it is not sufficient to terminate the counselling of a child after the resolution of issues if some of the child's thoughts and behaviours continue to be unhelpful. In order to complete the counselling process, the counsellor has a responsibility to help the child to learn new ways of thinking and behaving so that they can function adaptively. If this does not happen the child's thinking patterns and behaviours are likely to result in further distress, with the child needing counselling again in future to deal with this.

Review of therapeutic outcomes

Final assessment and evaluation

Final assessment and evaluation is best done in collaboration with the child and family (see Chapter 9). The assessment is to confirm that further work is not required or appropriate at the time. Evaluation is required to assess the effectiveness of the work which has been done and to make recommendations.

Case closure

After the final assessment and evaluation, the counselling process can be terminated and the case can be closed. Counselling skills for termination are discussed in Chapter 17.

In describing the process of child therapy, our greatest emphasis has been on inviting and enabling the child to tell their story. If this becomes central to the process, then we believe that the possibility of therapeutic change occurring is maximized. In order to engage the child in the telling of their story, we use not only child-counselling skills but also play and/or media.

In the next chapter we will look at other processes which also occur. These are the internal processes of therapeutic change that occur within the child.

KEY POINTS

- Inviting and enabling the child to tell their story are essential if the child is to benefit from counselling.
- Referral information is generally useful although it cannot be assumed to be accurate.
- It is essential to join and contract with parents so that they are fully informed and comfortable with the counselling process.
- The child needs to be aware of the reason they are being brought for counselling.
- The counsellor first joins with the child before inviting them to tell their story.
- Considerations when selecting media are age, gender, personal characteristics and the type of emotional problem.
- After addressing emotional issues and attending to the empowerment of the child it is usually necessary to use strategies to help the child to think and behave differently.

7

The Child's Internal Processes of Therapeutic Change

In the previous chapter we dealt with the processes which the counsellor sets in motion and facilitates in order to bring about therapeutic change in a child. In a sense these are external to the child because they involve action by the counsellor, not by the child. As those processes occur, there will simultaneously be processes occurring within the child. These directly result in the child experiencing therapeutic change. These internal processes either occur spontaneously in the counselling environment or they occur in direct response to the counsellor's interventions.

We will describe the child's internal processes by using a model which we have developed. We call this model the Spiral of Therapeutic Change. It is shown in Figure 7.1.

Because each child is different, and because human behaviour is complex, the Spiral of Therapeutic Change needs to be seen as offering only a general understanding of the types of processes which are likely to occur within the child; it is not intended to be an exact model of how therapeutic change occurs in all children.

We will now discuss each step in the process on the Spiral of Therapeutic Change, starting with 'Child is emotionally disturbed'. To illustrate our discussion we will use a fictional but typical case study. To protect the confidentiality of our clients we have combined information from several cases and have changed all identifying information.

A case study – background information

Amy is 11 years old, but immature for her age, and lives alone with her mother. She was brought by her mother for counselling help because she was depressed, anxious, over-sensitive and was getting into conflict at school. She cried easily, wasn't concentrating and was disobedient.

During an initial interview with her mother, it emerged that Amy was the result of an unplanned and unwanted pregnancy and at first Amy was rejected by her mother. However, for the last few years Amy had been treated like an adult companion to, and confidante for, her mother. It also became clear that Amy's mother had unrealistically

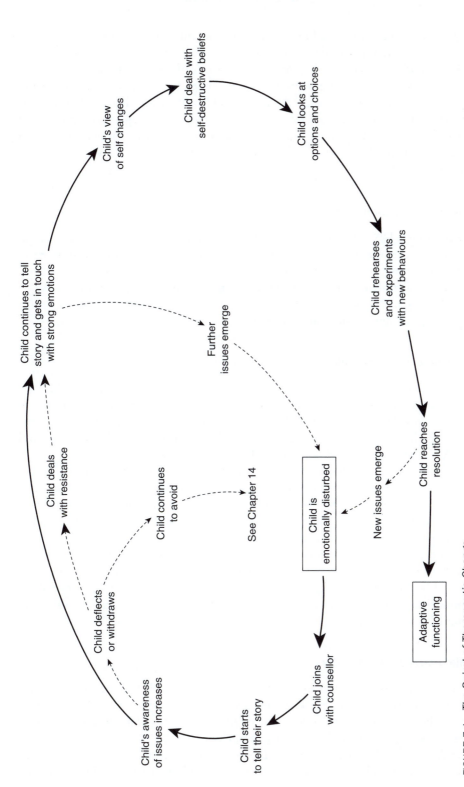

FIGURE 7.1 *The Spiral of Therapeutic Change*

high expectations with regard to Amy's behaviour and emotional maturity. When 18 months old, Amy was sexually interfered with by her maternal grandfather.

In the initial interview, it also emerged that Amy's mother had been neglected and physically abused by her own mother, sexually abused by her father, and subjected to rigid and strict rules in her family. Although Amy's mother was abused by her parents, her brothers and sister were not subjected to the same level of abuse. Amy's mother had decided that she did not want to parent Amy in the same way that her mother had parented her, and was making a determined effort to provide Amy with a better quality of life.

Child is emotionally disturbed

Children are unlikely to be brought for counselling unless they have emotional problems. However, sometimes referral sources may not recognize that the child is emotionally disturbed but may instead see the child as having behavioural problems.

In our case study, the mother recognized the behavioural problems, that is, the child's lack of concentration and disobedience, and also recognized the presence of emotional problems, including anxiety and depression.

Child joins with counsellor

The relationship between a child and counsellor is in some ways reciprocal, although in other ways it is unequal. It is reciprocal with regard to joining. If a child is to join with a counsellor, then the counsellor must join with the child. If joining is successful, then the child will experience a level of comfort with the counsellor, and this will enable the therapeutic process to proceed.

Initially Amy was encouraged in free play. The counsellor joined with her as the child played with the doll's house and the puppets. Through observation of Amy's free play and through interaction with Amy, the counsellor was able to discover Amy's strengths. She had a rich imagination, was good at abstract thinking, was friendly, but at times was over-compliant and eager to please.

At first, Amy expected to be reprimanded by the counsellor for the misbehaviour that her mother had described, and she agreed with her mother's negative descriptions of her behaviour. When the counsellor explained the nature and purpose of the counselling relationship, Amy was able to feel more comfortable and to allow the counsellor to join with her.

Child starts to tell her story

Given an appropriate environment, with suitable media available and with the counsellor using the required counselling skills, the child will become spontaneously involved in telling their story. This may be done in a direct way with the child openly recounting their story, or it may be done indirectly through play.

In Amy's case, the counsellor chose to use the miniature animals (see Chapter 22). The counsellor's choice was based on the assumption that the child's emotional problems might be related to her relationship with her mother. This assumption arose from the counsellor noting that the child had at first been unwanted and rejected by her mother, that the mother had experienced an unsatisfactory relationship with her own mother, and that Amy's impression was that she was being brought by her mother to counselling to be reprimanded for her misbehaviour.

By using the miniature animals, Amy was able to projectively demonstrate her relationship with her mother, her grandmother and her grandfather. She then moved on to discuss these relationships more directly. During this discussion her story started to unfold and it emerged that:

1   Amy believed that her mother continually pushed her away.
2   Amy was worried by her grandfather but was also curious about him.
3   Amy believed that she could only get near to her grandmother when she was good.

Child's awareness of issues increases

As a child recounts their story, their awareness of strong emotions and/or painful issues will be intensified. As a consequence the child may either continue to tell their story, thus enabling the therapeutic process to move forward, or may deflect or withdraw.

Work with Amy continued, using the puppets to role-play a fantasy story about a princess and fairies (see Chapter 28). As Amy developed the story, the princess took a mothering role. From this story, it emerged that Amy wanted a closer relationship with her mother based on positive warm interactions, with a lot of physical touching and cuddling. However, she realized that her mother did not respond to her attempts to achieve such a relationship. She also became aware that the times when her mother did respond to her was when she was naughty, or when she was being victimized by other children. This is understandable, because Amy's mother was responding to her own needs to parent in a particular way.

Amy also became aware of the fact that she couldn't satisfy her curiosity about her grandfather because her mother wouldn't let her get near to him. Her mother wanted to protect her from the threat of sexual abuse. She started to recognize that her grandmother and mother would fight whenever she got close to her grandmother, and that she felt to blame for their fighting. She also realized that she sometimes deliberately disobeyed her grandmother to distance herself from her grandmother and get closer to her mother.

Child deflects or withdraws

When children are dealing with strong emotions or difficult issues they may naturally deflect away from dealing with their pain or withdraw into silence. In their daily lives this behaviour may, at times, be adaptive because it helps the child to cope. Such avoidance is a normal part of the therapeutic process and is referred to as the child's resistance. When resistance occurs the counsellor is careful not to pressure the child to continue with the story, but instead helps the child to deal with the resistance in a way which is acceptable to the child.

As Amy's awareness of the importance of her relationship with her mother started to increase, she began to avoid talking about that relationship. If the relationship was mentioned she would move away and engage in some unrelated activity such as drawing on the whiteboard in order to avoid facing her pain.

Child deals with resistance

The nature of resistance and ways to deal with it are discussed in Chapter 14. The problem for a child in dealing with resistance revolves around the choice about whether to continue to tell their story or whether to avoid telling that story. While resistance is driven by subconscious processes, at a conscious level questions in the child's thoughts might include, 'Is it safe for me to talk about these issues?' and 'What might happen if I do?' Alternatively the child might be thinking, 'This is too scary', or 'This is too painful for me to talk about'. If appropriate counselling skills are used, the child may be enabled to continue talking about their troubling issues. However, it is equally possible that the child will continue to avoid doing this. If this happens, then the counsellor may feel they need to directly address the resistance as explained in Chapter 14. Additionally, it may be helpful for the counsellor to return to an earlier point in the process by creating a new opportunity for the child to tell their story in a different way. This new start can often be made easier if the media is changed so that the child's interest in the counselling process is aroused in a different way.

When Amy started to deflect and avoid painful issues the counsellor drew Amy's attention to her deflection by saying, 'It seems to me that you find it very hard to talk about the way you feel about your mother. I've noticed that when we start talking about her you stop talking and do something different, like drawing on the white-board. I'm wondering what it would be like for you if you did start to talk about your mother?' Amy responded by saying that she didn't know. The counsellor continued, 'I'm wondering whether it would be a bit scary for you to talk about your mother?' Amy agreed that it would and it was clear that she wasn't ready to continue talking about her relationship with her mother. The counsellor then made a decision to work differently in order to enable the child to continue telling her story but in a different way. The counsellor invited the child to use clay (see Chapter 24). Once the child was familiar with using the clay, the counsellor invited the child to make a clay baby. Amy was then encouraged to experience nurturing and separating from her creation (the baby). She was invited to put the baby in a part of the room remote from herself and encouraged to explore what that felt like. This activity enabled her to move into the next stage of the Spiral of Therapeutic Change.

Child continues to tell story and gets in touch with strong emotions

If the outcome of dealing with resistance is positive, then the child will continue to tell their story and is likely to get in touch with strong emotions. Having done this, the child might continue around the spiral or might return to the beginning in order to address new issues.

When Amy had moved the baby away from herself, she started to experience what it was like to be close and to be separate from her baby. The counsellor then encouraged Amy to dialogue with the baby and during this dialogue to reverse roles so that, as the baby, she could say things to 'the mother figure' (Amy). While role-playing the baby she was able to express her fear to the 'mother' that the 'mother' did not love her and might never love her. She expressed her fear that her mother might abandon her and her concern about who would look after her then. While participating in the dialogue between the baby and mother, Amy started to talk about her own personal experiences with her own mother, to cry and to get in touch with her own sadness. She continued by talking about her experience of being rejected by her mother and her fear of being abandoned.

Amy explored possible reasons why her mother might not like her. She believed that her mother did not love her because she wasn't a good child and wasn't lovable.

Child's view of self changes

Because of the messages that Amy had internalized from her mother and grandmother, Amy believed that she was not a good child and was not lovable. Before she could move on to make choices about the future which would not be undermined by low self-esteem and feelings of incompetence, Amy needed to feel good about herself. The counsellor invited Amy to think about and draw herself metaphorically as a fruit tree growing outside. By exploring the nature, strengths, activity, resilience and so on of the tree, Amy was invited to make comparisons between herself and the tree and produce an alternative and preferred image of herself. She was invited to remember instances where she provided 'shelter' and 'fruit' for other people and instances where she was able to 'weather the storm'. Gradually Amy built a picture of herself that was based on real events in her life but which was different from the image she had acquired. This preferred image of herself enabled her to have confidence in her ability to build on her strengths and make decisions and choices for the future.

Child deals with self-destructive beliefs

Once the child has changed their picture of themselves it is likely that the new picture will lead them into questioning some of their beliefs. At this point the counsellor can support the child to recognize those beliefs which are self-destructive and to replace them with more adaptive beliefs.

Amy's self-confidence improved but she continued to believe that her mother and grandmother saw her as a bad child and that this could be why she experienced feelings of rejection from them. This belief was clearly self-destructive and was reinforced by Amy's recognition that she didn't have friends at school and that her relationship with her grandmother was dependent on her being good. The counsellor encouraged Amy to look at other children's behaviours and to recognize that all children are sometimes good and sometimes not. Worksheets were used to provide further opportunities for psycho-educational work around challenging beliefs that were unhelpful and that did not contribute to her preferred image of herself.

Child looks at options and choices

The child is now in a situation where options and choices for the future can be considered.

As a result of the work that had occurred up to now, Amy started to look at her options and choices and to explore different ways of relating to her mother and to the children at school. She realized that her mother was either not able, or not willing, to provide her with physical closeness a great deal of the time. Amy saw that one option was for her to continue to struggle to gain the closeness that she would have liked, in the way that she would have liked, with her mother. An alternative option was for her to negotiate with her mother to achieve a different sort of relationship where she joined with her mother in different ways. She decided to do the latter.

Amy also looked at her choices with regard to her relationships with peers at school. She decided that she did want to improve her relationships but didn't know how to do this (because she lacked the basic social skills).

Child rehearses and experiments with new behaviours

During this phase, the child is able to act on selected options by rehearsing chosen behaviours or by putting these behaviours into practice.

Amy found that she could engage with her mother in some common interests. This turned out to be satisfying for both Amy and her mother, with the consequence that their relationship changed and Amy felt more secure.

The counsellor also helped Amy to develop social skills through the use of worksheets and role plays where direct verbal communication was rehearsed and practised (see Chapter 32). These role plays were based on unsatisfactory incidents that had occurred at school with other children and which had been recorded in Amy's diary. Amy was later involved in a social skills group to enable her to develop her skills further.

Child reaches resolution and moves towards adaptive functioning

Having completed the journey around the Spiral of Therapeutic Change, a child reaches resolution. She can now either move into normal adaptive functioning or return to the beginning of the spiral in order to deal with new issues.

Amy had now resolved her issues relating to her fear of rejection and abandonment by her mother. Her relationship and ability to communicate with her mother improved because she was no longer afraid to express her feelings openly. Consequently, Amy was also able to resolve issues relating to her grandparents by talking these through with her mother. She was now functioning adaptively, having discovered that she could talk directly to her mother instead of having to deal with issues in counselling sessions.

Using the Spiral of Therapeutic Change

We have illustrated the use of the Spiral of Therapeutic Change by using an example where all of the stages were involved and required. We would caution readers that the treatment described might suggest that counselling is an easy process without the complication of related issues. In practice this is rarely the case. Counselling is often complicated, with new issues being raised during the process.

Sometimes only parts of the spiral will be needed to achieve desired goals, and sometimes the child will travel around the spiral more than once. However, we find that it can be useful for us to refer to the spiral when we are evaluating the progress of our work with a child. By doing this we make decisions regarding changes which might be needed during the therapeutic process in order for the child to reach the point of resolution of issues.

KEY POINTS

- A sequential process of counselling as shown in Figure 7.1 is usually helpful.
- The counsellor needs to take time to join with the child before expecting that the child will start to tell their story.
- As the child tells their story and their awareness of issues arises they are likely to get in touch with strong emotions.
- When strong emotions start to arise the child may deflect or withdraw.
- Resistance can be addressed as discussed in Chapter 14.
- Strategies can be used to help the child change their self-perception.
- Generally children need to deal with self-destructive beliefs, look at their options and choices, and make behaviour changes in order to complete the therapeutic process.

8

Sequentially Planned Integrative Counselling for Children (the SPICC model)

The Spiral of Therapeutic Change (Figure 7.1) described in the previous chapter provides a general understanding of the types of processes which are likely to occur for a child during counselling. The spiral incorporates the assumption, identified by Vernberg et al. (1992), that the central goal of child counselling is to help children to return to, or achieve, healthy adaptive functioning relevant to their developmental stages. Thus, the spiral illustrates the way in which a child starts therapy in an emotionally disturbed state but leaves at a point where resolution has occurred so that the child may function adaptively in the world around them.

As well as understanding the processes that occur within the child it is important for us, as counsellors, to have a clearly defined model of practice. This includes having a clear understanding of the theories relevant to the therapeutic approaches that we will use to enable the child to move around the spiral.

We have developed a model of practice, which we use to help children move around the spiral of change. We call our model Sequentially Planned Integrative Counselling for Children, and will refer to it as the SPICC model. This model is an integrative model that makes use of a number of well-established therapeutic approaches in a deliberately sequential process.

Being an integrative model, the SPICC model makes use of, and is informed by, ideas, tenets, concepts and frameworks belonging to a variety of therapeutic approaches. Additionally, it makes use of strategies and interventions that come from a variety of therapeutic approaches. In order to be able to do this, the model relies on the following assumptions:

1 Positive therapeutic change in a child will occur more quickly, will be more effective, and will be more enduring, if the therapeutic approach used is deliberately and purposefully changed at particular points in the therapeutic process.
2 When using an integrative approach a counsellor can make use of some of the ideas, tenets, concepts, strategies and interventions taken from a particular therapeutic approach, without needing to accept in its totality all of the ideas, tenets and concepts of that approach.

Thus, we may make use of symbolic work while counselling a child but it is not necessary for us to be limited to, or restricted by, Jungian interpretation about that work or the symbolic representations involved. We may use the narrative therapy concept that relates to discovering a preferred 'story' and 'thickening' that story. While doing this we do not need to feel obliged to follow the clinical practices of the narrative therapy approach, which is to 'thicken' the child's story by building on unique outcomes, using outside witnesses or writing letters. Instead, we might use an experiential method to enable the child to thicken their story. Similarly, we may acknowledge the existence of defence mechanisms which help children to cope with the anxiety arising from intrapsychic conflicts as described in psychoanalytic psychotherapy. Although we may observe these in a child and use our observations to guide our subsequent interaction and interventions, we do not need to adopt the clinical practices of the psychoanalytic approach of providing a corrective emotional experience for the child through the use of transference in the relationship.

The process of change in counselling

In order to understand the theoretical basis for the SPICC model, a clear understanding of change processes relevant to counselling children is essential. Most of the literature is concerned with counselling adults, but the theories described also have relevance for children when they are sequentially integrated into an overall change process.

Most counsellors believe that the primary goal of counselling is to help clients to change (Lambert, 1992). Dene (1980) points out that there is no commonly held opinion about what constitutes change and what brings it about. Thus, in the relevant literature, we find that there are a number of ideas about how change occurs.

Change related to stage-matched therapy

Prochaska (1999) suggests that there are common pathways to change regardless of the therapeutic approach being used. When he investigated change, he found that ordinary people change by progressing through a series of stages. At different stages people apply particular processes to progress to the next stage and this process unfolds over time (Prochaska and DiClemente, 1982, 1983). This 'stage' effect suggests that if people are moved to immediate action before they are ready, the majority will not progress in therapy or complete the counselling process. Additionally, Prochaska and DiClemente (1983) suggest that particular processes of change need to be matched to specific stages of change. The SPICC model does this.

Change related to creativity and exploration

Several qualitative empirical studies support the notion that change is related to creatively exploring one's world (Corsini and Wedding, 2004; Duncan et al., 1997; Gold, 1994). Tallman and Bohart (1999) believe that the ultimate change process, inside and outside of therapy, is one wherein clients actively explore their worlds, both in thought and in behaviour, try out new ways of being and behaving, engage in creative variations on old learning, and solve problems as they come up. Martin (1994) and Bucci (1995) found that the degree to which clients connect verbal and non-verbal (experiential) aspects of processing is associated with change.

The SPICC model is consistent with these theories of change as it incorporates strategies which actively assist the child to creatively and experientially explore their internal and external worlds. This occurs in Phase 2 of the SPICC model, as will be discussed later.

Change related to the client's change in perspective

Osel (1988) suggests that the change process in counselling is related to the client's 'view' of events and often involves a client's change in perspective. Perspective can be defined as a mental view and it is this mental view of events that the client has the power to change. Often the events cannot be altered – either they are already past or beyond the client's control – however, the client's view of them can change. If the client changes their interpretation of events, then their perspective is changed and they have a greater range of choices. Oldham et al. (1978) support this theory of change, stating that if a client is able to make a small change in their perspective, then it follows that the situation in the client's internal world changes.

The SPICC model is consistent with this theory of change as it helps the child to change their interpretation of events by gaining insight into the issues confronting them and building on preferred ways of being, thinking and behaving. This occurs in Phases 2 and 3 of the SPICC model, as will be discussed later.

In summary

Perhaps the most important factors which have been suggested as being relevant for promoting change include the client's readiness for change, a change in the client's perspectives, the client's creativity, and the connection between experiential and verbal aspects of processing. It can be seen that although there are differences between the views of different authors, their theories are not mutually exclusive as they each focus on different aspects of, and different influences on, the change process.

The advantages of having a systematic approach to integrative counselling

It is clear from both relevant literature and knowledge of clinical practice, that although some counsellors work within one particular therapeutic framework, many others use an integrated approach, drawing on ideas from a variety of sources. In practice this often involves using ideas from differing approaches in an ad hoc and unplanned way without regard to the overall requirements of the change process. Unfortunately, there can be problems with working in this way. Theoretical concepts may become confused and overall treatment programmes may lack clear direction. In contrast to this, we believe that considerable advantages in therapeutic outcomes can be achieved by using the sequentially planned SPICC model. As explained, in the SPICC model a particular planned sequence of therapeutic approaches is deliberately used.

Are integrative approaches justified?

There is strong support in the literature for the use of integrative approaches to psychotherapy (Alford, 1995; Braverman, 1995; Davison, 1995; Goldfried and Castonguay, 1992; Jacobson, 1994; Pinsoff, 1994; Powell, 1995; Scaturo, 1994; Steenbarger, 1992). Similarly, many contemporary psychotherapists subscribe to an eclectic/integrationist approach (Watkins and Watts, 1995). In particular, Culley (1991) suggests an integrative approach based on the sequential use of strategies, each of which incorporates specific counselling skills. Culley's approach provides practical ideas for counselling and is useful in identifying processes that occur during counselling.

The SPICC model is conceptually different from Culley's integrative approach and is specifically related to counselling children. Whereas Culley provides a sequence in which to use particular strategies involving individual counselling skills, the SPICC model makes sequential use of particular theoretical models of psychotherapy.

The SPICC model

The SPICC model draws on theoretical concepts and practical strategies from a variety of well-established psychotherapeutic approaches. These include Client-Centred Counselling, Psychodynamic Psychotherapy, Gestalt Therapy, Narrative Therapy, Cognitive Behaviour Therapy and Behaviour Therapy.

As explained previously, we do not need to be constrained by total acceptance of the entire theoretical basis or practical methodology of any particular therapeutic model. However, it is important to recognize that each of the well-established psychotherapeutic approaches has its own unique theory of change. The SPICC model respects and makes use of the underlying theory of change for each therapeutic model in order to preserve the integrity of the counselling process.

An integrated theory of change

We recognize that counsellors who prefer to use one therapeutic approach believe that the therapeutic approach they use is sufficient in itself to achieve all the goals required in therapy. However, we have noticed that when working with children some therapeutic approaches work more quickly and effectively than other approaches in achieving particular goals during the counselling process. For example, Client-Centred Counselling is particularly helpful in enabling a child to join and tell their story, Gestalt Therapy is very useful for raising a child's awareness and helping the child to get in touch with strong emotions, Narrative Therapy is eminently suitable for helping a child to change their view of themselves, Cognitive Behaviour Therapy and Behaviour

Therapy are recognized as being most appropriate for producing changes in a child's thinking and behaviours.

In the SPICC model, a number of different therapeutic approaches are used sequentially in a particular order. Each of these therapeutic approaches has its own unique and specific theory of change. As a consequence, the overall theory of change in the SPICC model is made up of a number of differing theories of change used one after the other in a particular sequence. This makes sense, as by using a model which sequentially integrates a number of differing change processes, differing goals can be achieved in the various phases of the counselling process and the effectiveness of the overall process is likely to be enhanced. Thus, in the SPICC model, the child progresses through a series of phases each with its own change process. Generally, but not always, the child's movement to a new phase occurs when the child has completed the previous phase.

The overall change process in the SPICC model is similar to the process of change described by Watson and Rennie (1994). They describe a cyclic process of change that begins by disclosing information with regard to specific troubling issues, focusing experientially on one's experience, trying to articulate it in words, followed by changes in thinking and shifts in perception. This may then lead to behavioural experimentation and providing new experiences, which then feed back into the cycle. This cyclic process of change is appealing as a paradigm when counselling children, as it contains all the elements that are characteristic of children's play and the way they learn about interpersonal relationships (Heidemann and Hewitt, 1992). As explained, the stages in the process of change described by Watson and Rennie (1994) are consistent with the stages of the internal processes of change in a child as described in the Spiral of Therapeutic Change (see Figure 7.1).

Table 8.1 shows how the stages in the spiral compare with those proposed by Watson and Rennie (1994).

TABLE 8.1   *Processes in the Spiral of Therapeutic Change*

Stages in the counselling process (as proposed by Watson and Rennie, 1994)	Processes required as described by the Spiral of Therapeutic Change
Disclosing information with regard to specific troubling issues.	The child joins with the counsellor. The child begins to tell their story.
Focusing experientially on one's experience.	The child continues to tell their story.
Trying to articulate the experience in words.	The child's awareness of issues increases. The child gets in touch with emotions and may experience some catharsis. The child deals with deflection and resistance.
Making changes in thinking and shifts in perception.	The child develops a different perspective or view of themselves. The child deals with self-destructive beliefs. The child looks at options and choices.
Engaging in behavioural experimentation. Having new experiences, which then feed back into the cycle.	The child rehearses, experiments with and evaluates new behaviours.

How the SPICC model integrates a number of therapeutic approaches

The SPICC model fits around the Spiral of Therapeutic Change in five phases as described in Table 8.2 and as illustrated in Figure 8.1. In each phase a different therapeutic approach is used to enable the child to progress through the stages of the spiral.

Relying on particular processes of change at particular stages during the counselling process has been identified as relevant for promoting change (Prochaska and DiClemente, 1983). Because each therapeutic approach suggests a particular theory of how change occurs, it seems logical to apply these theories to the relevant stages in the counselling process so that the needs of the child are fully addressed.

In the SPICC model, as explained previously, we have chosen the following therapeutic approaches to support and inform the counselling process at specific stages of that process: Client–Centred Psychotherapy, Gestalt Therapy, Narrative Therapy, Cognitive Behaviour Therapy and Behaviour Therapy.

We will now look carefully at the phases of the SPICC model. We will illustrate how being informed by and using strategies and techniques from a particular therapeutic approach at specific points in time around the spiral of therapeutic change enables the child to move freely around the spiral.

TABLE 8.2   *Phases of the SPICC model*

SEQUENTIALLY PLANNED INTEGRATIVE COUNSELLING FOR CHILDREN (SPICC)		
Phase	**Processes required as described in the Spiral of Therapeutic Change**	**Therapeutic approach used in the SPICC model**	**Method of producing change and desired outcome**
Phase 1	The child joins with the counsellor. The child begins to tell their story.	CLIENT-CENTRED PSYCHOTHERAPY	Sharing the story helps the child to begin feeling better.
Phase 2	The child continues to tell their story. The child's awareness of issues increases. The child gets in touch with emotions and may experience some catharsis. The child deals with deflection and resistance.	GESTALT THERAPY	Raised awareness enables the child to clearly identify issues, get in touch with and release strong emotions.
Phase 3	The child develops a different perspective or view of themselves.	NARRATIVE THERAPY	Reconstructing and thickening the child's preferred story enhances their self-perception.
Phase 4	The child deals with self-destructive beliefs. The child looks at options and choices.	COGNITIVE BEHAVIOUR THERAPY	Challenging unhelpful thoughts and thinking processes produces behaviour change.
Phase 5	The child rehearses, experiments with, and evaluates new behaviours.	BEHAVIOUR THERAPY	Experiencing new behaviours and their consequences reinforces adaptive behaviours.

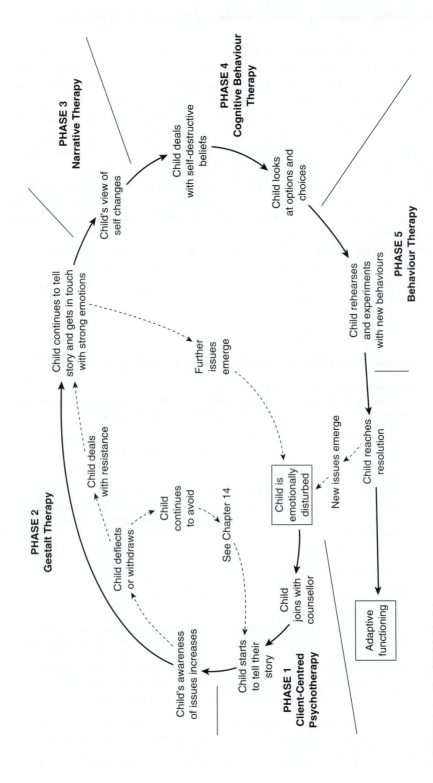

FIGURE 8.1 *The SPICC Model*

Phase 1 Client-Centred Psychotherapy

In the first phase the processes occurring in the child are those of *joining with the counsellor and beginning to tell their story*. As this is the relationship-building phase, we think that it is sensible to be informed by and choose strategies and interventions from a therapeutic approach whose theories of change are strongly focused on enabling the child to talk freely about their issues and to feel comfortable, safe, valued and respected.

This is the stage where the child discovers the nature of the counselling relationship and establishes a positive relationship with the counsellor. During this phase we use concepts and strategies from client-centred counselling as they are very well suited to this process. Joining is accomplished by creating a warm, empathic counselling relationship where the therapist is congruent and relates to the child non-judgementally with unconditional positive regard (Rogers, 1965).

The counsellor is seen as a facilitator who does not view themselves as a superior expert but who listens without judgement. While these characteristics of establishing a therapeutic relationship with the child may be common to many therapeutic approaches, the inherent beliefs in client-centred counselling about the relationship are made explicit through the use of counselling micro-skills specific to this therapeutic approach. In client-centred counselling great emphasis is placed on the use of specific counselling micro-skills, particularly the skills of reflection, summarizing, giving feedback and the use of open questions. Reflection of content and open questions are particularly important in the joining phase so that the child believes with confidence that they are being both heard and understood.

Additionally, an essential component of this phase is for the child to be able to 'tell the story' of how they perceive the current situation. The child is invited and encouraged to 'tell their story' either directly or indirectly, through the use of play and/or activity using media. The child is invited to communicate freely through the use of Rogerian (1965) counselling micro-skills. Reflective counselling skills enable the child to feel comfortable and safe. Additionally, an emphasis on reflection of emotional feelings enables the child to begin to get in touch with the emotions which relate to their story.

Psychodynamic principles can also inform the counsellor's practice in this phase. Psychodynamic formulations inform the counsellor about the way in which the child relates to the world and the mechanisms they use to ward off the anxiety that results from intra-psychic conflicts. Consequently, the counsellor has an idea of what the child is concerned about and how they defend against those concerns. Additionally, observing and developing hypotheses or hunches about the child's projections and free associations can help the counsellor in understanding the child.

While using a client-centred and/or psychodynamic approach, activities using miniature animals, symbols in the sand tray, storytelling and art provide excellent opportunities for the child to tell their story either directly or indirectly. Observations of the child inform the counsellor about possible internal processes occurring for the child and provide a guide for future exploration.

In this phase important issues for the child will emerge that provide the counsellor with specific targets for therapeutic exploration and intervention.

Phase 2 Gestalt Therapy

Phase 1 enables the child to feel safe and to trust the counsellor so that the child will now be ready to enter a new phase where a more dynamic approach can be used. Having disclosed information with regard to specific troubling issues in Phase 1, the change process requires the child to focus experientially on their experience and to try to articulate that experience in words (Watson and Rennie, 1994). In other words, the child's awareness of issues needs to increase as they tell a story so that they may get in touch with emotions and experience some catharsis. We believe that a Gestalt Therapy approach, which primarily focuses on experientially exploring the child's internal and external worlds and which is based on the notion that change occurs as a result of raised awareness, provides the most appropriate way to promote change in this phase. Gestalt Therapy can be used to enable the child to continue to tell their story as they experience raised awareness. Through raised awareness they are likely to get in touch with, and release, strong emotions. In emphasizing raised awareness, Gestalt Therapy enables the child to get in touch with their current experiences with regard to somatic or bodily sensations, emotional feelings and thoughts.

Important issues and themes which emerged in Phase 1 can be developed and provide the counsellor with specific targets for therapeutic exploration and intervention. Exploring these issues and themes, and then helping the child to experience, understand and articulate their experience, is instrumental in helping them to change and feel better. As the child's awareness rises, the release of strong emotions enables the child to experience catharsis.

Sometimes in this phase the child may deflect or withdraw, and in this case it will then be necessary to address resistance. As we know, most children come for counselling help when they are experiencing a level of emotional distress. For some children their emotions are clearly expressed, either verbally or non-verbally. For other children, although they may exhibit levels of anxiety or confusion, their emotional expression is more contained. Many children are unable to identify with clarity the emotions they are experiencing. In addition, most children will resist getting in touch with powerful emotions. Gestalt Therapy specifically addresses resistance and enables the child to get in touch with their resistance in a way that results in the expression of emotion (see Chapter 14 with regard to dealing with resistance). When feelings are expressed fully, they lead to new ways for clients to view themselves and the world (Pierce et al., 1983), thus preparing the child for Phase 3 of the change process.

Gestalt Therapy proposes a paradoxical theory of change. It suggests that change occurs by fully owning who one is, not by trying to be different or denying unacceptable parts of self. By helping the child to accept who they are, they are likely to experience clarity instead of confusion.

Many creative techniques can be used in this phase, including the use of metaphor, symbols, art, clay and psychodramatic techniques involving puppets and/or figurines.

Phase 3 Narrative Therapy

During Phase 3 the child is supported to develop a different perspective or view of themselves so that their self-image and self-esteem improve. We suggest that the most useful therapeutic approach at this stage is Narrative Therapy. Narrative Therapy is based on the concept that narrative therapists call 'storying'. Stories are told about how the child's problems have influenced their life and retold by creating an alternative story which the child prefers. Thus, the narrative theory of change is based on the client deconstructing old stories and reconstructing preferred stories about themselves and their life (Morgan, 2000; Parry and Doan, 1994; White and Epston, 1990). As a new and preferred story begins to emerge, it is important to help the child to hold on to, or stay connected with, the new story.

Many creative strategies such as symbols in the sand tray, art, clay and metaphorical conversations can contribute to a richer description of the alternative story.

Phase 4 Cognitive Behaviour Therapy

Engaging the child so that they are able to tell their story, helping to raise the child's awareness so that they can get in touch with, and release, strong emotions and then helping the child to improve their self-image, are important components of the healing process, but they are not sufficient. In our experience, many children who undergo such a process continue to use unhelpful ways of thinking and behaving unless they receive direct help to enable them to deal with their thoughts and behaviours. This is inevitable because all human beings, including children, develop patterns of thinking and behaving, which over time become entrenched. In particular, when children are emotionally disturbed they find ways of thinking and behaving which are responses to their disturbance. Often these are dysfunctional and maladaptive.

Even though the therapeutic processes described in the previous phases might reduce a child's stress, anxiety, depression or other emotions, it is quite likely that unhelpful ways of thinking and behaving will persist. Unfortunately, children who are unable to make changes in the way they think and with regard to unhelpful behaviours are likely to re-experience ongoing problems in the future as troubling situations arise. It is therefore appropriate in Phase 4 to help the child deal with self-destructive beliefs and look at their options and choices with regard to their behaviours.

We believe that the most appropriate therapeutic approach in this phase is Cognitive Behaviour Therapy because this therapeutic approach directly addresses thoughts and behaviours. Thus, in this phase the child learns how to change beliefs, attitudes, thoughts and ideas that are unhelpful for them and/or to experience relief from cognitive dissonance which may have resulted as a consequence of trauma and emotional distress.

The child can be supported to learn new ways of thinking so that self-destructive beliefs do not continue to cause emotional distress and/or maladaptive behaviour. Additionally, the child can be encouraged to explore options and choices with regard to behaviours which might lead to more adaptive functioning. It is important to remember that without this cognitive restructuring phase the child is likely to continue to repeat past behaviours which may result in new or repeated emotional trauma.

Ellis's Rational Emotive Behaviour Therapy (Dryden, 1990, 1995) and Glasser's Reality Therapy (Glasser, 2000) are particularly useful cognitive-behavioural approaches relevant for many childhood issues.

Phase 5 Behaviour Therapy

It is naive to believe that children who have decided that they want to engage in new behaviours can necessarily do this without further help. They may need to rehearse, practise and experiment with new behaviours before these behaviours can become established. Thus, in Phase 5, the child is encouraged to rehearse, experiment with and evaluate new behaviours. By rehearsing new behaviours in a counselling setting, the child is able to experiment with these in everyday-life situations. It is here that Behaviour Therapy can be used to help children to obtain the skills needed to extinguish old behaviours and to engage in new behaviours. This process is assisted by receiving from others, and/or giving themselves, rewards or other consequences. Clearly, systematic recording of positive and negative outcomes when using and experimenting with different behaviours can be helpful in enabling the child to acquire more adaptive behaviours. By adopting motivational and incentive strategies, the child is able to change and generalize new skills to the wider social environment.

Summary

The SPICC model offers a brief, cost-effective therapeutic counselling approach for children between the ages of six and twelve. Moving sequentially from being informed by the principles of Client-Centred Psychotherapy, to Gestalt Therapy, Narrative Therapy, Cognitive Behaviour Therapy and then to Behaviour Therapy can provide a brief therapeutic intervention with positive outcomes for many children.

We have noticed that often when Cognitive Behaviour and Behaviour Therapy programmes have failed, the SPICC model has succeeded. It has enabled children firstly to deal with their underlying emotional issues, to express emotions and to feel better about themselves. Then continuation of the SPICC process by reintroducing Cognitive Behaviour and Behaviour Therapy has been effective. Similarly, we have noticed that children who had been helped through a counselling process where their issues had been addressed and emotions released often continued to exhibit maladaptive behaviours because their behaviours had not been directly addressed. Thus, we find that the integrative SPICC model is more complete as it not only addresses emotional issues but also continues by addressing the need for cognitive restructuring and help in achieving behavioural change.

We have found that generally, when using the SPICC model, therapeutic interventions will consist of not more than six to ten therapy sessions. However, we recognize that there are a small percentage of children who require long-term help. During all phases of the SPICC model it can be helpful if the child's family, parents or significant others are involved in the therapeutic process in the ways described in Chapter 9.

KEY POINTS

- Positive therapeutic change in a child will occur more quickly, will be more effective, and will be more enduring, if the therapeutic approach used is deliberately and purposefully changed at particular points in the therapeutic process.
- When using an integrative approach a counsellor can make use of some of the ideas, tenets, concepts, strategies and interventions taken from a particular therapeutic approach, without needing to accept in its totality all of the ideas, tenets and concepts of that approach.
- The SPICC model sequentially involves processes of joining, listening to the child's story, raising their awareness to help them get in touch with emotions, and then promoting change in self-perception, thoughts and behaviours.
- The SPICC model makes use of strategies from Client-Centred Counselling, Gestalt Therapy, Narrative Therapy, CBT and Behaviour Therapy.

9

Counselling Children in the Context of Family Therapy

Many of the children who come to see us for counselling are brought by parents or carers who are concerned because they have noticed that these children are emotionally troubled. However, many others are brought not because they are seen to be emotionally troubled but because their parents, carers, teachers or other adults are concerned by the child's inappropriate, disruptive, developmentally different, destructive, anti-social or other unacceptable behaviours. We believe that these children are also emotionally troubled. For many of them, their poor behaviour is a result of external stressors such as abuse, trauma, crisis or interpersonal relationship difficulties. For others it is a result of disturbing internal processes. In both instances it is the child's response to the stressors that results in behaviours that are maladaptive and/or unacceptable. The resultant behaviours reflect the child's attempts to cope with anxiety and maintain emotional equilibrium.

Inevitably a child's unacceptable behaviours will impact on other members of the family. Additionally, if the behaviours are driven by unresolved emotional issues, these issues may well be related to the family environment, as that is the environment in which the child spends most time. We have found that in many instances information about, and observations of, family interactions provide us with clues to the way in which a family system manages, contributes to and/or maintains emotional and behavioural disturbances in a child. Also such information and observation of family interactions sometimes suggests how the troubling behaviour may have been shaped initially. It is clear that a child's parents and family provide a strong emotional influence in a child's life. Consequently, when counselling a child individually, we think that it is also useful to engage the family in the counselling process. Additionally, we believe that if we are to actively facilitate change quickly, we are likely to be more successful if we integrate individual work with the child with family therapy.

You may have noticed as you have been reading this book that the model and practice framework we present is primarily a short-term approach that focuses on the child's capacity to change and to connect with their internal resources to promote adaptive responses. Our rationale for this approach has been outlined clearly in Chapter 8. We recognize that there will be children who require long-term, intensive psychotherapy because the issues troubling them are deep and/or entrenched. However, we do not believe that intensive, long-term therapy is necessary or appropriate for most children who come for counselling help. Hence, we adopt methods that are convenient with regard to the time involved and are cost-effective because they do not involve lengthy therapeutic programmes.

Individual counselling compared with family therapy

We have noticed that in the past there have been two differing traditions in counselling children and young people. One tradition involves individual counselling of the child or young person, whereas the other involves family therapy.

Many counsellors who belong to the individual counselling tradition believe that it is sufficient to work with the child alone in helping the child to address and resolve troubling issues. Similarly, many counsellors who are committed to the family therapy tradition believe that family therapy alone is sufficient.

Some family therapists argue that working individually with a child is undesirable because the child becomes scapegoated, stigmatized and pathologized. On the other hand, some counsellors who work with children individually believe that family therapy does not provide an opportunity for the child to address intensely personal and sensitive troubling issues. We certainly agree with the latter position, as we have noticed that when we work with a child individually, the child will be likely to reveal personal information, which would have been too difficult to disclose in the context of the whole family. However, we have found that once troubling information has been disclosed by a child in an individual counselling session, subsequently the child is often able to share this information with the family. If family therapy alone is used, this information is unlikely to surface, with the consequence that the child's troubling issues are likely to persist. For this reason we believe that if we are to actively facilitate change quickly, we are likely to be more successful if we integrate individual work with the child with family therapy.

Integrating individual counselling with family therapy

We believe that by using the integrative approach suggested in this chapter we can blend individual counselling for the child with family therapy. In doing so, the child and family are offered a more comprehensive therapeutic process from which to experience positive outcomes. If this integrative approach is used appropriately and with sensitivity, we have found that the child does not become scapegoated, stigmatized or pathologized. On the contrary, we have found that as the child has started to change, other members of the family have recognized their own need to make changes in their thoughts, beliefs and behaviours.

In our experience, integrating individual counselling with family therapy is an approach that can be used when either children or adolescents are involved. However, we should point out that there are significant differences in the strategies used when counselling children individually compared with those used when counselling adolescents individually. This is because children and adolescents are in quite different developmental stages. Those readers who are interested in counselling adolescents might like to read our book *Counselling Adolescents: the Pro-active Approach* (Geldard and Geldard, 2004).

To help in understanding the process that occurs when working with a child individually but within the context of family therapy, we will describe a model for integrating individual and sub-group counselling with family therapy. In order to appreciate the value of this model we will first consider the following:

- What is a family?
- How the child functions as an individual within a family.
- The value of family therapy.

What is a family?

In this new millennium, and in our Western society, the idea that the traditional nuclear family is the only sort of family in which to bring up children is undergoing considerable change. In our experience, many children are being raised successfully in single-parent and blended or step-families. We have also noticed that families of same-sex partners are capable of raising happy children. In some communities and cultural systems the extended family is especially important and plays a significant part in how the family system functions. Whatever the family structure, we believe that the following can be said of most families where there are children:

- A family, usually but not always, is multi-generational.
- A family holds within it the history of each adult.
- A family is influenced by the history of each adult.

A family, usually but not always, is multi-generational
A family may consist of children, parents and grandparents. It may also include aunts, uncles, cousins and other people who are in close relationships with family members. Families can be enriched by the contribution that each member from a different generation has to offer. For example, grandparents and older members of the family in some cultures are highly valued members of the family and community. They are often an important source of wisdom and stability and give families and communities a sense of who they are. Children of various ages can contribute excitement, fun, experimentation, opportunities for nurturing and caring to the family system. Parents and other adults contribute much in the way of providing role-models for younger members of the family. It is useful to remember that a family is made up of individuals, each with their own developmental needs and tasks, which they perform so that they can mature comfortably and adaptively.

A family holds within it the history of each adult
As children grow they incorporate and integrate those values, beliefs and attitudes from the world around them which they find appealing and useful. As adults, however, they may find that they have also absorbed beliefs, attitudes and values which may not be as appealing as others, which they find difficult to ignore but which in some way have

become a part of them. Additionally, each adult will have had earlier experiences which impact on their ability to deal adaptively with later tasks. Each adult in the family will have a different set of beliefs, attitudes and values and a different set of experiences from the past from other adults in the family. Sometimes, values, beliefs, attitudes and experiences from the past are similar for a number of adults within a family, but sometimes they may be markedly different.

A family is influenced by the history of each adult

Because the family is the primary provider of the emotional, intellectual and physical environment in which the child lives, this environment will impact on the child's views of the world later in life and on the child's ability to cope with future challenges. Clearly, the ability of a family to function healthily will depend on the adults in the family. Each adult in the family has a personal history that will inevitably influence how they raise their children, how the family will develop and mature, and how the family will function as a whole. Family connectedness and structure will impact on a child's later adjustment.

How the child functions as an individual within a family

We think that it is important to remember that a family is not a single monolithic entity but is made up of a group of individuals. Each of these individuals, including the child's parents, are likely to provide a strong emotional influence in the child's life because children generally spend most of their time in the family environment.

Figure 9.1 illustrates the way each individual in a family (including the child being helped by counselling) functions within the family. Each individual family member's

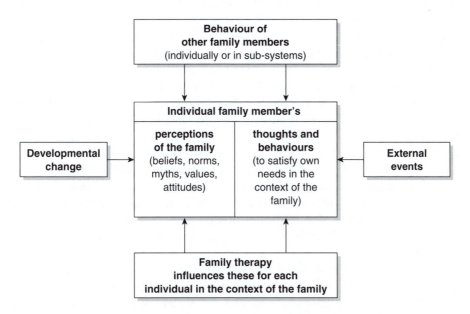

FIGURE 9.1   *Influences on an individual family member's perceptions, thoughts and behaviours*

thoughts, behaviours and perception of the family are clearly influenced by the behaviour of other family members, developmental changes within the family and external events. Additionally, family therapy is likely to influence individual family members' perceptions of the family and their thoughts and behaviours.

Each individual in the family, including the child, will have thoughts and behaviours to help them exist in the family unit. These thoughts and behaviours help them to get their emotional and physical needs met in a way that reduces their personal anxiety and helps them to feel comfortable within the family system. We have already mentioned that sometimes the way in which the child endeavours to get their needs met may not be appropriate or adaptive and may be problematic for them and other members of the family. Nevertheless, the child thinks and behaves in the best way they know how.

How the family culture influences the thoughts, behaviours and perceptions of the child

The child will have perceptions about the family in which they live. These perceptions of the family will be based on family beliefs, norms, myths, values, attitudes and cultural influences that have been either implicitly or explicitly transmitted to the child. For example, they might be aware that an important rule in their family is to keep personal information about the family private, or they may believe that closeness and physical touching in their family should be kept to a minimum. Consequently, they will behave in ways which preserve such perceptions.

How developmental changes within the family influence the thoughts, behaviours and perceptions of the child

All families experience change as a natural part of life. For many families, most of the time these changes are anticipated and expected. Events such as the birth of a baby, teenage independence, a career move and the death of an elderly parent are experiences that are likely to occur at some time. Despite the amount of preparation, it is likely that these experiences will bring changes that will influence the thoughts, behaviours and perceptions of each individual member in the family. For example, when a couple decide to have a child it is highly likely that they will anticipate major changes in their lifestyle. When the couple decide to have subsequent children, the arrival of a sibling is likely to impact on the first child in the family. The first child may experience thoughts about being displaced, and consequently behave in ways that aim at retaining their place in the family. Depending on how the parents respond, the child will then create a new perception or understanding about their changed family. When teenage siblings become independent of the family, the developmental change will influence the way the remaining children think, behave and understand their family. Similarly, a decision by parents to care for elderly parents in the family will strongly influence a child's thoughts, behaviours and perceptions of the family.

It is inevitable that families will face the challenge of confronting and managing normal developmental family experiences. How these challenges are managed will inevitably influence the thoughts, behaviours and perceptions of the child.

How external events impact on the family and influence the thoughts,
behaviours and perceptions of the child

While there are events that can be anticipated and prepared for in a family, there are many experiences that are unexpected. Global events such as war, being displaced from home or country, flood, fire and other similar disasters cannot be controlled by a family. More personal events such as motor vehicle accidents, serious illness and hospitalization are generally unexpected, so can't be anticipated. For children many events will be experienced as not being within the child's control; for example, moving house, changing schools and parental separation. The occurrence of any of the events we have described will impact on the child's thoughts, behaviours and perceptions about the family.

As a result of interacting with other members in the family, experiencing developmental changes in the family over time and adapting to unexpected events which may impact on the family, the child will create a 'picture' of the family which will be unique to them and different in some ways from the 'pictures' that other family members have.

How the family's interaction with the child influences the thoughts,
behaviours and perceptions of the child

The family may inadvertently reinforce unhelpful behaviours in the child in different ways. Here are some examples of the way in which a family's interaction with the child can influence them:

- The parents may wish to protect their child from experiencing painful emotions and this may lead them to avoid talking about disturbing experiences from the past. As a result, the child may cut off many emotions so that they are not reminded of troubling past events.
- One or both parents may identify with the child and take pleasure in the child being able to express emotions that they themselves find difficult to express. Therefore, instead of shaping behaviour that will be useful for the child, the child will be encouraged to act out in ways that may not be helpful.
- A fairly common situation arises where parents are determined to parent their children differently from the way their parents raised them. As a result, they will try particularly hard to encourage their children to behave in ways that reflect their desired parenting. This can often lead to the child developing behaviours that prove unhelpful in the family and in wider systems.

The patterns of interaction that occur in the family such as those described in the above examples may encourage and/or sustain the child's difficult behaviours and may even exacerbate the problem.

Clearly, the way in which the child thinks and behaves within the family will have much to do with the way other members of the family, as individuals and sub-groups, behave toward them. For example, bullying of a child by older brothers or sisters may influence the child so that they begin to think of themselves as being inferior and develop self-defensive behaviours. If the child is unsuccessful in soliciting support from adults or others in the family when they are being bullied, then the child may have a perception that in their family people defend themselves and do not rely on others for support.

The influence of the family on the child's behaviour

Sometimes it can be useful to look at the child's behaviour from a more general systemic point of view. In this case we might ask, what role does the child play within the family? We might ask questions such as:

- Is the child openly acting out feelings that are being expressed more covertly within the family?
- Does the child's behaviour distract the family from looking at more serious or threatening issues affecting the family?
- Is the child reflecting the tension in the parental relationship by being extremely demanding, angry or anxious?
- Is the child acting out the myths or strong belief systems of the family? For example, in families where the child is witnessing domestic violence, a strong belief may be that it is important for family business to be kept private and within the family. The child will then behave in ways that honour this belief.

Some children will manifest family assumptions and concerns about acceptable and non-acceptable behaviour at the expense of expressing themselves freely. In each case the child may, as a result, have difficulty developing healthy ways of coping with their anxiety and self-regulation.

The value of family therapy

We believe that initially it is helpful if we can discover how the child's problems fit within the context of the family. Next, it is essential for the family to recognize and understand how behaviours and interactions within the family contribute to and/or maintain the child's behaviours. Finally, we are strongly supportive of the concept that the family have the resources to discover their own solutions so that each individual and the entire family become more adaptive and comfortable.

It is not appropriate for us to describe in detail our own model of family therapy in this book, as this is a book on counselling children. We recognize that there are many different models of family therapy and each of these can be used in conjunction with individual counselling for the child. While we do not intend to describe in detail our model of family therapy, you may be interested to know that our approach is an integrated approach. Central to the model is Gestalt Therapy theory and practice and an understanding of systems theory (Resnick, 1995; Yontef, 1993), while at appropriate times during the therapeutic process we may make use of ideas from Solution Focused Counselling (De Shazer, 1985), Narrative Therapy (Morgan, 2000; White and Epston, 1990) and Cognitive Behaviour Therapy (Jacobson, 1994). Additionally, we make extensive use of circular questions as used in the Milan Systemic Family Therapy model (Selvini-Palazzoli et al., 1980). In our model we place significant emphasis on identifying processes and interactive patterns in the family.

Identifying processes and interactive patterns in the family

Regardless of the model of family therapy used, family therapy influences the thoughts, behaviours and perceptions of each family member. Either directly or indirectly, depending on the model used, family therapy invites each family member to observe and understand their own current thoughts, behaviours and perceptions with regard to their relationships with other members of the family, and to replace these with more helpful thoughts, behaviours and perceptions. Thus the picture they have of themselves and others in their family will change. These changes occur within family counselling sessions, within individual counselling sessions for members of the family, and between counselling sessions. In our model of family therapy, identifying interactive patterns in the family involves:

- sharing an individual's perceptions of the family;
- giving feedback;
- awareness raising.

Sharing an individual's perceptions of the family
Each individual in a family is likely to 'view' themselves and experience their family in different ways. Thus, it is as though each individual family member has monocular vision, as if they were looking through their own individual lens. If the family are to understand how the child's problems fit within the family, it is useful for each individual family member to understand the ways in which the other family members see the family. By inviting each member of the family to share their own individual perspectives of the family and how it functions, we begin the process of helping the family to identify differences within the family. They will also start to recognize patterns of interaction that occur which may be contributing to or maintaining undesirable behaviours in the child.

In our family therapy process we invite each family member to describe their individual perceptions of what is happening in the family. They are encouraged to share their individual points of view so that the whole family can learn how other members of the family see their family. In this way, instead of individual family members having monocular vision and looking at their family through one lens, they will hopefully start to look through multiple lenses. Often during this process family members will disagree with each other or re-evaluate their original descriptions. This can be encouraging as it is an indication that each individual is listening to the various descriptions provided by other family members.

We have found that some children are initially reluctant to talk openly in individual sessions for fear of betraying family secrets or appearing to be disloyal to members of their family. However, if they participate in a family therapy session in which other members of the family are talking openly about the family, they are more likely to feel as though they have permission to talk freely later in individual counselling sessions. Sometimes a family therapy session will provide the child with information which is new for them about relationships within the family. The information can later be discussed openly in individual counselling sessions with the child.

We think that it is important during family therapy sessions to validate each individual's point of view in order to join with them. By validating the picture that each individual member of the family has of the family, family members are likely to view the counsellor as an independent person. They are likely to recognize that the counsellor is able to see things from each individual member's perspective. By doing this, the counsellor avoids issues of betrayal and disloyalty arising in later individual sessions with the child. Through this process the child is also less likely to feel scapegoated in the family and is able to engage in a process that is empowering and helpful as they are able to see themselves as much the same as other family members.

While individual members are sharing their perceptions of their family, the counsellor is able to observe interactional patterns as they occur and learn about relationships in the family. Additionally, the counsellor can contribute to the concept of looking through multiple lenses by providing feedback.

Giving feedback

It can be helpful for a family to receive feedback of the counsellor's perceptions of the family. Giving feedback preserves the transparency of the counselling process and is usually received positively by a family. We have found that families are curious to know how others see them.

The counsellor's perceptions of the family will have been obtained by listening to the family's perceptions and observing the family's patterns of relating and interacting. Feedback of the counsellor's perceptions can be given by using either a representational or metaphorical description of the family. Thus the counsellor provides an additional picture of the family, seen through the counsellor's lens. Family members can then accept, reject or use this new picture in developing their own new pictures. It is not important whether the family accept or reject the counsellor's feedback because even if they reject it, it will still provoke them into reviewing their own pictures. It is useful, however, to encourage the family to discuss their response to the feedback and to feel free to modify and/or disagree with any of the counsellor's impressions that don't fit for them. In doing this, it is important for them to express their disagreement by explaining to other members of the family how they do see things.

What the feedback does is to provide an additional lens that comes from outside the family system and which may be useful in influencing individual family members' own pictures. In presenting feedback it is important to:

- stress that every family member is doing the best they can – their behaviour is a response to the system and environment;
- affirm the family's resources and competencies;
- comment on individual family members' strengths.

It is also useful to:

- give positive feedback about the way the family has responded to any developmental or physical changes;
- comment on what has been noticed within the family session with regard to processes and interactive patterns.

The family's response to, and discussion of, the counsellor's feedback picture helps in raising the family's awareness of what is happening in the family. The family's responses provide an opportunity for family members to move closer together and possibly to gain a shared point of view. Their responses may also highlight important differences that will provide material for further exploration and discussion in future counselling sessions.

Awareness raising

Raising the family's awareness of their current interactive patterns and enabling them to experiment with and experience new interactive patterns provides the family with an opportunity to change. In order to raise awareness, a number of interventions in conjunction with some creative strategies can be used. When creative strategies are used, children are more likely to become engaged in and enjoy the process.

During the awareness-raising process, family members have an opportunity to express how they view one another, to express how they feel about current relationships, and to say how they would like relationships to be different. Most importantly, the family can be encouraged to find solutions to the difficulties they are experiencing.

Sometimes as a result of the awareness-raising process it will be clear that one or more members of the family could benefit from individual counselling where they would have an opportunity to resolve personal issues, explore interpersonal relationship issues in a private setting, and experience personal growth and development.

A model for integrating individual and sub-group counselling with family therapy

Whenever children are referred to us for counselling we prefer to meet with the whole family first, provided that the family are prepared to attend and to be involved in a counselling process. Consequently, when a child is referred to us we will frequently start the counselling process by engaging the family in a family therapy session. This is the start of a process that may involve some family therapy sessions and some individual counselling sessions for the child and any other individuals in the family who need help to address personal issues privately. Additionally, we may have some counselling sessions for sub-groups. For example, we may work with the parental dyad, or with one parent and child, or with two or more siblings in a group. The way in which we integrate individual and sub-group counselling with family therapy is illustrated Figure 9.2.

As can be seen from Figure 9.2, we generally start the counselling process by working with the whole family in a family therapy session. During that session we will make decisions about the most sensible way to continue working. Frequently we will offer individual counselling for the child who has been identified as troubled, and may also offer individual or sub-group counselling to one or more other family members. We will openly discuss counselling options with the family so that they are actively involved in deciding whether to continue with family therapy or whether it is more sensible for us to work with the child individually, with other individual family members, or with one or more sub-groups.

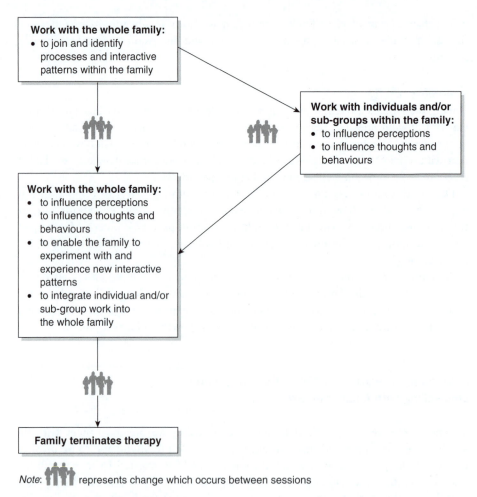

Note: represents change which occurs between sessions

FIGURE 9.2   *Practice framework*

Individual and sub-group counselling for family members

As a result of raising awareness in a whole family therapy session, it is likely that issues will emerge that relate specifically to one or more members of the family. For example, it may be that the family have become angry and resentful with regard to a particular child's aggressive behaviour towards their siblings. During the whole family session, the family might have discussed the way this behaviour impacts on each of them. However, the child might be unable to understand and/or explain their feelings or behaviours in a way that makes sense to the rest of the family. In a situation like this, it can clearly be advantageous for the child to be offered an individual counselling session. In the individual session the child may be able to be more open in telling their story of their experience of living in the family. For example, it might emerge that the child is worried because they believe that their parents' relationship is unsatisfactory, something they were unable to mention in the whole family setting. In the individual setting the child might get in touch with their fear with regard to possible parental separation, and then will help make some decisions about how to deal with their anxiety in a constructive way.

Work with individuals and/or sub-groups may include:

- Individual counselling:
  - for an adult, to address personal issues and behaviours
  - for a child, to address personal issues and behaviours.

- Parent/couple counselling:
  - for relationship issues
  - to address parenting style (including the influence of the family of origin)
  - to address parenting problems.

- Sub-group counselling:
  - to address relationship issues
  - to address emotional responses to past trauma.

Some reasons for working in sub-groups or individually rather than in the whole family setting may be that in the whole family setting we may not be able to focus on the specific needs of individuals or sub-groups, as we are working to keep the whole family engaged. Sometimes individuals may not be able to address sensitive personal issues in front of the whole family. Individuals may not feel safe in disclosing information in the whole family setting. For example, this typically happens in domestic violence situations where a child or parent is too frightened to talk about what is actually happening in the family.

Integrating individual or sub-group work with whole family work

After working with a child, other individual family members or a sub-group, we like to integrate this counselling work into the wider family system. This provides an opportunity for redressing individual issues of the child and at the same time address-ing problems in the family that contribute to the child's emotional and psychological condition. In this integration process we involve the whole family in a counselling session, where the individual or sub-group concerned can share information, which is appropriate for sharing, that has arisen from their counselling session. Naturally, there is often information that is disclosed in an individual or sub-group setting which is not suitable for sharing with the whole family. Because of this, we are very careful to maintain confidentiality and not to pass information from an individual or sub-group counselling session on to other members of the family. What we do instead is to encourage the individual or sub-group members to share what information they wish with the whole family.

In some cases, we will realize that because of confidentiality issues arising from an individual or sub-group counselling session, rather than involving the whole family, additional work may need to be done involving just the parents and a particular child or sub-group. This involves bringing the child and other members of the family together to share information, beliefs and ideas, which may have evolved in individual or small-group work. For example, a child may have used the miniature animals in an individual session to explore their discomfort with regard to living with their step-family. The issues underlying the child's discomfort may be important for their parents to know so that they can help the child to feel more comfortable within the family, but may not be useful for the rest of the family. As a result, bringing the child together with just their parents may be a sensible way to integrate the work.

While working with a child or small group, it is important for the counsellor to pre-pare the individual and sub-group for the work of integration. Consequently, discussion can be encouraged regarding what information is to be shared in the wider family context and what is to remain private. The implications of sharing with regard to likely consequences can also be explored. Sometimes, it is satisfactory for family members to carry out the work of integration in a setting where the therapist merely acts as a facilitator. In this situation the therapist can invite family members to share whatever they wish to share, making it clear that there may be things that they wish to keep pri-vate. At other times, it may be unnecessary to carry out the work of integration within the therapeutic setting; this is because, as a consequence of individual or sub-group work, family members may spontaneously resolve issues between counselling sessions.

When integrating individual work into work with the whole family, the goals are generally to focus on solution building and to identify change.

Focusing on solution building

The work of integration will often occur as a result of the counsellor acting as a facilitator. In this situation the counsellor invites family members to share whatever they wish to share. As a result of this sharing process, the family and individuals within the family will be encouraged to embark on a process of solution building. During this process the counsellor creates a climate where respect will be shown for the feelings, needs and roles of all family members.

We have often found that many of the underlying issues confronting family difficul-ties stem from conflicts of power and intimacy within the family. Many solutions will include ways to enable family members to feel empowered and at the same time have an opportunity to get their emotional needs met comfortably within their family.

Identifying change and the influence of circular processes

An important reason why we choose to work with the whole family as well as with the individual child relates to the influence of circular processes within the family system. If we work with the child alone, then the therapeutic gains we achieve may be limited.

Consider the circular process shown in Figure 9.3. In this example, the child initially feels rejected and misbehaves in order to get attention. Because of the mis-behaviour, the parent becomes angry and withholds affection. This increases the child's feelings of rejection. Consequently, there is an escalation of both the child's acting-out

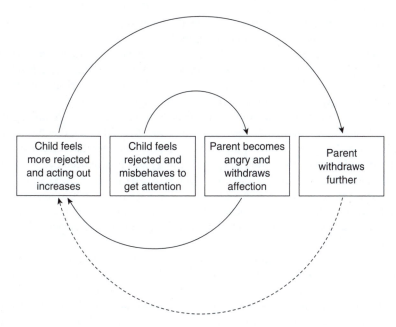

FIGURE 9.3   *A circular process*

behaviour and the parent's withdrawal behaviour. The process is circular, with each behaviour being a response to the previous behaviour. Because of the inevitability of circular processes occurring, it is often advantageous for siblings as well as parents to understand the changes that a particular child is making, and sometimes the issues that have confronted that child during individual therapy. Clearly, because of circular processes, change by one individual in the family may be restrained by the actions of other members of the family who continue to use familiar, unhelpful behaviours.

Often when change occurs, family members may either intentionally or unconsciously resist this change even though they believe that the change is what they want. It can be helpful for families to understand that they may inadvertently interfere with or block the change process. Additionally, it is important to inform the family that sometimes a child may experience periods of setback and regression during a counselling process before positive enduring change occurs. By informing the family in advance, they can be prepared for this and recognize that it is part of a change process. Involvement of the family in the therapeutic process provides the opportunity for individual family members to express their emotional feelings regarding the process of change and to be actively and positively involved in the process.

Recognizing that change occurs between counselling sessions

Much of the change that occurs in families engaged in counselling occurs between counselling sessions. This is inevitable, because during counselling sessions individual perceptions of family members change due to raised awareness and the possibility of using new behaviours is discussed. It is important to capitalize on this between-session change so that it is recognized. By recognizing the change that has occurred between sessions, further change is likely to be promoted.

Often families will minimize changes that have occurred between sessions, for example by saying, 'Oh yes, but Jason was away on camp for several days in the last week', thereby minimizing the change which occurred on the other days. To ensure that change is recognized, valued and will continue, we can make change newsworthy.

Change can be made newsworthy by deliberately looking for and identifying change. For example, at the beginning of a new session it may be useful to ask the question, 'How have things been better since we last met?' This question presumes that positive change has occurred and encourages the family to look for things which have been better, rather than focusing on the problem. An alternative approach is to ask the question, 'Have things been better or worse since we last met?' An advantage of using this question is that members of the family who are focusing on problems have an opportunity to express their point of view and this can then be incorporated into a wider picture where positive changes have occurred.

Particularly with young children it can be useful to use scaling questions accompanied by diagrams on a whiteboard. For example, the counsellor might ask, 'On a scale of one to ten, where one is very unhappy and ten is very happy, where does your family fit?' The scale can be drawn on the whiteboard and family members asked to mark on it how they saw the family before counselling started and how they see the family now.

Seeking witnesses who can confirm change is also useful when helping a family to consolidate change. For example, it may be useful to ask the question, 'Has anyone else noticed this change?' and to explore 'how' the change was achieved, by asking, 'What did you do differently?' or 'Did anyone else do anything different?' Asking these questions can help the family to identify and feel good about individual and family resources which have helped them to change.

Congratulating the family on the changes they have made is important as often, positive changes can get overlooked, especially in chaotic families.

The need for advocacy

Sometimes children may need the help of an advocate in order to be able to share relevant information with others in the family. This is particularly relevant when children are unable to articulate their feelings or needs in front of their parents. In the above example, for instance, following the individual work the child may be able to share more easily if the counsellor is first able to summarize the individual sessions so that the process that helped the child reach their current position is understood by the family.

When acting as an advocate for a child, it is important to have first spent some time with the child so that their issues can be understood. Next, it is essential to have discussed with the child the implications of advocating for them in the family and to have agreed with them about what is to be said and how and when it is to be said. This enables the child to have some level of control over the process of disclosing personal or sensitive information. Where there are issues with regard to the child's safety, we follow the guidelines set out in Chapter 2.

Feedback to referral sources

Following a period of therapy, after a child has resolved issues and become empowered in some ways, it may be desirable for a counsellor, with the parents' permission, to integrate the therapeutic work with the child's wider environment. Referral sources such as schools and community organizations may benefit from feedback about the child's movement through therapy. It is important that general feedback is provided which does not break confidentiality by divulging specific information of a private nature. A child can benefit if significant others understand past behaviours and are able to cooperate constructively with regard to changes in behaviour. Such cooperation can enable the child to continue experimenting with new behaviours and to practise newly discovered adaptive skills.

KEY POINTS

- Children may not feel free to disclose troubling issues to a counsellor while other members of the family are present.
- If a child changes, encouraging change within the family will help to support the child's change, rather than undermine it.
- Family therapy is the best way to enable a family deal with unhelpful circular processes.
- Integrating individual counselling with family therapy allows individual family members, and in particular children, to deal with personal issues which may impact not only on them but also on the family as a whole.
- Sometimes children need the counsellor to act as an advocate in order to be able to share important information with other family members.

10

Counselling Children in Groups

While you have been reading this book we are sure that you, the reader, will have recognized the value of working individually with a child to allow them a safe, private and confidential situation in which to tell their story, address their issues and make changes to their thinking and behaviour. For many children individual counselling is the best option. However, for some children with particular problems or in specific situations there can be significant advantages in including them in a counselling group with other children.

Readers who are especially interested in the possibility of counselling children in groups might wish to read our book *Working with Children in Groups: A Handbook for Counsellors, Educators and Community Workers* (Geldard and Geldard, 2001). In that book we fully discuss the issues related to running groups for children and include programmes specifically designed for counselling children who have experienced domestic violence, have self-esteem problems or social skills difficulties, or have been diagnosed with ADHD (Attention Deficit Hyperactivity Disorder).

When deciding whether or not to use group work, the personalities of the children concerned, the nature of their problems, and their own and their family's preferences are important considerations. It is important for leaders to be aware of the advantages of group counselling, and have a conviction that group work can be used to foster healthier functioning and development and become a catalyst for growth (Kymissis, 1996). Because groups can mirror the wider social environment they are often able to promote change, which may be difficult to achieve through individual counselling.

Advantages in counselling children in groups

Where a counsellor has a number of children as clients who have similar problems or have had similar experiences it can be advantageous to work therapeutically with them in a group setting. By working in a group setting the children discover that they are not alone but that other children have also encountered similar problems or experiences. This discovery can be very empowering in enabling the children to open up and talk freely with their peers in the group about their personal issues. This can be very useful therapeutically.

Establishing a group of children with common problems or experiences is usually not difficult, because among children who come for counselling there are certain to be children who have had similar experiences. For example, there will be those who have experienced family dysfunction, family break-up, domestic violence, the problems of blended families, the loss of significant others through death or separation, or who have suffered neglect or physical or emotional abuse. Including children who all fit into one of these categories in a counselling group enables them to share with each other, learn from each other, and learn from the input of the counsellors who are leading the group.

Another significant advantage of counselling children in a group is that a group provides a social setting which helps the children to learn from their social interactions within the group. This can be particularly useful for children who have problems with social skills, as they can receive feedback from the other children in the group and from the group leaders about the effect of their behaviours on their interactions, and thus learn to use more helpful behaviours. Although some gains can be made through individual counselling in helping a child to improve their social skills, the benefit of learning social skills through practising new behaviours within a group setting has considerable advantages. In our experience it is likely to produce change more quickly and more effectively than working individually with a child who has poorly developed social skills.

Like working with children who have social skills deficits, counselling groups can be used to facilitate personal growth in children who have a poor self-image, low self-esteem, or particular behaviour problems. Groups can be particularly useful in addressing self-esteem issues, because poor self-esteem is often the result of a child's failure to interact positively with peers. The intended outcome of groups targeting self-esteem is to enable the children to identify with others in the group, to value and enhance their personal abilities, strengths and skills, and to learn more effective ways of relating. A group can provide the opportunity for a child to experiment with new behaviours in a safe and supportive environment, and then to experience success in interacting positively with other children. As such a group develops it is likely to provide the participants with a sense of belonging, and this can have a positive effect on the children's feelings of self-worth.

Counselling groups can also fulfil a supportive role for children who live in difficult situations. Examples of children who might benefit from belonging to a counselling support group are the children of alcoholics, latch-key children, children in foster care, and children with parents who have mental health problems.

Limitations of group work with children

Unfortunately, group work may be unsuitable for particular groups of children, for a variety of reasons. Certainly, counselling children in a group setting would be problematic for children who lack impulse control and cannot control their exuberance and aggressiveness (Kraft, 1996), and for children who quickly display aggressive behaviour and are destructive to property. Additionally, working in a group is unlikely to be successful with children who suffer from psychotic disorders which might predispose them to decompensate as a result of the stress of the social exchanges required in a group, or those children who have expressive or mixed receptive-expressive language disorder and may have difficulty expressing their frustration other than with aggressive outbursts (Gupta et al., 1996).

Another limitation of the work is that it is not feasible to spend a significant amount of time addressing the individual and personal needs of one child in a group. Children who have high levels of emotional disturbance are likely to need individual counselling, although in some cases it can be useful to include a child in a group programme while concurrently counselling them individually.

Types of counselling groups for children

There are two common types of counselling groups for children, depending on the particular membership needs and aims of the group. One type of group is basically a therapy group, which aims to bring about change through the use of the group. Such groups enable the participants to work through troubling emotional issues by talking about them in the group setting, and engaging in activities which allow them to express their feelings and then change their thinking and behaviour. The other type of group aims to bring about change primarily through the use of psycho-educational input. Additionally, there are those groups that combine group counselling with the psycho-educational input, followed by group discussion of the input.

Therapy groups

Therapy groups are particularly useful for those children who have been diagnosed with a mental health disorder or are suffering from severe emotional distress and/or psychiatric disturbance; for example, children suffering from post-traumatic stress disorder (Shelby, 1994), children with schizophrenia (Speers and Lansing, 1965), children with anxiety disorders, depressive disorders, disruptive behaviour disorders, conduct disorder, oppositional defiant disorder and specific developmental disorder (Gupta et al., 1996).

Therapy groups are also useful for those children who do not have severe emotional distress or psychiatric disturbance but are experiencing some difficulty in coping with the stressors produced by life's challenges. In these groups the primary focus is usually on the exploration and resolution of troubling issues. These groups enable the children involved to get in touch with and release disturbing emotions, and then modify their beliefs, attitudes and behaviours. Such groups are extremely useful for preventing the development of more serious problems, as participants have the opportunity to share their personal experiences, thoughts and feelings, before major issues develop. They may receive support, encouragement and feedback, relating to their issues, behaviours, beliefs and attitudes, as a result of which they may discover more about themselves and realize that they have more choice than they imagined with regard to changing attitudes and behaviours.

As when counselling children individually, counsellors running therapy groups for children will usually make extensive use of media and activity to engage the children in ways that enable them to talk about difficult issues.

Psycho-educational groups

Other counselling groups for children might be more specifically psycho-educational in nature. The purpose of these groups is to provide the children with information, which will help them adjust their responses to their life situations and to behave in more adaptive ways. Because psycho-educational groups emphasize the acquisition of information and knowledge, these groups are generally more structured than therapy groups. They may develop content in accordance with a structured curriculum. They usually have specifically defined goals and explicit expectations of group members. Although the focus is on learning, the process usually involves group interaction, with members of the group sharing and discussing thoughts, feelings, experiences, attitudes, beliefs and values, particularly as these relate to relevant topics.

As with therapy groups, counsellors running psycho-educational groups for children will usually make extensive use of media and activity to engage the children and to help them in their discussion of the psycho-educational material presented.

Planning to run a group

Before planning to run a particular children's group, a decision needs to be made as to whether running a group for the children concerned will be more appropriate than working individually with each child. Some children are best helped individually whereas others will benefit more by participating in a group programme, or by simultaneously engaging in individual counselling and a group programme.

When counselling a child individually a significant relationship is purposefully developed between the child and the counsellor. Although such a relationship is helpful for children who can cope with a degree of intimacy with an adult, other children may act out, much as they would in other close relationships. For such children group counselling may be the best option, as it diffuses the intensity of the relationship with the counsellor. Strong relationships do develop in a group, but for many children these tend to be directed more to peers than to the leaders (Swanson, 1996).

Some parents worry about their child entering into a one-to-one relationship with an adult in a situation where they are not present themselves. In these cases the parent's anxiety is likely to be an obstacle to effective outcomes. In such cases it may be advantageous to include the child in a group, as a similar level of parental anxiety is less likely to occur in this situation.

Sometimes it can be useful to include a child in a counselling group while personal counselling for the child is also being undertaken. This can enable the child in the individual counselling sessions to deal with emotional issues which might arise for them as a result of the group interaction. Often such issues might be too difficult for the child to raise within the group setting.

It is important for counsellors who plan to run groups for children to have a very clear idea of the needs of the children, the aims of the group, and make decisions about the therapeutic process to be used. If appropriate, a specific programme of topics and activities can be designed to run over a series of sessions.

Assessment of children for inclusion in a group programme

There is a view that, at best, selecting group members may be 'guesswork' (Henry, 1992). However, experience suggests that by looking at specific factors in composing children's groups it is possible to avoid a catastrophe, a dysfunctional group, or at least a major conflict that may prove destructive to the group (Fatout, 1996). Consequently, it is sensible to use a formal assessment process in deciding which children to include in a particular group.

The assessment process determines whether the child's needs match the identified needs of the target group, whether the child will be likely to benefit from the planned group programme, and whether the child's inclusion will lead to the formation of a group of balanced or compatible composition. Group composition can take into account age, gender, culture, and the purpose of the group and type of activity planned.

It can be useful to include children in a group who have different personal resources, experiences and behaviours. This may have a positive influence on the way the group functions. Additionally, their inclusion may result in the generation of useful material that can be processed to the benefit of the group.

The assessment process determines whether the child will be likely to be able to function in the group and seeks answers to the questions:

1 Does the child have the necessary ego-strength and skills to cope in a group?
2 Will the child be able to fit in with other group members?

During the assessment process it is essential to consult with parents. It is important to include a child in a group only if the parents are clear about the nature of the group, the aims of the group, the activities that the group is likely to engage in, and are comfortable with the choice of leaders for the group.

Assessing whether a child is suitable for a particular group can be done either through clinical assessment or through psychometric assessment, or both, depending on the nature of the group.

Clinical assessment might involve assessing the suitability of the child for a group in terms of behaviour, intellectual functioning, speech and language, motor skills, and the child's self-perception. Particularly with groups for children with mental health problems it can be useful to include psychometric assessment.

Planning to run a counselling group

Initially, when deciding to run a group, it is important to make decisions about how many children will be involved in the group, the location, the length of individual sessions, and the overall duration of the group programme.

There is no general rule regarding group size, because this will depend on the goals of the programme, the age of the children, degree of acting out, manifestation of disturbance and the activities that are planned. Rose and Edleson (1987), referring to therapy groups, suggest groups usually range in size from three to eight children, as larger groups make it difficult for every member to get their personal needs met in a group session. However, it is fairly difficult to work with fewer than four children in a group, because with three children there may be joining between two of the children to the exclusion of the third.

Considerations for setting up the group room include: sufficient space and furniture to allow the planned activities to be carried out; free from visual and auditory distractions from outside; and free of materials which could be distracting or be a danger to the children.

The length of each group session will depend on the needs of the target group, the activities to be undertaken, and the age range. Schnitzer de Neuhaus (1985) suggests that generally young school-age children can only handle 45 minutes in a group, while for older children 60 to 90 minutes may be acceptable. While agreeing that this may be true for those groups which rely heavily on verbal interaction with little activity, we have found that, for most children, one-and-a-half hours or even two hours can be a comfortable length for a group. We believe this is true provided that the group programme is designed appropriately to include the use of media and activity, and allow for appropriate changes in tasks for the children, and changes to the pace at which the group is operating.

For most counselling groups with children we find that eight to ten weeks' duration seems to be the minimum useful period for a group if they meet for one or two hours each week. This timeframe allows for the development of group processes such as the establishment of group cohesion, and maximizes the opportunity for group processes to contribute to positive outcomes of the group.

Designing a group programme

Once the needs of a particular target group of children have been recognized, it can be both useful and satisfying for counsellors running groups to design specific programmes to meet the needs of the particular target group in question. In this process, we suggest starting by developing an overall programme for a series of group sessions and then designing specific programmes for each individual session.

A number of authors including Malekoff (1997) and Rose (1998) support our belief that, as with counselling children individually, it is important to use activities and media when counselling children in groups. The range of media used might include art materials, games, worksheets, puppets, miniature animals, videotapes or DVDs, craft materials, clay and construction materials. Activities might include free play, playing organized games with rules, and role play. The use of media and activity helps to engage the children's interest and can promote a sense of competence, a sense of belonging to the group, self-discovery, invention and creativity. As a result of the children's interactions while engaged in an activity, they can learn about the way their behaviours affect their personal relationships with their peers, provided that the group leader uses the appropriate counselling skills.

An important point to remember is that it is not the particular activity or outcome from the activity that is important in a group, but rather the way the activity is processed in terms of resulting behaviours and emotions. Skills for processing an activity will be discussed in Chapter 18.

Varying the programme for a particular group session helps to maintain the children's interest. If you intend to run counselling groups for children you may wish to read our book *Working with Children in Groups* (Geldard and Geldard, 2001), as this includes detailed information about how to design a group programme.

Counselling skills and facilitation skills required in children's groups

Counselling children in groups is clearly very different from counselling children individually. The counsellor not only draws on knowledge about how to use those particular counselling skills which are relevant for use in a group situation, but also knowledge on how to facilitate the group process. An outline of information relating to group facilitation and group counselling skills is provided in Chapter 18.

KEY POINTS

- Where a number of children have similar problems or have had similar experiences it can be advantageous to work therapeutically with them in a group setting.
- Group work is particularly useful for children with social skills problems as a group provides a safe environment in which the child can experiment with, practise, and learn new ways of relating.
- Counselling groups can fulfil a supportive role for children who live in difficult situations.
- Therapy groups are particularly useful for many children who have been diagnosed with a mental health disorder or are suffering from severe emotional distress. They are also useful for children who do not have these severe problems but are experiencing difficulty in coping with the stressors produced by life's challenges.
- Psycho-educational groups are useful in providing children with information that will help them to adjust to life situations and behave in more adaptive ways.
- As when counselling children individually, counsellors running children's groups will usually make extensive use of media and activity.
- The suitability of a child for inclusion in a particular group can be assessed through clinical observations and/or psychometric measures, or both.
- Planning to run a counselling group includes consideration of goals for the group, programme design, group composition, group size, length of the group sessions, and the suitability of the environment in which the group is to be held.

Part 3

Child Counselling Skills

Children come to therapy with different personalities and different problems, and at different ages, so for each individual child we, as counsellors, will choose what we think will be the best way to work if we are to be of help to the child. With some children we may choose to be active and direct in our approach, whereas with others a gentle self-discovery style may be more useful. However, regardless of the differences between children and any differences in working style, there are a number of basic child counselling skills which are generally useful.

Different counselling skills will be relevant for the various stages of the therapeutic process. Generally this therapeutic process will span a series of sessions, during which the counsellor will perform a number of different counselling functions:

- Joining with the child (Chapter 2)
- Observation of the child (Chapter 11)
- Active listening (Chapter 12)

- Awareness raising and the resolution of issues to facilitate change (Chapters 13–16)
- Dealing with the child's self-concept and self-destructive beliefs (Chapter 15)
- Actively facilitating change (Chapter 16)
- Termination of counselling (Chapter 17).

Each of the above functions involves one or more counselling skills. In this part we will deal with each function and related skills, starting with *Observation*. (The function of joining was covered during our discussion of the child–counsellor relationship.)

11

Observation

Observation begins early in the joining phase when the counsellor observes the child's relationship with their parents, the ease with which the child separates from their parents and the child's general behaviour. The observed information is valuable in helping the counsellor to make a decision as to how to proceed.

One way to carry out effective observation is to refrain from interacting actively with the child and instead to stand back and observe unobtrusively. When observing in this way, we usually invite the child to play with the toys, games and materials set out in the play therapy room and tell the child that we will sit quietly while they play. While observing the child, we monitor our own behaviour to ensure that we are refraining from making judgements and interpretations about the child's presentation.

Other ways of making valuable observations are to watch what happens when you, as the counsellor, intrude on the child's space, or insist on interacting with the child, or act in a directive way.

If you were asked to observe a child, what sort of things would you observe? We suggest that before reading the following pages you might like to try to draw up a list of useful things to observe.

We believe that some of the most important things to observe when counselling children are as follows:

- general appearance
- behaviour
- mood or affect
- intellectual functioning and thinking processes
- speech and language
- motor skills
- play
- relationship with counsellor.

Observing general appearance

Observation of general appearance includes observation of the way the child is dressed, the child's level of alertness and any obvious discrepancies from normal – for example, physical differences. The degree of attractiveness of the child may be relevant, as well as information relating to physical development and level of nutrition. Peculiar mannerisms of the child may also be noted (for example, facial tics).

Observing behaviour

When observing the kinds of behaviour the child exhibits, a counsellor might ask any of the following questions:

- Is the behaviour quiet and careful, or noisy, boisterous, aggressive and destructive?
- Is the child distractible, or does the child have a good attention span?
- Does the child try to engage in behaviour that is dangerous?
- Is the child willing to take risks?
- Is the child affectionate and dependent on the interaction of the counsellor?
- What is the child's response to physical contact?
- Is the child defensive, responsive or searching for contact?
- Does the child have appropriate boundaries?
- Does the child show approach–avoidance tendencies; for instance, by showing initiative and then waiting for cues?

During observations of behaviour the counsellor may note the presence of defence mechanisms such as suppression, avoidance, denial and indications of dissociation.

Observing the child's mood or affect

Observing the child's mood or affect during the session gives clues to the child's underlying emotional state. Generally, children can be observed to be happy, sad, angry, depressed, excited and so on. Some children will be observed to show little or no emotion, being flat in affect. Others will be self-absorbed. Sometimes, behaviours already observed will also give information about the child's internal mood or emotional state (for example, aggressive play might indicate that the child is angry).

It is also useful to observe any changes in mood during the counselling session and to observe the child's awareness of their own moods and their level of emotional reactivity during the session.

Observing intellectual functioning and thinking processes

For a young child between the ages of four and eight, an initial indication of intellectual functioning can be obtained by inviting the child to engage in specific tasks such as doing puzzles, naming body parts and identifying colours. With an older child, general conversation will point to the ability of the child to solve problems and to conceptualize, and will give an indication of level of insight. Whether or not a child is oriented with respect to time, place or person can be determined by asking about recent events. By checking a child's sense of reality, and organization of thoughts, the counsellor may become aware of any abnormal thought patterns, including the presence of delusions and hallucinations.

Observing speech and language

Engaging in conversation with a child enables the counsellor to make an initial assessment of speech and language skills. For example, a counsellor might notice that a child experiences frustration at not being able to communicate adequately, or that the child tends to rely on non-verbal methods of communication. Additionally, it may be observed that a child's speech is not clear or that the child lisps, stammers or stutters.

Observing motor skills

Gross and fine motor coordination can be observed during the child's involvement with activities in the play therapy room. Observe whether the child sits most of the time, or walks, jumps, runs or squats, and observe how the child moves in and out of positions – with ease, or with difficulty. Observe whether the child appears constricted in their physical expression or free. Anxious children sometimes show differences in their breath control, so take note of breath-holding, sighing or gasping.

Observing play

Children's play differs according to age and development, so an understanding of the play of typically developing children is essential when making comparisons through observation. Generally speaking, it is helpful to observe whether or not a child's play is age-appropriately creative or is stereotypic, repetitive and limited. An example of the latter would be if a child were to repeatedly pour sand in and out of a container in the sand tray and do little else.

If a child can initiate play, then the counsellor does not need to be involved in the play except when wanting to influence it. The counsellor is then free to withdraw and observe the development of themes that arise in the content of the play. Additionally, the counsellor can observe the quality of the play and can notice whether the play is goal directed and following an understandable sequence and whether play materials are being used appropriately.

Whether play is creative or stereotypic will give an indication of the child's level of developmental maturity. For example, the counsellor might notice that a child can use object substitution in play by using a box as a shopping trolley. The counsellor may also make note of whether the child's play is regressed, infantile or maybe pseudo-mature.

The normal play of three- to five-year-olds is highly imaginative and creative. When observing the play of children of this age, it is important to keep in mind that the expression of fantasies and themes may well be a developmentally appropriate behaviour. The child's mode and intensity of affect in play is also an important observation.

Observing the child's relationship with the counsellor

An important aspect of observing the child's relationship with the counsellor is related to the issue of transference (see Chapter 14).

The child's warmth and friendliness, eye-contact, social skills level and predominant interactional style all contribute information which the counsellor may require during the therapeutic process. The counsellor may also notice whether a child is mainly withdrawn, isolated, friendly, trusting, mistrustful, competitive, negativistic, cooperative and so on. Much of this information can be obtained by observing the child's relationship with the counsellor.

While the counsellor is observing the child, the child may be starting to tell their story. If so, it is important that the child be made fully aware of the counsellor's interest in that story. In order for this to happen, the counsellor will make use of active listening skills.

KEY POINTS

- Observation can provide valuable information, which can be useful to the counsellor when deciding how to work with the child.
- In observing general appearance note any discrepancies from normal.
- Observations of behaviour may include noticing the presence of defence mechanisms.
- Observing mood or affect can give information about the child's underlying emotional state.
- Observation of intellectual functioning provides information about the child's intellectual abilities and the presence or absence of abnormal thought patterns.
- Observation of the child's speech and language can give an indication of the child's ability to communicate adequately.
- Observation of motor skills can reveal whether a child is constricted in their physical expression or free.
- Observation of play gives the counsellor an indication of the child's development.
- The ability of the child to relate to the counsellor can give information about the child's general emotional state and social skills.

12

Active Listening

The skills involved in active listening come from Client-Centred Counselling and are especially important in Phase 1 of the SPICC model, as explained in Chapter 8 (see p. 73).

As counsellors, we gain information about the child by observation and by listening. By performing these counsellor functions we are able to help the child to tell their story and to identify troubling issues. In doing this, it is important for the child to know that we are paying attention and valuing the information that we are receiving.

How will the child know that we are paying attention? How will the child know that we are taking in, and valuing, the information that they are giving us?

Unfortunately, some children are used to spending time alone and to being treated without respect, or ignored, by adults. How can we let these children know that we are willing to enter into their world and to respect their view of that world? We can do this by active listening.

There are four major components to active listening:

1 Matching body language
2 The use of minimal responses
3 The use of reflection
4 The use of summarizing.

Matching body language

An effective way to enhance the child–counsellor relationship is for the counsellor to match the child's non-verbal behaviour. This matching helps to give the child a message that the counsellor is listening attentively. For example, if a child is sitting on the floor beside the sand tray, then it may be helpful for the counsellor to sit on the floor with the child and to mirror the child's posture. This works best when done in a way which is natural and comfortable for the counsellor, otherwise it will look contrived and the child may well be disconcerted by incongruent behaviour on the part of the counsellor.

Matching the speed of talking and tone of voice of the child is also useful in enhancing the child–counsellor relationship. When the child talks rapidly, it may be helpful if the counsellor joins with the child's style of relating and responds similarly. Then, when the child slows up, the counsellor can match the change by being more leisurely.

There is an additional advantage to be gained if a counsellor is able to match a child's non-verbal behaviour and posture when appropriate. Not only will the child feel that the counsellor is joining with them and attentively listening, but also after a while the situation can be reversed: after the counsellor has been matching the child for a while, the child is likely to follow the counsellor in any significant change. Imagine that a counsellor has been matching the speed of speaking, tone of voice and rate of breathing of an agitated child. When the counsellor wants to do so, they can slow down their breathing and speaking speed and sit more comfortably. It is quite likely that the child will follow the counsellor's behaviour and start to relax.

Matching behaviour includes matching levels of eye-contact. Eye-contact is important in establishing rapport with children, but each child will be different with regard to the amount of eye-contact which they find comfortable. Therefore, it is important for the counsellor to observe the child's behaviour in this regard and to respond appropriately. Some children feel more comfortable and are able to talk more freely if they avoid making eye-contact and instead engage in an activity while talking.

The use of minimal responses

The use of minimal responses is something that happens automatically in our conversation when we are predominantly listening rather than talking. Minimal responses indicate to the talker that the listener is attending. These responses are sometimes non-verbal and include just a nod of the head. Verbal minimal responses include expressions such as 'Ah-ha', 'Uh-hm', 'Yes', 'OK' and 'Right'.

Some longer responses serve a similar function. For example, the counsellor might say, 'I hear what you say', or 'I understand'.

Both minimal responses and this type of longer response are very useful in encouraging the child to continue to tell their story. It is important when making both verbal and non-verbal minimal responses that they are not likely to be interpreted as judgemental in either a positive or negative way. If the child is to tell their story accurately, it is important that their story is not significantly influenced by the child's perception of the counsellor's approval or disapproval. For example, powerful exclamations like 'Wow!' may lead the child to draw conclusions about the counsellor's beliefs and attitudes. These conclusions may inhibit the child, or may influence the child into distorting their story in order to gain the counsellor's approval, or to avoid the counsellor's disapproval. In a similar way, some non-verbal minimal responses may be perceived as expressions of judgement about the content of what the child is saying.

As a counsellor, space your minimal responses appropriately. If you give them too frequently, they will become intrusive and distracting. Remember that minimal responses are not just an acknowledgement that the child is being heard. They can also be a subtle way of passing on other messages. As such, it is important to use minimal responses with care, otherwise messages which are not useful therapeutically may be communicated inadvertently.

The use of reflection

Matching and minimal responses set a climate in which the child gains a sense that the counsellor has joined with and is attending to them. It is also important that the child is assured that the counsellor is attending to the content and detail of the story that is unfolding. Generally, the most effective way of giving the child this assurance is by using the skill called 'reflection'.

There are two types of reflection: *reflection of content* (sometimes called *paraphrasing*) and *reflection of feelings*. We can combine these two types of reflection and *reflect both content and feelings*.

Reflection of content (paraphrasing)

Using this skill, the counsellor literally reflects back to the child what the child has said to the counsellor. The counsellor does not just parrot or repeat word for word what the child has said but instead paraphrases it. This means that the counsellor picks out the most important content details of what the child has said and re-expresses them in a clearer way and in their own words rather than in the child's.

It is important to note that reflection does not necessarily occur during conversation with children but can happen during the therapist's observation of the child in play.

The following are some examples of paraphrasing.

Example one

Child statement: 'My Mum and Dad are always working. My Dad leaves home a lot to go to work, he goes to Cairns and all over the place. Mum is the boss where she works and has to stay back sometimes and tell other people what to do.'
Counsellor response: 'Sounds like your Mum and Dad aren't around very much for you.'

Example two (child playing with miniature animals in the sand tray)

Child statement: 'Come on dinosaur, jump over the fence; it's nice over here. Come on, watch me, look, come on Spiky, come over here, I'll help you, I'll come back and get you, look.'
Counsellor response: 'Looks like your animal wants Spiky to come and join him.'

Example three (child playing in the doll's house, with the doll's family)

Child statement: 'I told you not to make that mess on that floor. You'd better clean it up. You've put stuff all over the floor, you naughty boy.'
Counsellor response: 'That mother wants the little boy to clean up the mess.'

Example four

Child statement: 'I got all my spelling words right in my test but Tiffany didn't. She got into trouble for talking, too. When you get naughty you have to go to the time-out room. I never go to the time-out room.'
Counsellor response: 'Somehow you don't seem to get into trouble but Tiffany does.'

What the counsellor does, when reflecting content, is literally to tell the child clearly and briefly the most important things that the child has just told the counsellor. When the counsellor does this, the child feels as though they have been heard. By using reflection of content the counsellor also makes the child more fully aware of what they have just said, thereby intensifying the child's awareness of this. The child is then able to more fully savour the importance of what they are talking about and to sort out any confusion. Thus, reflection of content is useful in helping the child to move forward in their exploration.

Reflection of feelings

As well as reflection of content, the counsellor may also reflect feelings. This involves reflecting back to the child information about emotional feelings that the child is experiencing. When a child is involved in play, reflection of feelings can also be used in relation to emotional feelings, which the child attributes to imaginary people, symbols or toy animals involved in the play.

Reflection of feelings is one of the key counselling skills because it raises the child's awareness of feelings. It encourages the child to deal with significant emotional feelings rather than to avoid them.

It is important for a counsellor to be clear about the difference between thoughts and feelings and not confuse the two. If we were to ask you, the reader, to tell us the difference between thoughts and feelings, what would you say? If we said, 'We feel that caring people make better counsellors' we would be expressing a thought; it would have been better if we had said, 'We *think* that caring people make better counsellors'.

Thoughts generally require a sentence to describe them, whereas feelings usually only need one word. Feeling words such as the following describe an emotional state:

happy	sad	angry
confused	disappointed	surprised
despairing	overwhelmed	frightened
worried	contented	insecure
rejected	betrayed	helpless
responsible	powerful	

When you look at this list you might notice that most of these feelings have opposites. As therapists, we may help children to deal with negative and uncomfortable feelings in ways which will be adaptive for them. However, it is important to be realistic and to recognize that it will not be possible to 'take away' a child's negative feelings. Nevertheless, we can help the child to deal with these, so that they either change or can be managed appropriately.

Reflecting feelings involves making statements that include 'feeling' words, such as 'You're sad', 'You seem to be angry', or 'You look disappointed'. The following are some examples of statements made by children with the appropriate reflection of feelings by the counsellor.

Example one

Child statement: 'Every time I ask Mum if I can go to Aunty Karen's, she says "No". Kelly's going this weekend, and it was my turn.'
Possible counsellor responses: 'You're disappointed' or 'You sound angry.' (The correct response would depend on the context and on non-verbal cues.)

Example two (child's brother was killed in a car accident)

Child statement: 'My brother didn't even have his favourite dog with him when the car was hit.'
Counsellor response: 'You're very sad' or 'You sound very sad.'

Example three (child is involved in imaginary pretend play)

Child statement: 'Let's get out of here before they find out. Quick, they're coming.'
Counsellor response: 'You sound scared.'

Example four (child is playing in the doll's house, with the doll's house family)

Child statement: 'I told you not to make a mess on that floor. You'd better clean it up. You've put stuff all over the floor, you naughty boy.'
Counsellor response: 'That mother sounds very angry.'

Frequently, children will try to avoid exploring their feelings because they want to avoid the pain associated with strong emotions such as sadness, despair, anger and anxiety. However, getting in touch with feelings usually means moving forward to feeling better emotionally and then to being able to make sensible decisions.

Sometimes children will tell us directly how they are feeling. For example, a child might say, 'I'm very angry with my brother.' However, usually children will not tell us directly how they are feeling emotionally, but instead will give non-verbal cues and will talk indirectly about their situation.

If you, as a counsellor, attend closely to a child, your own feelings will begin to match those of the child and it will become easier for you to identify what the child is feeling. With practice, it is possible to notice feelings such as distress, sadness or anger from the child's posture, facial expression, movements and play behaviour.

Be aware that if you correctly reflect a child's feelings, then the child is likely to get more fully in touch with those feelings. If the feeling is a painful one, the child may start to cry. As a counsellor, how will that be for you? For us it is sometimes difficult. Certainly, it is important for counsellors to be able to deal with the feelings generated in themselves by children's tears.

Reflecting back anger to a child can sometimes have a dramatic outcome. If the counsellor reflects back the anger by saying, 'You're angry' or perhaps 'You sound very angry', then the child may respond by angrily snapping back, 'I'm not angry', followed by a period of acting out in the play room. If this happens, the counsellor may feel alarmed; however, the child's reaction reflects their ability to express anger, which they did not wish to own openly. The counsellor may then encourage the child to direct their anger more appropriately through the use of media.

In summary, reflecting feelings allows the child to fully experience their emotions and to feel better as a result of releasing these feelings. Once feelings have been released, the child is then able to think more clearly and be able to consider constructive options and choices about the future. Reflection of feelings is therefore one of the most important of the counselling skills.

The use of reflection of content and feelings

With experience you will find that you can quite often combine the reflection of content with the reflection of feelings. For example, you might combine 'You feel sad' with 'You're telling me that Dad wasn't around for you at the weekend' into the response, 'You're sad because Dad wasn't around for you at the weekend'. Here are some examples of combined reflection of content and feelings.

Example one

Child statement: 'Steven and I used to play princes and princesses in the garden. He always wanted to be the king and sit on this rock which was the throne. He can't do that now he's in heaven.'
Counsellor response: 'You're sad because you can't play with Steven anymore.'

Example two

Child statement: 'Even when you walk away the big kids just follow you. If you tell the teacher they get you after school. Nothing really works.'
Counsellor response: 'You feel helpless because you can't deal with these bullies.'

Example three (an older child)

Child statement: 'I wrote all my subjects down with my preferences next to them. I posted it off to my mother so that it would get there in time, and she still hasn't taken it up to the school.'
Counsellor response: 'You're angry because your mother has let you down.'

In reflecting content and feelings, it is desirable for a counsellor to keep their responses short so as not to intrude unduly on the child's inner processes. Long statements will take the child away from their current experience and will bring them out of their own world and into the counsellor's.

Counsellors will use their judgement in deciding when it is best to reflect content, or to reflect feelings, or to reflect both. Sometimes it will be more appropriate in the interests of brevity to use either reflection of content or reflection of feelings, rather than both.

It can be useful, in helping a child to own a feeling which they are trying to suppress, if reflection of feeling alone is used. The child may then focus on that feeling, and be better able to deal with it. For example, if a counsellor says to a child 'You are really sad', then that statement focuses on the child's pain rather than encouraging the child to escape from the experience of the pain by dealing with the content of what has been said. The pain is not avoided by the child moving into a cognitive rather than a feeling mode: instead it is appropriately addressed in the therapeutic situation.

Whenever possible, help children to experience their emotional feelings rather than to suppress them by operating at a 'head' or cognitive level. Experiencing feelings fully is often painful but is cathartic and consequently therapeutically desirable.

The counselling skills of matching body language, minimal responses, and reflection are those which are most useful for creating a good counselling relationship. Through the use of these skills the child is encouraged to open up and to share with the counsellor the issues that are causing emotional distress.

From time to time it is helpful for the counsellor to provide the child with a review of the ground that has already been covered. This review is carried out by using the skill of summarizing.

The use of summarizing

The counsellor summarizes by reflecting back to the child information from a number of statements which the child may have made over a period of several minutes. The summary draws together the main points in the content and also takes into account the feelings that the child has described. The summary is not a complete re-run of the ground covered, but it picks out the most salient points or the most important things that the child has been talking about. Frequently, children can become confused by the detail of their own stories. Summarizing clarifies what the child has been saying and puts the information into an organized format so that the child has a clear picture and can be more focused.

Imagine that over a period of a few minutes a child gave you a lot of information. Included in this were several specific examples of times when the child would have liked one of their parents to be present, but they were absent. Further, the child gave more than one example of their father breaking promises and the child's tone of voice and facial appearance indicated to you that the child was very sad. How would you summarize what you had learnt from the child?

A possible summary would be to say: 'You have told me how you are sad because your Mum and Dad aren't around very often when you need them, and because your Dad promises things and doesn't seem to be able to keep his promises.'

This kind of summary enables the child to put a lot of confusing information together to create a clear picture. The child can be more focused and thus has an opportunity to move towards finding some resolution of the issues.

Summarizing is also useful when a counsellor wishes to move towards terminating an individual counselling session. It allows the child to integrate what has been shared and experienced during the session before leaving.

The active listening skills described in this chapter encourage and enable the child to tell their story. In the next chapter we will look at those skills which are required to raise the level of the child's awareness, so that the possibility of emotional and behavioural change is increased.

KEY POINTS

- Actively listening by matching body language and using minimal responses, reflection and summarising, lets the child know that the counsellor is paying attention, taking in and valuing the information that the child is sharing.
- Matching body language involves matching the child's non-verbal behaviour, posture, speed of talking, tone of voice and level of eye-contact.
- The use of minimal responses confirms that the counsellor is listening and encourages the child to continue telling their story.
- Reflection of content involves reflecting back to the child in the counsellor's words the content of what the child has said.
- Reflection of feeling involves reflecting back the emotional feeling that the child is expressing.
- Sometimes it is useful to reflect back both content and feeling.
- Summarizing involves picking out the most salient points in the child's story and reflecting these back to the child together with any feelings that may have been expressed.

13

Helping the Child to tell their Story and get in Touch with Strong Emotions

The skills of active listening described in the previous chapter are useful in Phase 1 of the SPICC model in helping to create a good counselling relationship and in enabling the child to tell their story as explained in Chapter 8 (see p. 73). Indeed, much of the information that a counsellor needs to know about a child will emerge naturally and spontaneously if the counsellor uses these active listening skills. Having used these skills to build a relationship with the child and to hear their story, the counsellor can move into Phase 2 of the SPICC model. In Phase 2 it is useful for a counsellor to continue to use observation and active listening while introducing additional skills, particularly those taken from Gestalt Therapy, to help raise the child's awareness and to enable them to get in touch with, and release, strong emotions. The additional skills important in Phase 2 include the use of questions and statements. As in Phase 1, the counselling skills are used in conjunction with the child's involvement with media and activity.

Unfortunately, many children who come to counselling have issues which are too painful for them to confront without help. Sometimes these issues are known to the child but often they are hidden, or partially hidden, in the child's unconscious. Some children have misconceptions about past traumatic events as a result of information which has been repressed and is missing from their consciousness because it is too painful. If a child is to become aware of issues which are partially or fully buried in the unconscious, then the counsellor may support the child to raise awareness of these issues. This support is provided with skill and care so that the child is allowed to confront painful issues at a pace which is acceptable to them and which does not produce further trauma. It is important to recognize that some children who are brought to see a counsellor may not be ready to work through their issues and need to be respected by not being pressured to do so. Having acknowledged this we also recognize that children are natural experts at deflecting away from emotional pain and at avoiding the issues which relate to that pain. Because of this a counsellor may make use of appropriate skills, which will enable the child to address and resolve difficult issues. We believe that for therapy to be effective it is important for a child to focus on the relevant issues with raised awareness and to experience and release the associated emotions.

Because children often find it difficult to talk freely with an adult about troubling issues, the counsellor attempts to not only join with the child and to invite the child to tell their story, but also to create an environment in which the child is enabled to continue telling their story even when to do so is difficult or painful. This environment is created by the use of the following:

- observation and active listening skills
- questions
- statements
- media.

Use of observation and active listening skills

Observation and active listening have already been discussed in Chapters 11 and 12. They are useful in inviting and enabling the child to tell their story. However, the use of these skills alone will usually not be sufficient to raise the child's awareness of the underlying issues so that the child can get fully in touch with the related emotional feelings.

Use of questions

Children generally live in a world where adults expect them to have answers to many questions. However, if you observe children at play, you will notice that they rarely ask each other questions. Instead, they make statements about what they are doing or what they observe their playmates are doing.

When children are confronted by adults they are usually required to answer many questions. Inquisitive aunts and uncles, school-teachers, mothers and friends of the family, all with the best of intentions, ask children questions. Many children, in response to such pressure for answers, become very adept at producing what they consider to be the 'right' answers. These are answers which the child thinks will satisfy the questioner. They are not necessarily what the child believes to be true and they may not fit with the child's experience or with what the child is thinking. Consequently, if a counsellor relies on asking questions they may never discover what the child is really thinking and/or experiencing, but instead may be given misleading answers which are useless in the therapeutic process.

A further problem with asking questions is that the direction in which the counselling session heads is likely to be influenced and controlled by the questions the counsellor asks, instead of following the direction in which the child's energy leads. What is worse, if a counsellor asks too many questions, the child will quickly learn to expect questions and will wait for more questions to be asked instead of thinking for themselves and talking about what is important for them. The counselling session will then degenerate into an interrogation session, with the child being less likely to be open and communicative and more likely to avoid distressing issues.

If, as a new counsellor, you find yourself repeatedly asking questions, then it is important for you to discover what your goal is in asking these questions. If your goal is to stimulate the child into talking, then you are almost certainly using the wrong approach. More often than not, reflective counselling skills will encourage a child to continue telling their story without the need for questioning.

Having given the above warnings, we need to say that questions are a powerful tool for raising awareness if used appropriately and sparingly. There are two major types of questions: *closed questions* and *open questions*.

Closed questions

Closed questions are questions which lead to a specific answer. Usually, the answer will be very short because closed questions invite answers such as 'Yes' and 'No', or answers which give a small piece of specific information such as 'Twenty-three'. Let us look at some examples of closed questions:

1 Did you come here by car today?
2 How old are you?
3 Would you like a felt pen?
4 Are you frightened of your brother?
5 Are you angry?
6 Do you like school?

The answers to the above questions might be as follows:

1 Yes
2 Six
3 No
4 No
5 Yes
6 Yes.

Obviously, some children might choose to expand on these answers, but other children might not. The problems with asking closed questions are as follows:

• The child may give a short factual answer and may not enlarge on that answer.
• The child may feel limited and may not feel free to answer the question in a meaningful way.
• The child may wait for another question instead of feeling free to talk openly.

Sometimes it is appropriate to ask a closed question in order to obtain some factual information. However, generally our intention as counsellors is to encourage children to talk openly about important issues without feeling restrained by our agendas. This is where the open question is useful.

Open questions

Open questions are usually very different in their effect. They give the child lots of freedom to explore relevant issues and feelings, instead of inviting a single-word answer. Consider the following open questions:

1 What is it like living with your brother?
2 Can you tell me about your family?
3 How do you feel?
4 What can you tell me about your school?

Each of these open questions allows the child to think freely about the question and invites the child to give a full and expansive answer without being restrained by the counsellor's agenda. For example, answers to the question 'What can you tell me about your school?' could include:

- My school is large and crowded.
- Some of the boys at my school are wimps.
- My school is a long way from home.
- School is good fun.
- My school is very hot in summer.

Notice that with the open question, a wide range of different answers is possible. Compare these answers with the answer to the closed question, 'Do you go to a big school?' With the closed question, the answer may simply be 'Yes' or 'No', and if the child does expand on their answer, the range of answers is likely to be limited by the question.

Not only are the answers to the open questions likely to be rich in information, but they often include information which allows the counsellor to use reflection of content and/or feelings to encourage the child to continue. Open questions allow the child to talk about those things which are of most interest or of most importance to them, rather than those things which are of most interest to the counsellor. For example, in responding to the open question 'Tell me about your brothers and sisters', a child might focus on one particular sibling. Such a response might give rich information, which the counsellor did not directly seek, about the significance of that sibling in the child's life.

If we were to ask you the closed question 'Are you finding this book useful?', your answer would probably be less helpful in providing us with feedback than if we asked you the open question 'What can you tell us about this book?' However, both the open and closed questions might equally stimulate an open and informative response. But we need to remember that you are an adult and are not being invited to discuss intimate personal details with us. Children in therapy are in quite a different situation. They are often reluctant to talk, particularly about very personal matters, so we are wise to use those counselling skills which are most likely to encourage open communication.

There are times when closed questions are *more* suitable than open questions. Closed questions lead to a specific answer, confine the child to a limited response, help the child to be more precise, and are useful in eliciting specific information.

We have found that it is generally wise to try to avoid asking questions that begin with 'Why'. The problem with asking 'why' questions is that the child is likely to respond with an intellectually contrived answer, rather than giving an answer which is centred on what is happening to them internally. 'Why' questions tend to generate answers which relate to matters or events external to the child, aren't connected to the child's inner experience, are lacking in emotional content, and are often trivial or unconvincing. The answers to 'why' questions frequently fall into the categories of excuses or rationalizations.

When working with children, we are generally most successful in enabling them to tell their stories if we stick to the following rules:

1 Ask only those questions that are needed.
2 Whenever appropriate, use open questions in preference to closed questions.
3 Avoid using 'why' questions, unless there is good reason to do so.
4 Never ask questions just to satisfy your own curiosity.

With regard to the fourth rule, as a counsellor, before you seek information, check whether you really need it. Before you ask a question, ask yourself 'If I don't have this information, will I still be able to help the child effectively?' If the answer to that question is 'Yes', then asking the question is unnecessary. The desire to ask the question probably stems from your own needs and/or curiosity.

When questions are used sparingly and appropriately, they can be powerful in help-ing to raise the child's awareness of important issues so that they can move forward around the Spiral of Therapeutic Change towards resolution.

Questions to raise awareness

Gestalt therapists see human beings as holistic. They believe that the body, emotions, and thoughts are inter-related and inter-dependent. Using this paradigm, we believe that somatic or bodily sensations are directly related to emotional feelings and thoughts. Consequently, it can be useful when helping a child to become fully aware of troubling thoughts and emotions for a counsellor to use questions or feedback statements which will enable the child to make connections between the way they feel internally physically, and their emotional feelings and thoughts.

Here are some examples of suitable questions that can be useful in helping to raise a child's awareness so that they get more fully in touch with the issues involved and the related emotional feelings:

• Can you tell me how your body feels right now?
• Which part of your body is most uncomfortable?
• When you think about what happened how does your body feel?

- Where do you experience the tightness (or other feeling) in your body?
- Now that you notice that your body is uncomfortable, how do you feel emotionally?
- If your uncomfortable body (the tightness in your chest) could say something to you what would it say?
- If your tears could talk what would they say?
- Can you tell me what you are thinking right now?

These questions from Gestalt Therapy can often be used to help the child to get in touch with, and release, strong emotions that are connected to troubling issues.

Use of statements

Statements made by a counsellor can be very valuable in helping a child to stay on track in telling their story and in helping to raise the child's awareness of important issues and associated emotions. Statements can be used in a number of different ways:

- Statements give permission for the child to feel and express a particular emotion. For example, a counsellor might say to a child who is suppressing their anger and talking quietly, 'When I am angry I talk in a loud voice.' This might give the child permission to get in touch with their anger and to express it.
- Statements help a counsellor to float ideas about what might be happening for the child at a particular moment. For example, a counsellor might suspect that a child is experiencing embarrassment and say, 'If I were you, I would feel embarrassed.'
- Statements provide counsellors with a tool with which to affirm a child's strengths. For example, the counsellor might say, 'You must be really brave to have done that.'
- Statements can be used to highlight significant events during an activity. For example, if a child is having difficulty in choosing objects for the sand tray, the counsellor might make a statement like 'You have a hard time choosing objects' or 'It's really hard for you to find the objects that you want'. By making this statement, the counsellor gives the child feedback about the difficulty they have in making choices, and the opportunity has been created for the child to explore this aspect of their behaviour.
- Statements can be used to give feedback, without judgement, about what the child is doing. For example, the counsellor might say, 'I see that you have made a cave with the clay.' In a similar way to reflecting content, this feedback invites the child to talk about what they have done.
- Statements can be used to raise the child's awareness of an element of their activity, and/ or to float an idea which the counsellor has about the child's issue. For example, if a child was working with puppets, and a mouse puppet was hiding, and the counsellor suspected that the child was feeling vulnerable, the counsellor might say, 'That mouse is hiding. I wonder if he is afraid of being caught?'

Statements to raise awareness with regard to important issues

Earlier in this chapter we explained that in Gestalt Therapy there is a recognition of the way that the body, the emotions, and the thoughts are inter-related and inter-dependent. As a consequence of these inter-relationships, counsellors can use questions like those which we suggested earlier in this chapter in order to raise the child's awareness of important issues and related emotions. Often, before asking such questions, it can be useful to give feedback statements such as the following:

- I notice that you are clenching your fists (or doing something else physically).
- You are breathing very quickly now.
- You look sad (or any other emotion that is relevant).
- You put that animal down in a hurry.

These statements can be used on their own, but often it is useful to follow them up with a question related either to somatic experience, emotional feelings, or thoughts. For example, if we were using the feedback statements listed above we could follow up with questions, as in the following examples:

- I notice that you are clenching your fists, and I am wondering how you are feeling as you do that? (The question raises the child's awareness of their physical behaviour and then inquires about the related emotion.)
- You are breathing very quickly now. Can you tell me what you are feeling?
- You look sad. Can you tell me what you are thinking? (This question moves from raising awareness of an emotion to inquiring about the related thought.)
- You put that animal down in a hurry. What would you like to say to that animal?

The last question 'What would you like to say to that animal?' might encourage the child to be expressive in talking to the animal. For example, the child might say something to the animal in an angry voice in which case the counsellor could follow up with another feedback statement by saying 'You sound angry'.

Can you see that either by using feedback statements or suitable questions we can help a child to get more fully in touch with their emotions and hopefully release them?

Use of media

In Part 4 we will discuss the use of media in some detail. While doing this, we will also consider the ways in which counselling skills and media are used together to help the child to tell their story, and thus to raise the child's awareness of both current and past unresolved issues.

The media provides the child with activity to hold their interest and to help them to stay focused. Through using them, the child tells their story either directly or indirectly. They may do this by talking directly about issues which are troubling them, or indirectly by projecting elements of their story on to the media. Media may also allow the child to connect with their emotions and may act as a vehicle through which they can express these emotions. This is a two-stage process: the child first gets in touch with their emotional feelings and then expresses them.

During the therapeutic process, the counsellor may initially invite the child to talk about how it feels to use the media, and will also focus directly on what the child is doing with the media. Later in the therapeutic process, the focus will move away from discussion of the content of the activity involving media and instead will focus directly on the child's life situation and unfinished business. Sometimes, when a child is working with media and telling a story through the media, it is appropriate for the counsellor to ask directly 'Does this fit with your life?' or 'Does this sound like something that might be happening to you?'

Sometimes, though, a child will spontaneously recognize the association between the story they are telling through the media and their own life story. At other times a child may suddenly become very silent. When this happens we might ask them: 'What has just happened?' The child may then begin to talk about something they have remembered which relates in some way to their present life.

In some situations it is useful to go with the opposite of what the child is discussing, or with what may have been omitted. For example, if a child is discussing the excitement and pleasure of a situation, it might be appropriate to say, 'Maybe your life doesn't have much fun in it.'

Often it is easier for children to share the happy experiences in their lives. Once they have told us about the happy ones, then they can often talk about the sad ones.

As the child continues to talk, they may find that they have expressed contradictory feelings related to their memories. They may become puzzled, troubled or confused by the variety of different feelings which they have expressed. Helping the child to recognize that it is OK to have differing, varied and apparently contradictory feelings can help the child express themselves more clearly and accurately.

It can be useful to invite the child to engage in a dialogue between different parts of their story, or their drawing, or whatever other work they are involved in.

Watching for cues from the child's tone of voice, body posture, facial and body expression, breathing and silences can give the counsellor information. For example, the child may be censoring, remembering, thinking, repressing anxieties or fears, or becoming aware of something new. As a counsellor, if you observe the non-verbal behaviours mentioned, you may be able to use these as cues to promote further expression. For example, if a child sighs while telling their story you might say, 'I noticed that you just gave a big sigh. What's it like when you let all that air out at once?'

Many children who experience emotional difficulties seem to have some impairment in their contact functioning. The tools of contact are looking, talking, touching, listening, moving, smelling and tasting. Sometimes by focusing on a contact function we can encourage a child to put their feelings into words. Helping the child to get in touch with bodily feelings and sensations may enable them to connect with the emotional feelings they may be experiencing. For example, we might say to a child, 'Watching you move around quickly and being very busy makes me feel exhausted. I imagine that you must feel very tired, being so busy.'

To summarize: we can help the child to tell their story and thus to get in touch with important issues and emotions by using media, together with appropriate counselling skills. In this process we might do any of the following:

- Encourage the child to talk about what they are currently doing in the therapy session.
- Help the child to relate current experiences in therapy to current and past life issues.

- Encourage the child to explore important unresolved issues.
- Encourage the child to fully experience and express their emotional feelings.
- Explore opposites and absences in the child's story.
- Give permission for contradictory feelings to exist.
- Focus on contact functions to help the child to access suppressed emotions.
- Give the child affirmation.

As a result of this process the child may get in touch with strong emotions (see Figure 7.1, p. 59). We will then help the child to move further round the Spiral of Therapeutic Change by dealing with self-destructive beliefs, options and choices, and rehearsal for subsequent action, as will be discussed in Chapters 15 and 16.

KEY POINTS

- The child will be enabled to continue telling their story, and to get in touch with and release emotions, if the counsellor uses observation, active listening, appropriate questions and feedback statements, in conjunction with the use of media.
- Closed questions usually invite a one-word answer.
- Open questions usually invite the child to talk freely and to expand on what they are talking about.
- Statements can be used to give the child permission to feel and express an emotion, to help the counsellor float ideas, to affirm a child's strengths, to highlight significant events during an activity, to give feedback and to raise the child's awareness.
- Media and activity enable the child to be interested and stay focused while they are telling their story either directly or indirectly.

14

Dealing with Resistance and Transference

In the previous chapter we mentioned the way in which children tend to avoid emotional pain and the way in which painful information is sometimes partially or completely repressed into the child's unconscious. As a child's awareness starts to rise, they may start to become aware of repressed material or of other emotionally painful material. When this happens, the child may become spontaneously blocked from further exploration. This is known as resistance, and is illustrated on the diagram of the SPICC model in Figure 8.1 (see p. 72) by the broken arrow pointing to 'child deflects or withdraws'.

Another problem which can intrude on helping a child to satisfactorily travel through the five phases of the SPICC model to reach resolution is the problem of transference. Consequently, as counsellors it is important for us to know how to deal with both resistance and transference.

Dealing with resistance

In practical terms, when a child becomes blocked, the counsellor is likely to realize that the child is deflecting away from discussing something connected with emerging painful or troubling issues. This deflection may involve the child becoming silent and withdrawn, or may involve the child avoiding the issues by becoming loud and boisterous. It may also involve the child using coping behaviours, which we will describe below. When a child becomes blocked in this way, psychodynamic counsellors and Gestalt therapists refer to this as the child's *resistance* to the therapeutic process. We believe that resistance may either be conscious or it may happen without the child realizing that it is happening, with the process occurring at a subconscious level.

Nearly every child in counselling will be resistant at some time. When a child is resistant we know that it is their way of protecting themselves and coping with a situation which they find stressful. Sometimes this coping behaviour works and the child is able to avoid dealing with uncomfortable feelings; however, the behaviours they use when coping are often considered inappropriate by the adults around them and sometimes make the situation worse. Additionally, using these same behaviours repeatedly is exhausting and usually only masks the more important underlying issues.

Resistance is often a sign of important material or significant issues which would be helpful for the child to explore and work through.

Some behaviours that children use to deal with anxiety and stress

It is important for us, as counsellors, to understand what issues are important to the child and need to be resolved, and also to understand how the child protects themselves from experiencing the anxiety of those issues. A useful question to ask, when you notice that the child you are working with is resisting, is: 'What is it that this child is having difficulty talking about, and what are they protecting themselves from?' We list below some behaviours, generally referred to as defence mechanisms, that children use to protect themselves from experiencing painful or troubling issues.

Regression
Younger children use more primitive ways of coping with their anxiety than older children. For example, a younger child might deal with anxiety by regressing to earlier stages of development. They may, for example, feel threatened by and worried because of strong feelings of anger and jealousy that arise when a new baby arrives in the family. Knowing that it would be unacceptable to their parents, who may reject them, to express a high level of hostility, the child may instead resort to 'babyish' behaviour as a way of coping with the stress of repressing the unacceptable anger. By doing this, the child believes that they will continue to be valued and cared for, despite the arrival of the new baby.

Denial
When the reality of a situation is very disturbing, young children may deny this reality by distorting it and fantasize about a scenario which is more acceptable to them. For example, when parents separate, the father's absence from the home may be described by the child in terms of him having a job that takes him away for long periods of time. Distorting the truth protects the child from uncomfortable feelings. As children get older, this way of coping does not work quite as well because the reality of the situation cannot be disguised in fantasy. Older children usually find alternative ways to cope with troubling feelings without distorting reality.

Avoidance
When a child starts to experience uncomfortable emotions they may deflect the conversation from a painful or troubling topic. For example, a child may move to the doll's house and offer to tidy it for you when asked about their relationship with an abusive mother.

Repression
For older children, ways of coping with anxiety arising from intrapersonal uncertainties and conflicts are more complex. When repressing painful experiences from earlier

years, the memory of these experiences may be completely displaced from the child's awareness. Thus the child will have no memory of these experiences and will use denial and avoidance when confronted by triggers which might normally remind them of the initial painful experience. For example, you as the counsellor may know that the child with whom you are working has experienced a particular trauma. However, during counselling the child may simply not remember the trauma and consequently be unable to talk about it. When invited to remember, the child may invent logical alternative reasons to explain the events.

Projection

Sometimes a child will project unwanted emotional feelings on to another person or object. By doing this the child is able to feel absolved from owning the uncomfortable and possibly unacceptable emotion. However, the child does this at a considerable cost. For example, a child may, while playing, take on the role of an imaginary friend. During this play, the child may talk, while pretending to be the imaginary friend, about destructive and angry things they will do because their imaginary mother and father have separated.

Many of the activities mentioned in later chapters make use of *projection* to help the child express uncomfortable and unacceptable feelings. Projection can be rather like a stepping stone that enables the child to move from denying feelings to owning them. By doing this they are likely to become more emotionally robust and developmentally adaptive.

Intellectualizing and rationalizing

Both of these behaviours help the child to talk about experiences without making contact with the emotions accompanying the experiences. For example, to avoid the painful emotion of not being accepted by peers, a child may talk about their preference for befriending animals. The child may strongly believe that they would rather have animals for friends than other children.

Reaction formation

Sometimes children will become worried by overwhelmingly strong, usually negative, emotions. They may be concerned that if they expressed these feelings they might lose control or behave in ways that are unacceptable to others and to themselves. As a consequence they will, without recognizing what they are doing, change these feelings into feelings which are diametrically opposite. Reaction formation occurs in older children and adults and is a normal and useful way of coping for young children. Unfortunately, when this way of coping is used frequently it can result in the child losing touch with congruent emotions.

The use of defence mechanisms

During counselling, it is important to pay attention to defensive behaviours and to try to determine whether the diversion created reflects anxiety about the current situation or anxiety about internal conflicts arising with regard to issues from the past.

The use of defence mechanisms in young children is quite normal. For older children, provided that defence mechanisms are not used to excess, they may help the child experience a level of emotional equilibrium so that they can more easily learn and interact with others. However, it is maladaptive for an older child to make use of defence mechanisms as a predominant way of coping.

When a child consistently does this in order to cope with anxiety, it is likely that acquiring normal age-appropriate skills, establishing satisfactory personal relationships and having fun will be compromised.

Other defensive behaviours

Sometimes, in contrast to children using to excess the defence mechanisms described above, children will instead develop undesirable behaviours in order to enable them to cope. Often these children will exhibit intense feelings which they find difficult to regulate. Intense feelings can be seen when a child has difficulty controlling emotional outbursts, in taking turns, or in delaying gratification. Additionally, the child might exhibit extreme distress when certain issues are discussed, or show poor concentration when learning a new game or while playing alone. Being able to self-regulate and to have ways to calm and reassure oneself when tasks become difficult are absent in these children.

The need to deal

Again we suggest that you might like to refer back to the Spiral of Therapeutic Change (see Figure 7.1, p. 59). Notice how some children will continue around the spiral to tell their stories and to get in touch with strong emotions without meeting resistance, as shown by the thick dark arrow which forms the top of the spiral. Other children will deflect or withdraw, as shown by the dotted arrow. It is important for these children to deal with their resistance if they are to gain from the therapeutic process. It is the counsellor's job to help them to do this.

Consider an example of how a child might become blocked in therapy and consequently resist further exploration of painful issues. During therapy a child's awareness might have been raised with regard to issues of rejection by their parents who have put them into foster care. It could be too scary for this child to face these issues and the child might demonstrate resistance by deflecting, withdrawing or acting out. It is tempting for the counsellor to pressure the child to continue talking about the painful matters they are avoiding, but to do this will usually be therapeutically disastrous.

If, as counsellors, we try to pressure a child into talking about painful issues, we will raise the child's level of anxiety. The result will be that the child will almost certainly withdraw further and will shut down meaningful communication with us. What is worse, the child may no longer feel safe in the counselling situation, so the possibility of engaging them in further useful work is minimized.

If a child meets a block it is important to help the child to deal with the block, rather than to try to ignore the resistance, and to push on. This may be achieved through raising the child's awareness of the resistance by identifying the resistance and giving the child feedback about it. For example, in the case mentioned previously, the counsellor might identify the resistance as being related to the child being scared to talk about issues of rejection. Having identified the nature of the resistance, the counsellor then gives the child feedback. For example, the counsellor might say to the child, 'It might be a bit scary to talk about not going home to Mum and Dad', and 'When I get scared I like to run away, just like you.' The counsellor has validated the child's fear, made it clear that it is legitimate to feel that way and that it is acceptable to respond by withdrawing.

Paradoxically, once a child has permission to withdraw, they will be more likely to continue. This is because the child knows that their wish to withdraw will be respected, if it intensifies or recurs, and thus they will feel safer about continuing.

If the child is able to continue, then the counsellor might ask a question to help the child to understand and work through the resistance. Using our previous example, the counsellor might ask: 'When you think about Mum and Dad, what is the scariest thing that you think about?' This question is designed to help the child to fully confront the fear associated with the resistance and to deal with it.

The child might respond by saying, 'I'm scared that Mum and Dad won't love me anymore.' The counsellor has now enabled the child to face the most painful issue underlying the resistance and can help them to get in touch with the sadness related to this issue. The child has moved around the spiral to the point labelled, 'Child continues to tell story and gets in touch with strong emotions'.

Directly identifying the resistance

It is possible that the process described above, in which the child moves through the resistance and continues to tell their story, may not occur. Instead, when the counsellor draws the attention of the child to the resistance by giving the child feedback, the child may continue to withdraw. This situation is shown on the Spiral of Therapeutic Change by a dotted line leading to the words 'Child continues to avoid'. The child we have described might say 'I'm not scared' (denial) and continue to avoid talking about useful material. If a child does continue to resist in this way, the therapist can take the pressure off the child by allowing the child to withdraw into free play and focusing on maintaining a positive relationship with them. Then, at an appropriate time, the counsellor can provide the child with a new opportunity to tell their story in a different way. Often this can be achieved by introducing new media. Thus the child is invited to return to the earlier point on the spiral entitled 'Child starts to tell their story'. Because the child has been given time to process what has happened, and has been provided with a new opportunity to tell their story, they may, on this journey around the spiral, be able to confront and deal with the resistance.

The processes described above for dealing with resistance are used in conjunction with the reflective and summarizing skills described in Chapter 12. By using these combined skills to confront the resistance, the child may then be enabled to move through the resistance and to continue telling their story.

When a child is not able to confront resistance

As counsellors it is important for us to recognize that we do not always have success in achieving our goals. Particularly when using a brief therapy model, there will be a small percentage of children who are unable to confront and deal with resistance. In such a case we have two options. One option is to recognize the child's predicament, acknowledge it, and then talk to the child and also the parent/s or carer/s. We might say to the child, 'It seems to me that it is too difficult [or scary, worrying, and so on] for you to talk about ... [whatever the issue relates to], and if you don't feel able to talk about these things, that is OK.' The counsellor might then help the child to discover practical strategies for dealing with day-to-day problems. Clearly, this approach deviates from our preferred Spiral of Therapeutic Change approach, as important emotional issues are not addressed. However, in the short term this may not be possible. Additionally, the counsellor might talk to the parent/s or carer/s about the child not being ready to talk about sensitive troubling issues, so that the parents are informed of the limits to counselling outcomes and made aware that, at some time in the future, the child may need to restart the counselling process when they are able to talk about the difficult issues that are currently blocked.

Another option when a child is blocked and unable to deal with the resistance is to engage the child in long-term psychotherapy involving free play, with the counsellor focusing on maintaining a positive relationship with the child. In this way, the issues may be worked through indirectly, enabling the child to progress round the spiral to the point of 'Continuing to tell their story and getting in touch with strong emotions'.

Dealing with transference

The nature of transference was discussed in Chapter 2 (see p. 14). Although we have not specifically included it on the Spiral of Therapeutic Change, the process of the child telling their story can be affected not only by resistance but also by transference.

As discussed earlier, it is inevitable that transference and counter-transference will occur at times during the counselling process. Unfortunately, if transference and counter-transference are ignored when they occur, then the quality of the child–counsellor relationship will be changed. This change in the quality of the relationship will then interfere with, and undermine, the therapeutic process.

When we, as counsellors, suspect that transference and/or counter-transference is occurring, it is helpful to step back from the immediacy of the counselling relationship and to be as objective as possible. This is best done by talking to a supervisor about the transference so that we can deal effectively with those issues of ours which predispose us to move into the counter-transference position. Within the counselling situation it is then important to be vigilant so that we can remain sufficiently detached and objective to avoid behaving like a parent. It is also important for us to raise the child's awareness of the transference process.

We have noticed that in the transference process there are often two dimensions in which material is projected on to the counsellor. These dimensions involve the child's experiences and fantasies with regard to first a 'good' mother, and second a 'bad' mother. Naturally, transference relating to a mother figure generally occurs with female counsellors; for male counsellors, transference will generally relate to the father figure. Additionally, there are a number of different scenarios for male counsellors, some of which strictly relate to transference and some of which relate to broader issues of projection.

Consider transference related to the child's experiences and fantasies of a 'good' mother. In this case, the child may have expectations that the counsellor will meet all their needs. Clearly, the counsellor cannot do this. However, the counter-transference might involve the counsellor *wanting* to meet the child's needs by, for example, protecting, cuddling or nurturing the child. If a counsellor were to respond in this way, the child would be set up for disappointment in the long term and diverted from facing the painful issue of not getting their needs met by their real mother.

Now consider transference related to the child's experiences and fantasies of a 'bad' mother. In this case, the child will project the negatively perceived behaviours of their mother onto the counsellor. As a consequence, the child might be aggressive or abusive to the therapist, and counter-transference might result in the counsellor becoming angry or punitive to the child. Alternatively, as a consequence of transference, the child might be withdrawn, submissive or compliant, and counter-transference might result in the counsellor becoming impatient or exasperated.

The appropriate counsellor behaviour for dealing with either type of transference is for the counsellor to:

1 Recognize and deal with their own feelings and issues as they arise in response to the child's behaviour.
2 Resist the temptation to respond as a parent and try to remain objective (without compromising safety – see rules in Chapter 2).
3 Raise the child's awareness of their behaviour. For example, the counsellor might say, 'It seems as though you want me to be like a good mother to you', or, in dealing with the negative case, 'I'm wondering if you are angry with me [or frightened of me] because you think that I am like your mother.'
4 Use the situation to explore the child's perceptions about mother–child relationships in general, and then to look at the mother–child relationship that the child actually experiences at home.

Steps 1 and 2 deal with the counter-transference and its associated behaviour. Step 3 raises the child's awareness of the transference behaviour and makes it clear to the child that the child–counsellor relationship is different from the mother–child relationship. Thus the child is less likely to have unrealistic expectations of the counselling relationship. Instead of escaping into an inappropriate relationship with the counsellor, in step 4 the child is encouraged to focus on the real-life issues relating to their own mother's relationship with them.

We need to point out that sometimes, at step 3, children will deny the truth of the transference projection. In this case we explore what the child's feelings are related to, and/or move on to step 4.

Transference behaviours will inevitably recur during the counselling process. Therefore, it is important to remain vigilant to ensure that the issues are consistently being effectively addressed.

KEY POINTS

- Resistance is said to occur when the child avoids talking about troubling issues.
- Resistance may be conscious or may occur at a subconscious level.
- Resistance provides the child with a way of protecting themselves from experiencing emotional pain.
- Resistance is often a sign that it might be helpful to explore and work through important material or significant issues.
- Defensive behaviours used by children to deal with anxiety and stress include regression, denial, avoidance, repression, projection, intellectualizing and rationalizing, and reaction formation.
- Some children develop undesirable behaviours in order to cope with stress instead of using defence mechanisms.
- Pressuring a child into talking about painful issues will raise the child's anxiety, with the consequence that they are most unlikely to continue talking about those issues.
- It can be useful to talk to the child openly about any identified resistance and to give them permission to withdraw.
- Transference and counter-transference interfere with the quality of the child–counsellor relationship and, if unaddressed, undermine the therapeutic process.
- In dealing with transference it is important for the counsellor to resist the temptation to respond as a parent, and to raise the child's awareness of the transference behaviour.
- When a counsellor recognizes that they are having difficulty coping with counter-transference it is helpful to address the issue with their supervisor.

15

Dealing with Self-Concept and Self-Destructive Beliefs

In previous chapters we have described the skills which help to enable the child to tell their story, and to get in touch with strong emotions and release them. In this chapter we will discuss the skills appropriate to Phase 3 of the SPICC model (see p. 72) to help the child to change their self-perception. These skills come from Narrative Therapy. Additionally, we will discuss the skills helpful in the first part of Phase 4 where we use Cognitive Behaviour Therapy to help the child deal with self-destructive beliefs.

As children grow up, they naturally and adaptively absorb ideas and beliefs from the adults and children around them. These ideas and beliefs that the child acquires are strongly influenced by the culture the child lives in. The child begins to develop a view of themselves within a context of a family and a wider community. This is the normal way in which children develop their self-concept and learn what is acceptable, and what is not acceptable, with regard to personal and social behaviour. Unfortunately, some beliefs which children absorb may not be appropriate or useful, but instead may result in emotional problems. Because this view or picture that the child has of themselves is unhelpful, instead of enabling the child to live a satisfying life the picture that they have of themselves and how they should behave causes problems for them. For example, a parent might teach a child to be polite to all strangers. As a consequence, the child may see themselves as a polite and obedient child. That child may then find themselves in a situation where, because of their beliefs that they should be polite, it becomes difficult or impossible for them to refuse the inappropriate advances of a stranger. Similarly, a child may receive repeated messages from those around them that they are useless, as they are unable to perform tasks that are required of them. As a consequence, the child may then see themselves as unlovable and also believe that they are incapable of performing new activities or tasks. It can be seen, then, that the way children see or view themselves is strongly related to the ideas and beliefs that they have about themselves. How the child sees themselves and their beliefs, thoughts and attitudes will reflect the child's self-concept. The extent to which the child values themselves is an indication of their self-esteem. We will discuss improving a child's self-esteem in Chapter 31.

As we have said, the child's self-concept is made up of how the child sees themselves and what they think and believe. It can be useful to initially address the child's ideas about themselves (their self-concept) and then to explore the child's beliefs, thoughts and attitudes which contribute to that self-concept.

Self-concept

As a result of the child experiencing strong emotions during the counselling process, often questions will spontaneously arise in the child's mind about their contribution to the troubling events which have brought them to counselling. Children are renowned for thinking that they are responsible when things go wrong. For example, when children live in violent homes they often feel responsible for the violence that occurs between adults. Similarly, in situations where sexual abuse has occurred children may often be troubled by their perceived collaboration in the event and blame themselves for the negative outcomes that occur.

In order to help the child to see themselves more positively we use concepts from Narrative Therapy. We have found that moving naturally and gently with the child's spontaneous questioning about themselves is a useful way to help the child develop a positive self-concept.

A negative self-concept can develop when the child interprets their participation in past and subsequent experiences as sneaky, incompetent, inept, disloyal, secretive, naughty, nasty or stupid. Similarly, a positive self-concept can be promoted if the child can be helped to remember events or experiences in their past that have been different from those they are focusing on and which resulted in more positive outcomes for them. Looking for these 'exceptions' to negative events and experiences helps the child to build up an alternative picture of who they are. Thus they may start to see themselves positively and to describe themselves using positive adjectives such as brave, honest, skilful, caring, and so on. One very powerful way for the counsellor to help the child change their view of themselves and find 'exceptions' is through the use of metaphor combined with some creative medium such as art or clay.

A metaphor is a figure of speech containing an implied comparison; it expresses one thing in terms of something else. Rather than making a direct description of some specific aspects about the child, the metaphor provides an alternative description. It uses an alternative picture and its contents to represent the real-life picture symbolically. In using metaphor, there is an underlying assumption that if some aspects of the metaphor agree with reality, then other aspects will also agree. This assumption can be useful in enabling the counsellor to make use of metaphor with the child to explore the child's perceptions of themselves more fully. For example, the counsellor might invite the child to draw a picture of themselves as if they were a fruit tree. Once the child has completed the drawing the counsellor can process the child's picture by asking questions about the tree. Some useful questions might be 'Where does this tree grow; on its own in a field or in a garden with other trees, or in an orchard with similar fruit trees?' The answer to this question can give the counsellor information, which can then be compared with the child's life in terms of how they see themselves with regard to their social and interpersonal relationships. Other questions might be 'How does this tree manage in a fierce storm?' to explore the child's perception of themselves with regard to managing their fear, or 'What happens to this tree in the winter?' to explore the child's perception of their own inner strengths and resources. The counsellor can search for 'exceptions' by extending the metaphorical process. By doing this the child can be reminded of times in their life when they have behaved in ways that are positive, helpful and adaptive. The counsellor can invite the child to think of times when, for example, 'the tree's branches didn't fall off', and what would have to happen so that the 'fruit could grow all year round'. We have found that those children who may find it challenging to talk more directly about themselves can better explore concepts of self using this metaphor of a fruit tree (Geldard et al., 2009).

Self-destructive beliefs

By helping the child to see themselves differently, the counsellor is then able to help them explore any inappropriate beliefs that have supported a negative view of themselves. If a child holds on to inappropriate beliefs they may become disempowered, anxious and compliant, and also have difficulty with interpersonal relationships. Inappropriate beliefs will often be recognized by the counsellor when the child has moved around the Spiral of Therapeutic Change to the point where strong emotions are experienced (see Figure 7.1, p. 59). Clearly, for useful therapeutic change to occur the child is supported to discard those beliefs which are maladaptive. The counsellor uses strategies which will enable the child to replace inappropriate and/or self-destructive beliefs with more useful beliefs.

It may sometimes be necessary for the counsellor to involve parents/carers in helping the child to discard and replace unhelpful beliefs. This is because it is usually parents who have the responsibility for helping their children to learn beliefs which will be useful and appropriate for them. Further, it could be quite destructive, and might set the child up for failure, if the counsellor challenged beliefs that were important in the child's current environment.

Below is a list of beliefs, which in all or some situations would be inappropriate or self-destructive for a child:

- I'm responsible for my father hitting my mother.
- I don't have any control because I'm too little.
- Boys are better than girls.
- It's not fair when I get treated differently from my brother.
- I'm naughty; that's why my mother doesn't love me.
- You have to be tough to be popular.
- Parents split up when kids misbehave.
- My parents should never punish me.
- If you tell the truth you get into trouble.
- My Mum and Dad will always look after me.
- You should always be good mannered.
- You should always be polite to grown-ups.
- It's bad to show that you're angry.
- You should never say 'no' to a grown-up.
- I must never make mistakes.
- I must always win.
- I must not cry.

In addition to beliefs similar to those listed above, there is a common self-destructive belief related to the effect of trauma. Following trauma, children sometimes believe that an irreversible negative change has occurred which will prevent life returning to normal. Thus the possibility of something new and different is ruled out, and the child believes that there is no way in which to start living in an adaptive and comfortable way. This is a very destructive belief because it prevents the child from leaving the trauma behind and moving forward into a space where life can once again be enjoyed.

Challenging self-destructive beliefs

The idea of challenging self-destructive beliefs derives from Rational Emotive Behaviour Therapy in which the client is challenged to replace so-called 'irrational beliefs' by 'rational beliefs' (see Dryden, 1995). Our approach is to encourage the child to challenge inappropriate and/or self-destructive beliefs and to replace them by more helpful or adaptive beliefs. Once they have done this they can progress around the Spiral of Therapeutic Change to the next stage, which is where the child looks at their options and choices.

The first step in challenging an inappropriate belief is to reflect back to the child what the counsellor perceives to be the child's belief. We will use an example of a child who believes that they are to blame for their father hitting their mother. In this case the counsellor might say to the child, 'You believe that you are responsible for your father hitting your mother.'

The next step is to help the child to test out the validity of the belief. To do this it is important to identify to what extent the belief comes from the child's own experience and to what extent it comes from what others have told them. For example, the counsellor might ask, 'How do you know that it is your fault that your Dad hits your Mum?'

The child's reply might indicate that their belief has come from their parents, who have told them that it was their fault. In this case, it is best if the child's parents be involved in the therapeutic process so that this belief can change. Alternatively, the child's response may indicate that their belief relates to their own perceptions of the connection between their behaviour and their father's behaviour. The counsellor can then explore the logic behind the child's thinking and to invite the child to consider alternative beliefs. This could be done by asking questions such as, 'If you hit someone, would it be your fault or someone else's fault?' Thus the counsellor raises the child's awareness of other possible beliefs, which in some way the child is overlooking or failing to identify for themselves. The counsellor might also help the child to compare their experiences with their perceptions of other children's experiences.

Challenging self-destructive and/or inappropriate beliefs may involve bringing into the child's awareness, in an acceptable way, information which might be unpalatable to them and which is being avoided or is just not being noticed. The child may need to accept information they may not want to hear. For example, this child may not want to accept that their father is capable of behaving abusively and violently. Patiently, and with care, the counsellor supports the child to accept reality.

During this process a child may need to own and accept responsibility for some parts of the events which have troubled them. It is important to help the child to separate out those parts of the events for which they were responsible from those parts for which they were clearly not responsible.

To summarize: challenging inappropriate or self-destructive beliefs involves the following:

- reflecting back the child's current belief;
- helping the child to check the validity of that belief by identifying where the belief comes from;
- exploring the logic behind the child's thinking;
- helping the child to explore possible alternative beliefs;
- raising the child's awareness of unpalatable information;
- helping the child to separate out who is responsible for what behaviours – themselves or others; and
- enabling the child to replace maladaptive beliefs with more appropriate beliefs.

We will now consider two more examples of challenging inappropriate and/or self-destructive beliefs.

Example one

Imagine that a boy has been in a violent home in which there have been strong messages that females are inferior and should not have the same rights as males. The counsellor might reflect back the child's belief by saying, 'You believe that boys are better than girls.'

To help the child to check the validity of the belief, the counsellor might ask, 'How do you know that's true?' The child might give an answer which suggests that the males in his family get preferential treatment.

The counsellor might now float alternative ideas. For example, the counsellor might ask questions like, 'What things can Mum do that Dad can't do?' or make statements such as, 'Boys and girls are different'. The counsellor can then help the child to recognize that difference does not imply better or worse, but that each gender has different attributes. This information is likely to be unpalatable for the child when initially presented, but can hopefully be accepted after some exploration of the issues. Once the child has accepted the alternative belief, he can examine how his behaviour contributes to relationship problems for him.

Example two

Consider a child who believes that her parents should never punish her. In this case, the counsellor could reflect back the child's belief, then check its validity by finding out where the belief came from. The child might say, 'My Mum does things that she shouldn't do, and she doesn't get into trouble.' The counsellor could then explore the child's logic, which includes an underlying assumption that children and parents are equal. To do this the counsellor might ask questions such as 'Does your best friend, Trudy, get punished by her mother?' and 'Who makes the rules in families, parents or children?' Thus the child's awareness of unpalatable information is raised, and hopefully the child will realize that in reality parents control children. The counsellor can then help the child to see how her own behaviour inevitably results in punishment.

Two useful techniques which can be used in the processes described above for challenging inappropriate and/or self-destructive beliefs are *reframing* and *normalizing*.

Reframing

The idea behind reframing is to alter the way the child perceives their situation. This can be done by accepting the child's picture of their world and expanding that picture to include additional information so that the child will perceive their situation differently and more constructively. For example, a girl might be complaining that her older brother is continually telling her to keep her room tidy. A reframe might be: 'Is it possible that your brother cares about you so much that he wants to prevent you from getting into trouble because your room is untidy?'

Normalizing

Sometimes it is helpful for a child to know that their thoughts, feelings and/or behaviours are similar to those of other children. Giving a child this information is called normalizing the child's experience. For example, a counsellor might say, 'Many children whose parents have split up believe that it is their fault that their parents have separated.'

When normalizing it is important not to invalidate the child's feelings and associated discomfort.

KEY POINTS

- A child's beliefs, thoughts and attitudes contribute to their self-concept.
- Children often incorrectly believe that they are responsible when things go wrong involving others.
- Narrative therapy and/or metaphor can be useful in helping a child to develop a positive self-concept.
- Self-destructive beliefs negatively impact on a child's self-concept and behaviour.
- Challenging self-destructive beliefs can be done sensitively in a process which explores the logic behind the current belief and helps the child to explore possible alternatives.
- Reframing involves expanding that child's picture to include additional information so that the child will perceive their situation differently and more constructively.
- It can be helpful for a child to know that their thoughts, feelings, and/or behaviours are similar to those of other children.

16

Actively Facilitating Change

In previous chapters we described those skills which are suitable for joining, helping the child to tell their story, to get in touch with and release emotions, and to change self-concept. However, we do not believe that the therapeutic work is necessarily complete once these processes have been achieved. Often, as a result of troubling experiences and/or emotions, children will develop unhelpful ways of thinking and behaving, and these unhelpful ways of thinking and behaving will not necessarily change unless they are directly addressed.

We can address unhelpful ways of thinking by challenging inappropriate and self-destructive beliefs and encouraging the child to replace them by more helpful ones, as explained in the previous chapter. Having done this, the next step in Phase 4 of the SPICC model (see p. 72) is for the counsellor to continue to use Cognitive Behaviour Therapy to help the child to consider their options and choices. After this, in Phase 5, the child can be encouraged to rehearse and experiment with new behaviours through the use of Behaviour Therapy.

Exploring options and choices

As we have just indicated, as a result of a child's past experiences, they may have learnt behaviours which are unhelpful for them and unacceptable to others. For example, the child may have learnt to be excessively compliant, or aggressive, or deceitful, or to behave in a regressed way. Consequently, they may now need to learn how to behave differently and look at their options and choices.

One way to help a child to explore their options and choices is to use ideas from Glasser's Reality Therapy approach to help the child recognize that they can choose to use whatever behaviour they wish, but must take responsibility for the consequences of the behaviour they choose. Because we are counselling children we introduce this Reality Therapy idea through the use of a comic strip.

The comic strip exercise

Many comic strips that we see in the newspaper have a sequence of three frames, which tell a story as illustrated in Figure 16.1a.

In the comic strip exercise we use the three frames differently as shown in Figure 16.1b. In the first frame, at the left-hand end of the comic strip, the child is encouraged to draw sketches, or to use abstract symbols, to represent particular behaviours which are causing problems for them – unhelpful behaviours.

In the third frame, at the right-hand end of the comic strip, the child is encouraged to draw sketches, or to use abstract symbols, to represent alternative behaviours – helpful behaviours – which are likely to produce more positive outcomes and which could be used in place of the unhelpful behaviours that have been illustrated in the first frame.

In the centre frame the child is encouraged to draw a self-portrait.

A case study

Kathryn will now discuss an imaginary case to illustrate the comic strip.

Imagine that I, Kathryn, have been counselling a boy called Adam who is continually getting into trouble at home for punching his sister, and for deliberately throwing

FIGURE 16.1 *The comic strip*

things and breaking them when he is angry. Clearly, before using the comic strip, I would have helped Adam to tell me his story and to get in touch with and release his angry emotions. However, even though he had been through this counselling process, Adam might continue at times to hit his sister and to throw things and break them when he is angry, because this is the way he has learnt to respond to his frustration over a long period of time. Obviously, it is important for him to learn how to replace these unhelpful behaviours with more helpful ones.

The first step in the process would be for me to talk with Adam about those behaviours of his that I know get him into trouble. I would also check out with him whether there are any other behaviours that he could think of that get him into trouble. I would then ask him to draw sketches in the left-hand frame of his comic strip to illustrate these problematic behaviours. I would explain to him that I would like to help him to avoid getting into trouble and I realize that these behaviours are a problem for him.

The left-hand frame of Adam's comic strip might look like the left-hand frame in Figure 16.1c.

Notice in the left-hand corner of the frame that Adam has drawn a stick picture of himself punching his sister. Once Adam had drawn this, I would ask him what might have happened before he got angry and punched his sister. He might say, 'She takes my things, and she's always teasing me.' I would explain to Adam, that while I understand that his sister might be very annoying and provocative, that provocation does not justify abuse, and punching his sister is abusive. Moreover, I know that punching his sister gets him into an awful lot of trouble and I would like to help him to avoid getting into trouble.

I would then invite Adam to draw two other pictures in the left-hand frame. One to show his sister taking his things, and another to show her teasing him as shown at the top of the left-hand frame of Figure 16.1c.

I would remind Adam that his parents have told me that he will often throw and break things when he gets angry, particularly when his parents won't let him do what he wants, or won't give him what he is asking for. I would ask him to add a picture to the left-hand frame of himself throwing and breaking things, as shown in the bottom right-hand corner of the picture in Figure 16.1c.

Next, I would look at each of Adam's sketches in turn, and explore with him things that he could do that would have better outcomes for him; things that he could do instead of punching his sister, and instead of throwing and breaking things.

I would ask Adam to draw sketches in the right-hand 'helpful behaviours' frame to illustrate the alternative behaviours that he could use. I would initially encourage Adam to think of helpful behaviours himself, and after that I would tentatively make suggestions of other behaviours that I thought might be useful and would discuss these with him to see whether or not he agreed.

Adam might draw sketches like those shown in the right-hand frame of Figure 16.1c. In the bottom left-hand corner a sketch shows Adam walking away from his sister without responding to her when she teases him. In the bottom right-hand corner a drawing shows him talking to his mother, explaining that his sister has taken one of his possessions without permission. In the top left-hand corner Adam goes into his bedroom when he's really angry and shuts the door, lies on his bed imagining that the mattress represents his anger. The picture shows him pummelling the mattress while repeatedly saying, 'I hate being angry, I hate being angry'. This is a way for him to let his anger out without hurting anyone or damaging anything.

With regard to this last strategy, it is important for counsellors to use caution. Sometimes we are asked by new counsellors whether or not it is a good idea to encourage angry children or young people to release their anger by punching a punching bag. We believe that there is real danger in encouraging children or young people to do this to get rid of anger. Punching a punching bag is too similar to punching another person. By hitting the punching bag they may just learn to how to hit harder and may at some stage in the future hit a person instead of the punching bag when they become really angry. Throughout our work with angry children it is important to stress that hitting other people is not OK, and that it is also abusive to frighten people by throwing things, breaking things, slamming doors, yelling and banging things loudly.

Finally, in the right-hand frame of the comic strip, at the top centre there are two sketches; one of Adam visiting one of his friends, and the other of him going for a bike ride so that he can get right away from his sister.

When using the comic strip strategy in this way it is almost always important to suggest to the child that it would be a good idea to show their parents the comic strip, or at least to talk to their parents about the new behaviours they would like to use. If they don't do this, their parents might inadvertently undermine their attempts to use the new behaviours. The parents may also need to set in place some rules for both the child and other members of the family. In Adam's case, the parents may explain to his sister that it is not OK for her to take his things without his permission, and that if she did do this then they would expect Adam to tell them.

In addition, they might need to set boundaries so that his sister did not go into his room after he had shut the door, when he wanted to be on his own or to vent his anger privately. His parents may also be clear with him about how he would ask for permission if he wanted to go to visit a friend or to ride his bike in order to escape from a troubling situation.

Once a child has completed drawing pictures in the 'unhelpful behaviours' and 'helpful behaviours' frames, the next stage is for the counsellor to ask the child to draw a picture of themselves in the central frame. Thus, Adam's comic strip would finally look as shown in Figure 16.1c.

The final stage of the comic strip process involves helping the child to recognize that they have choice about what behaviours they use, but are responsible for the consequences resulting from those behaviours. Firstly, I help the child to explore the various consequences which might result from the behaviours displayed in all the pictures. I deliberately avoid trying to pressure the child into believing that they should always behave in the way that is described by the pictures in the 'helpful behaviours' frame. In fact, I will say:

Sometimes you might deliberately choose to do the things that you have drawn in the 'unhelpful behaviours' frame, knowing that by doing them you are likely to get into trouble. At other times, when you recognize that you are about to do one of the things described in the 'unhelpful behaviours' frame, you will recognize that you have a choice, that you can do this if you want to, but that you don't need to – instead, you can do something from the 'helpful behaviours' frame. The choice is yours! However, you will need to accept the consequences associated with the behaviour you choose.

I will fully explore with the child what it would be like to be about to engage in one of the unhelpful behaviours, and then to deliberately choose to engage in one of the helpful behaviours. I would be careful not to minimize the difficulty which the child might experience in letting go of the unhelpful behaviour and replacing it by a helpful behaviour.

Sometimes I encourage the child to draw a large comic strip on a roll of paper and then stretch it out and place it on the floor. I might then ask the child to initially stand beside the central self-portrait frame, and then, as we discuss particular behaviours invite them to move physically to stand at either the left frame or the right frame as they consider which choice fits best for them. This movement emphasizes the child's responsibility for choices by adding another dimension to the exercise. Whenever they choose a particular behaviour I ask them to remind me of the likely consequences of using that behaviour.

Once I have completed the comic strip process, I will ask the child: 'Would you like to show your comic strip to your Mum or Dad? Or would you like to keep it private?' I will explain that there might be an advantage in showing the strip to Mum or Dad as they may be able to help. For example, if Dad noticed that Adam was just about to use an unhelpful behaviour, he might be able to tip him off and suggest a helpful behaviour instead. I might ask Adam, 'Would you like Dad to help you in this way or not?' Once again the decision would be the child's.

You might wonder why I put such an emphasis on giving the child the opportunity to make choices. I do this because I believe that there is a much greater chance of success in changing behaviour if the child themselves believes that they have the choice and are capable of taking responsibility for the consequences of that choice. In this regard, I would give the child encouragement by saying, 'I think that sometimes it will be difficult for you to choose a helpful behaviour, but I think you will probably be able to do this quite often – what do you think?' At a later counselling session I might check the child's success in choosing helpful behaviours and, assuming that there has been a level of success, congratulate the child by saying, 'Well done, I thought you could do that!'

The comic strip process works well with many children. However, it's important to recognize that some children are extremely impulsive and may need help in managing their impulsive behaviour or they will not succeed in replacing unhelpful behaviours by helpful ones. There are two strategies that we can use with children to help them learn self-management skills. For younger children, the 'monster-in-me' strategy can be very useful, and for older children the 'stop–think–do' process can be effective. We will describe these strategies later in this chapter.

Making the decision to change

We might expect that parents, family members and others would be pleased if a child learnt to behave more adaptively. However, we human beings dislike change, and if a child changes their behaviour, then those who interact with the child may also need to change their behaviour. For example, if a child has been behaving in a compliant way, parents and others may have difficulty accepting the behaviour of the child if they become more assertive with regard to their own needs. The other people in their life may need to learn to respond differently and initially may not like doing this. Consequently, as the child's behaviour changes, they may have to deal with some unpleasant reactions by others. They may find that they are unable to cope with those reactions and that, without help, they lack the skills to carry out the newly discovered behaviours. One way of dealing with this problem is to integrate individual counselling for the child with family therapy as discussed in Chapter 9; however, this is not always possible.

If a child does decide to behave differently, then they take a risk because they cannot predict what will occur. It may well be easier for them to go on behaving as they did in the past. Certainly, if they make no changes they will continue to experience the pain they know, whereas if they take a risk and behave differently they will face new and unknown pain. Clearly, making a decision to change is hard: the child has to cope not only with their own feelings but also with other people's reactions.

Another difficulty is related to the loss or cost component, which may result from the decision to change. Frequently, we have found that deciding whether or not to accept the loss associated with a decision is more difficult than choosing between the positive gains associated with the decision. Consider a child who has behaved in an angry, aggressive way, and has been stubborn and uncooperative with adults. Because of these behaviours, the child may have gained the respect of peers and have assumed a leadership role. As a result of counselling, the child may have gained insight into their behaviour and may have recognized how destructive it is for themselves and for others around them. However, to give up their maladaptive behaviours would involve a loss: they might lose their leadership role, their power, and the respect and control of peers. The child may see the decision about whether to change or not more in terms of the things they would lose than the positive things they would gain. Unless the counsellor validates the importance of the child's losses, the child may be blocked from making the desired change in behaviours.

Some children have difficulty in making decisions because they have been taught that there is always a right choice and a wrong choice. Unfortunately, in real life, decisions are often complicated, with differing options having advantages or positive qualities, and also costs or disadvantages. Therefore, it is important for the counsellor to help the child to understand that making decisions does not generally involve deciding between right and wrong or between black and white. Most decisions involve a choice between shades of grey.

Consider again the child we have just been discussing. In considering their options, the child may initially decide to suppress their anger, to be more cooperative, compliant and submissive, and to become a follower instead of a leader. However, it is incumbent on the counsellor to introduce some new ideas so that the child has more choices. As an alternative to suppressing anger, the counsellor may raise the option of the child dealing with their anger differently and being assertive. The counsellor might introduce the concept of showing initiative, instead of submissiveness and compliance. Thus the child is offered options which will allow them to continue to gain respect from others, but in a different way, by using different behaviours.

Consequently, they may be able to continue to exercise a leadership role and to have an appropriate level of control in some situations. It is important to remember, however, that the counsellor can only suggest alternative options and never try to persuade the child. A child is only likely to carry through on choices which they have made themselves and which fit for them.

In summary, exploring options and choices involves the following:

- weighing up advantages and disadvantages of options;
- looking at the risks involved in making behavioural changes;
- being realistic about possible losses or costs;
- understanding that there may be reactions from others to changed behaviour.

It is the counsellor's job to help the child to work through the issues related to the above.

It must be clear from the above discussion that it will be difficult for some children to change their behaviour. In particular, we have discovered in our counselling practice that many children have problems in trying to control a tendency to react impulsively without thinking first. This tendency seems to be particularly powerful at times when the child is starting to become angry. Consequently, we often hear of children who become angry very quickly and act out inappropriately as a result. There are two useful strategies for helping children with this problem. One of these strategies is the 'monster-in-me' strategy, which is particularly suitable for use with younger children. The other strategy is the 'stop–think–do' strategy, which can be very helpful for older children.

The 'monster-in-me' strategy

Kathryn will explain how she uses the 'monster-in-me' process, which adopts a Cognitive Behaviour Therapy approach to help the child recognize that they have the ability to control their behaviour instead of letting their behaviour control them. This is done in conjunction with the Narrative Therapy idea of 'externalizing the problem'.

What I do when I use the 'monster-in-me' strategy is to explain to the child that, as they know, their parents have told me that they get into a lot of trouble. I explain that I don't think that it is their fault that they get into a lot of trouble. I think that it is the monster that lives inside them that gets them into a lot of trouble. It's the monster's fault!

Now when you hear this you might be troubled because you might think that I am absolving the child from responsibility for their behaviour. It certainly appears to the child that I am doing that, but in fact I'm not … because I will subsequently make it clear that it is the child's responsibility to control the monster!

I say to the child:

I think you get into trouble because there's this monster that lives inside you.
Usually the monster is sound asleep, and when he's asleep he shrinks and becomes very, very, small. So small that he's smaller than a pinhead. Now, I think that when you start to get angry the monster wakes up, and he starts to get bigger, and bigger, and bigger,

and bigger! He then takes over and does the most terrible things, he throws things around, he kicks, he punches, he yells, and he screams. And as a result you get into an awful lot of trouble, and that isn't fair!

The monster just goes back to sleep and doesn't get into any trouble at all, but you get into trouble!

Now I'd like you to draw me a great big picture of the monster that lives inside you with these coloured felt pens.

When the child has finished drawing a picture of the monster, I ask them to draw a picture of themselves on another sheet of paper. I then ask them to put a dot on the picture of themselves to show us where the monster lives inside them.

'Does the monster live in your stomach, in your head, or somewhere else?' I ask. I will usually say to the child, 'You seem like a pretty tough kid. However, I think this monster is pretty tough too. Is this monster tougher than you or are you tougher than the monster? Who's the boss – are you the boss or is the monster the boss?' Obviously, I encourage the child to believe that they are the boss, and usually they will tell me this anyway.

Next, I explain to the child that I think this monster is very sneaky. I remind the child that I think that it is the monster that gets the child into trouble, which doesn't seem fair. I suggest that the monster sneaks out all of a sudden without the child realizing until it's too late.

I will remind the child that the monster wakes up, grows big, and comes out, when they are starting to get angry.

I will ask: 'What's the first thing that happens when you're starting to get angry? Do you go red in the face, do you clench your fists, does your hair stand on end? What happens to you?' My goal is to help the child to recognize the physiological clues which precipitate an angry outburst.

At this stage I find it helpful to make use of Behaviour Therapy. To do this, the cooperation of a parent is required in monitoring the new behaviour and reinforcing it through giving or withholding a reinforcer. I suggest to the child that because the monster is so sneaky we need to have Mum's or Dad's help in order to make sure that the child remains the boss! I then invite the parent to come into the room and talk to them about my theory that the monster is to blame, but that I believe that the child is capable of being the boss and controlling the monster! I will ask the parent for their suggestions of ways in which they might be able to let the child know when they think that the monster is about to sneak out. Often this will be in the way of a secret symbol because the child will not want other members of the family to know that they are being tipped off by their parent that the monster is coming out.

Then I suggest the use of a star chart where the child gets a star in the morning, afternoon and evening, if they succeed in being boss of the monster during that period.

I make it clear, that if the monster is starting to come out and the child succeeds in controlling the monster, that they will definitely get the star, because even though the monster was starting to come out they were successful in being the boss.

I then encourage the parent and child to negotiate a reward which the child will get if they succeed in earning a certain number of stars during the week. I try to ensure that the number of stars required is not too high during the first week so that it is likely that the child will succeed.

I usually use a star chart for a second week also, but not for longer, because in my experience the effectiveness of star charts quickly diminishes after the first couple of weeks.

The 'monster-in-me' strategy can be very helpful with younger children, but will be seen as childish by older children. With older children it is better to use the 'stop–think–do' process in order to address impulsive behaviour.

The 'stop–think–do' process

David will explain this Cognitive Behaviour Therapy strategy, which has its origins in William Glasser's Reality Therapy and is an adaptation of processes described by Caselman (2005), Miller (2004) and Petersen and Adderley (2002).

I think that it is a good idea to start the 'stop–think–do' process by encouraging the child to make two lists. One is a list of those behaviours that result in negative consequences, and the other is a list of those behaviours the result in positive consequences for them.

As Kathryn explained when describing the comic strip exercise, I explain to the child that they can choose to engage in those behaviours that result in negative outcomes, or they can choose those behaviours that result in positive consequences. I will stress that they have the ability to make their own choices about how they behave. However, their choices inevitably have consequences, either positive or negative. I will let the child know that I believe that they will sometimes impulsively behave in a way which have negative consequences for them, and then wish they hadn't.

I will then write on the whiteboard in large letters the words:

STOP

THINK

DO

I will explain that if they are able to stop, and pause for a second or two before acting, they will have time to think about their possible choices and to make a choice about the way they want to behave, taking into account the likely consequences.

I will say that I know that sometimes it is difficult to stop, and in order to help them stop it is important that they are able to recognize when their emotions are building up to a level where they might act out without stopping and thinking first.

As in the 'monster-in-me' strategy, I will check out with the child the physiological indicators that can be used to let them know that they are about to act out.

I will ask what they notice about their body when their emotions are starting to rise? Do they clench their fists, go red in the face, feel their heart beating faster, or notice something else? I will write down what they tell me on the whiteboard.

I will reiterate that if they are able to stop before acting out, they will have time to think, to make a choice taking into account the likely consequences, and to do something which has positive consequences for them rather than negative ones.

In some situations it can be useful to involve parents, as in the 'monster-in-me' strategy, so that the parents are aware that the child is intending to try to use the 'stop–think–do' process. This puts the parents in a position where they can help their child to recognize the signs that they are about to act out.

Rehearsing and experimenting with new behaviours

After the child has made decisions about future behaviours, the counsellor can then help the child to rehearse and to practise the desired behaviours.

Some children find it helpful to use action plans when deciding how to experiment with, or to implement, new behaviours. By using an action plan, the counsellor can help the child to identify the goals they hope to achieve and can look at how these goals can be achieved. In doing this, the child may initially believe that they lack the skills to carry out the desired behaviours, and may need assistance from the counsellor to acquire these skills.

Using our previous example, as a result of counselling the child may have gained insight into how destructive their aggressive behaviour has been in the past. They may then have decided that they want to be less aggressive (goal one), but also want to maintain some control so that their needs can continue to be met (goal two). Now that they have identified their goals, it is desirable to work out a plan so that these goals can be achieved. That plan might include the following steps:

1 Identifying the signals which will warn of rising anger.
2 Learning how to deal with that anger (by challenging self-destructive beliefs and using other anger-control techniques).
3 Learning to be assertive.
4 Practising the above in role play.
5 Experimenting with the new behaviour in the family, school or social setting.
6 Adjusting their behaviour in response to other people's reactions.

Having made a plan, the counsellor can help the child to implement it. In the above plan, the counsellor would deal with steps 1 to 4 in counselling sessions. The counsellor would then help the child to make a decision with regard to the timing of step 5.

We wonder if you, the reader, are sometimes like us? When we have to carry out a new or difficult task, we often delay doing what we have decided to do by using the excuse that the time is not right. As a result, delayed action sometimes results in no action. When working with children it's important to be aware that they, too, may have a tendency to put off doing what is new and possibly difficult. It is useful to explore with children the desirability of choosing a suitable time and place for practising new behaviours. This exploration serves a dual purpose: it helps the child to avoid procrastinating, and it alerts the child to the risks of using the new behaviour at an inappropriate time.

For a child to use newly learnt assertive behaviour in the morning, when the family is preparing to leave for work and school, might be inappropriate. Use of the new behaviour at this time might prove unsuccessful because parents and other family members may not be expecting it and will probably be feeling pressured with regard to keeping to their normal routine. Therefore, it is important for the counsellor to discuss with the child the need for sensible timing when trying out new behaviours.

After the child has tried out the new behaviour, the counsellor can look at the outcomes and help the child to make necessary adjustments to the behaviour (step 6 in the plan above). The counsellor can support the child to feel good and to recognize that they have shown courage in trying out the new behaviour. A child who has attempted to use a new behaviour but failed to achieve a positive outcome is more likely to continue making further attempts to change if they receive praise for having had the courage to try out a new way of behaving. Frequent discussions with the child's parents can help to ensure that the child is affirmed and rewarded when using new and more appropriate behaviours.

Sometimes, as the result of counselling, children develop unexpected behaviours which were previously non-existent. These behaviours may well be adaptive, but they may not always suit the parents and family. The counsellor can respond by reminding the parents that the child is maturing and developing during the counselling process. Children are by their nature continually developing and changing, so it is almost inevitable that a child's behaviour will change significantly when participating in counselling. When unexpected behavioural change occurs, it may be necessary for counselling to focus on helping the parents to manage these behaviours. Sometimes, counselling strategies might need adjustment in order to address these changes.

KEY POINTS

- Children often develop unhelpful ways of thinking and behaving as a result of troubling experiences.
- After the child has told their story, and identified and released strong emotions, counselling can then address unhelpful thoughts and behaviours through the use of Cognitive Behaviour Therapy and Behaviour Therapy.
- The comic strip exercise is useful in helping a child to identify options and choices.
- The 'monster-in-me' strategy is useful in helping younger children to control outbursts of undesirable behaviour.
- The 'stop–think–do' strategy is useful in helping older children to control impulsive behaviour.

17

Termination of Counselling

The decision about when to terminate a series of counselling sessions can sometimes be a difficult one for a counsellor. If we look at the Spiral of Therapeutic Change (see Figure 7.1, p. 59), we might assume that the time for termination would be obvious. Once the child has reached the point of *Resolution* on the spiral, then counselling will no longer be required and the child will move ahead, functioning adaptively. However, in practice the decision is often not so easy. There are a few ways in which the question of termination can be made difficult for the counsellor. Any of the following may cause problems:

1 Regression, with the child relapsing into previous behaviours, sometimes occurs with children who are anxious about ending the therapeutic relationship.
2 As termination approaches the child may raise new and different issues.
3 The counsellor may have unwittingly become dependent on the counselling relationship.
4 The child may seem to have reached a plateau in the therapeutic process, with the counsellor believing that more change is required.

With regard to item 1 (the problem of the child regressing), the counsellor may respond by raising the issues of separation, abandonment and rejection with the child. This will enable the child to recognize their response to the impending termination and to explore new ways of managing their response now and in the future.

With regard to item 2, the counsellor will make a decision about whether or not to allow the child to re-enter the Spiral of Therapeutic Change, starting at the beginning again. This decision will depend on an assessment of the importance of the new issues, and an assessment of the child's ability to deal with them independently without the assistance of counselling.

Item 3 is a matter of ongoing importance to any counsellor. When counsellors do become dependent, they often have difficulty in recognizing this. The best way to identify such dependency is for counsellors to have regular supervision where their cases are discussed with an experienced counsellor.

With regard to item 4, reaching a plateau may be an indication that the child needs an opportunity to integrate and to assimilate the changes which are taking place as a result of the counselling process. This is often a good time to terminate counselling.

While a few children may require long-term therapy, we believe that generally children should not be engaged in a counselling process over a long period of time. Adults are different: they may have accumulated many years of unresolved issues. These tend to compound each other, so that the counsellor may need to help the adult client work through many layers of unfinished business. Because of their more limited life experience, children generally don't seem to accumulate the same complexity of neurotic or maladaptive behaviours.

Responsible counselling requires the counsellor to continually review the progress of therapy to check whether goals have been achieved and, if so, to terminate the counselling process. Certainly, except in unusual cases, if a child continues coming to counselling over a period of several months, then it is important for the counsellor to review the case and consider revising goals and moving towards termination. Generally, we work with children on a weekly basis over a period of two to three months. However, some children need only two or three visits before termination.

As counsellors we do have clues that the time is right for termination. Here are some possible clues:

1   The child may have reached a plateau (see earlier discussion).
2   Sometimes the child will remain blocked and unable to deal adaptively with resistance. This needs to be respected, so that the child does not feel pressured but can return to counselling later, knowing that they will not be forced to do work which is too painful.
3   Sometimes the child seems to have an inner sense that to continue would need more strength than they are able to provide at that time.
4   The child may have become involved and happily engaged in social activities with friends, in sport, or in a club. Further, they may be starting to see counselling as an unnecessary intrusion into their life and may not want to attend.
5   The focus of counselling may shift and the child may begin to 'play' instead of doing useful therapeutic work, with the counsellor recognizing that the counselling sessions no longer seem to be achieving therapeutic goals.
6   The child has gone far enough in the counselling process so that they can continue making progress on their own. This is especially true when parents are involved and committed to the process of change.
7   The child's behaviour may have changed, as reported by the parents or school.

With regard to the last item on the above list, it is important to point out that improved behaviour on its own may not be sufficient reason to terminate the counselling process. Changes of behaviour can also be due to the child opening up and expressing deeper material to the counsellor, so it is important to look at what is happening in the counselling process at the time.

Even though, as counsellors, we try to help children gain as much independence as we can, it is inevitable that many children will form a caring attachment to their counsellor. There will therefore be a loss for a child when the counselling relationship ends, so it is important that the child be adequately prepared for termination. In this preparation we talk openly with the child about the impending separation and explore the child's feelings with regard to this. It might be useful to engage the child in an activity that focuses on what it is like to be leaving the counselling relationship. Children might sometimes feel ambivalent about leaving and it is important to allow them to share their mixed feelings. Finally, to say 'Goodbye' we may want to have a special closing session so that the child is enabled symbolically to let go of the counselling relationship.

Sometimes a counsellor may decide to ease the situation for the child by maintaining contact for a limited period of follow-up. This could be in the form of further assessments, letters or phone calls.

During the termination process, it is important for the counsellor to be in touch with their own feelings and reactions so that these do not interfere with appropriate termination at the right time. Where a counsellor recognizes some dependency on their own part, they may need to talk with their supervisor.

KEY POINTS

- Generally it is not desirable to engage a child in a counselling process over a long period of time.
- It is good practice to continually review the progress of counselling in order to check whether goals have been achieved so that termination can occur at the appropriate time.
- Where a child does require long-term counselling it is important that the case be looked at regularly with a view to revising goals and moving towards termination.
- Because the child loses the counselling relationship at termination, it is important for the child to be forewarned so that they are adequately prepared.
- It is important for the counsellor to be in touch with their own feelings and reactions so that these do not interfere with appropriate termination at the right time.

18

Skills for Counselling Children in Groups

As explained in Chapter 10 it can sometimes be advantageous to run counselling groups for children. Counselling children in a group requires additional skills to those required when working with children individually, as the counsellor has to facilitate the group process as well as attending to the needs of individual children. Thus the counsellor has to do several things simultaneously while the group is running. While facilitating group activities they have to observe, notice and respond to issues concerning the group as a whole, while continuing to attend to the individual needs of group members. Consequently it is certainly preferable, and we think essential, to have two group leaders who work together in each counselling group.

Leadership

Two leaders offer two sets of observations, two perspectives and a broader expertise. They may complement each other's strengths and weaknesses, and their relationship can serve as a successful role model for relationships for the children (Siepker and Kandaras, 1985). Having two leaders is especially sensible for those groups where there is a high degree of disturbance in a group. It is a necessity for groups where there is the possibility of disruptive or violent behaviour. For children's groups in general, there are considerable practical advantages in having two leaders, as one can attend to the whole group while the other attends to individuals with specific needs.

Leaders and sweepers

Where there are two leaders, before the start of a group session it is essential that they agree about their individual roles and responsibilities. Our preferred model is for one leader to take the primary role of *leader* and the other to take the role of *sweeper*. Each time the group meets the leaders can, if they wish, reverse roles, so that the group does not associate the primary leadership with one person. We believe that this is particularly important when the co-leaders are of opposite gender.

The leader's role involves directly organizing and processing group activities. It is the leader who makes decisions about what to do next, and is generally seen to be in charge. The sweeper's role is different, but equally important. The sweeper's role includes being supportive of the leader, attending to individual problems when these cannot be dealt within the whole group setting, fetching and carrying materials, and attending to issues that may arise as a result of a group process. An example of an issue which might be dealt with by a sweeper is dealing with the difficult behaviour of one individual, if dealing with this in the whole group setting might be counter-productive for the child concerned, or might seriously intrude on an important group process.

Leadership style

Every leader will have their own personal leadership style, but that style is influenced by the counselling model to be used. For example, when running a group using Cognitive Behaviour Therapy, the style of leadership will tend to be didactic and directive, whereas when running a group using a humanistic/existentialist counselling approach the leader will be more likely to focus on the use of reflection and feedback of observations.

The leadership style also takes into account the needs of the particular group of children involved. For example, when running a group for children with Attention Deficit Hyperactivity Disorder (ADHD), leaders may need to contain behaviours and be predominantly authoritarian, whereas when running a group for anxious children a gentler approach might be more suitable.

Whatever style is used, the leader's role is to take action to ensure the emotional and physical safety of group members and to maximize the potential for achieving change.

It is important for leaders to take account of their own personality traits so that the style of leadership they use is authentic and genuinely matches their individual personalities. They can choose to use a predominantly democratic, or authoritarian, or laissez-faire leadership style. However, we prefer to use a proactive approach involving a combination of these. In the proactive approach, the leader is flexible, so that spontaneous movement from an emphasis on one style to another occurs. Thus, during a group session, and over the life of a group, we vary our style to maximize opportunities occurring in the group, and also to suit the mood and activity of the group at any particular time.

Usually our proactive approach to leadership will make use of a democratic leadership style as the predominant style to allow individuals in the group to feel free to make choices within limits set by the group, while at the same time providing safety. However, being proactive allows leaders to be authoritarian when appropriate, in order to ensure compliance with group rules, and to ensure that goals are met. At other times leaders may deliberately use a laissez-faire style for a while to allow children in the group more freedom. During this period of freedom, they can observe the group's interactions, behaviours and social skills, which can then be discussed or 'processed', as described later.

Debriefing and supervision

Naturally, when there are two leaders, it is essential that they have a good working relationship with each other. To achieve this, it is good practice to talk through any negative feelings which arise. Debriefing also enables leaders to provide feedback and support for each other and to deal with issues with regard to group processes. During debriefing leaders can discuss the emerging needs of the individual children and changes which may be required in the way the group is facilitated to meet these needs.

As applies for counselling generally, it is essential for leaders to have ongoing supervision from an experienced counsellor.

Group facilitation

While attending to issues which develop for the whole group, leaders also attend to the issues of individual children. Some individual children may have unexpected and excessive responses to a group programme. For example, they may demonstrate high levels of anxiety, become dissociative, regress, and/or withdraw as a consequence of the programme content and/or the responses of other children. For some of these children, it may be possible to attend to their needs in a whole group setting by using appropriate intervention strategies and counselling skills. For other children this may not be possible. In this case, while the leader continues to address the needs of the group, the co-leader (the sweeper) may need to attend separately to the child in question by exploring that child's personal feelings and issues which have been triggered by the group programme. As a consequence of such an intervention, the child may be able to readjust to the group programme, or the child's membership of the group may need to be reassessed.

When running a group, it is sensible to plan the group programme in advance so that activities can be deliberately selected to encourage the group to interact in ways that will promote the achievement of specific goals. Examples of group programmes for children in specific target groups are given in our book *Working with Children in Groups: A Handbook for Counsellors, Educators and Community Workers* (Geldard and Geldard, 2001).

During group sessions the leaders observe and influence the group processes so that goals for individual children and the group can be met. Central to a leader's role is the orchestration of the group programme in such a way that the children experience a process which has a natural and comfortable flow as they participate in meaningful activity and discussion. Effective facilitation creates an atmosphere of safety and containment so that the children become free to explore, express themselves and gain from their experience. The group leader gives directions and instructions, introduces and organizes activities, facilitates discussion, gives support to individual children when required, teaches, gives advice, and models appropriate behaviour. Additionally the leader also deals with group issues as they arise. For example, when a child drops out of a group or a new child joins the group the leader's role is to help the group to readjust.

Recognizing and dealing with confidentiality issues

In counselling groups for children the participants need to be able to trust that there will be some level of confidentiality. If this is not so, they may not be willing to participate freely and to disclose information which relates to their issues.

The confidentiality issue is complicated, as parents or carers have the right to information about their children. It is therefore sensible for leaders to discuss the issue of confidentiality with parents at the stage where the child is being assessed for suitability for inclusion in the group as discussed in Chapter 10. Also, it is important to acknowledge that group leaders cannot ensure that children in a group will respect the confidentiality of others.

When counselling children in a group there is a possibility that group members may disclose abusive behaviours by parents or others. If this happens, the information may have to be reported to parents/carers, and/or the appropriate authorities, to ensure the ongoing safety and protection of the child. In particular, it is imperative that any legal requirements regarding reporting are observed.

When discussing issues of confidentiality with children in a group it is important to be open about the limits to confidentiality, and early in the group programme to be clear about any conditions and exceptions that might apply with regard to confidentiality.

Introducing and organizing activities

When activities are organized or introduced it is important for group leaders to explain clearly what is expected. Often, some children in a group will be familiar with a particular activity, whereas others will not. While introducing activities, it is usually sensible to explain how the activity relates to the purpose of the group.

Facilitating discussion

To facilitate discussion, a leader's role includes guiding the verbal exchanges between and among the children in the group. While a discussion is taking place the counselling skills described later can be used to provide the children with the opportunity to share their thoughts, feelings and ideas on relevant topics. Leaders may need to deal with monopolizing behaviour and interruptions, and to encourage children who are not participating to contribute. Leaders may also need to deal with diversions and inappropriate contributions from children.

Counselling skills for use in children's groups

The counselling skills selected for use when running a group will depend on the type of group and the theoretical approach of the leaders. However, the counselling micro-skills most commonly used in counselling groups for children include:

- Observation
- Active listening

- Summarizing
- Giving feedback
- Using questions
- Confrontation
- Giving instructions
- Processing skills.

Observation

When using observation skills, as described in Chapter 11, leaders may usefully observe not only current behaviours and social skills, but also changes in these over the life of the group. The group programme may then be adjusted, if necessary, to meet changes in perceived needs.

Active listening

Active listening skills include non-verbal responses, minimal responses, reflection of content and feeling, and summarizing. These skills have been described in Chapter 12 and are particularly useful when encouraging children to self-disclose and share personal information with a group.

Summarizing

The skill of summarizing is especially useful when working in groups as it enables a leader to feed back to the group a concise synopsis of what has been discussed, so that the children are able to grasp the central themes of the discussion. Sometimes, where a child has rather poor communication skills, or has made a lengthy statement, it can be useful to summarize the content of what the child has said so that it becomes clear to other members of the group.

Giving feedback

Giving feedback helps individual members and the group as a whole become aware of the behaviours that are occurring in the group. Feedback may be given to the group as a whole by using a comment such as, 'I notice that there is a lot of interrupting in the group', or, by saying to an individual, 'Annette, you are very active'.

Sometimes, feedback will be given with the intention of drawing attention to a group process, which may be affecting two or more people. For example, a leader might say, 'Ann, I notice that whenever Jack says anything, you give a big sigh.' This might allow Ann to talk about her feelings towards Jack, might encourage Jack to look at his behaviour, or might give other members of the group the opportunity to comment on their perceptions and feelings related to the group process.

Rose and Edleson (1987) provide sensible guidelines for giving feedback to children who have been rehearsing new behaviours by role-playing. They suggest giving positive feedback first so that the child receives reinforcement for engaging in the role play and is then more open to receiving criticism. It is important for feedback to be specific, and that criticism is couched in terms of actions or statements that could have been used as alternatives. For example, a leader might begin by saying, 'Mary, you did well in that role play; it was difficult but you managed it', and then follow up by saying, 'You used a gentle approach by hinting at what you wanted. An alternative to what you did would have been to have asked Jimmy directly for what you wanted. That might have been more effective.'

Using questions

Whereas questions are best used sparingly when counselling children individually, they can be very useful in group work, where a range of suitable types of question from a number of different theoretical approaches can be employed. Examples of these are:

Questions to heighten a child's awareness: These questions help the child to recognize and own feelings and thoughts. Examples are: 'What are you feeling emotionally right now?', 'What is happening inside you right now?' and 'What are your tears saying?'

Follow-up questions to elicit more information: Questions such as, 'Can you tell me more?' and 'Is there anything else you can tell me about …?' are useful in encouraging children to continue in the disclosure of information which might otherwise be censored.

Circular questions: Circular questions are directed to one child, but ask that child about the thoughts or feelings of another child or other children. Thus, they invite individual group members to think about other children, and their behaviours, thoughts and feelings. Often, the use of circular questions will promote useful discussion between children and this may enhance group cohesion. Examples of circular questions are: 'Glenda, what do you think Tom feels when April ignores him when he is talking to her?' and 'Keith, if you had a guess, what do you think Billy might be thinking now that he's handed over the leadership of his team to Kate?'

Transitional questions: Transitional questions help children return to the content of a previous discussion which has been interrupted. They are particularly useful in children's groups where children easily deflect away from topics which may be difficult to talk about. Examples are: 'Earlier, Brenda, you talked about your Mum and Dad separating; I wonder how you feel about that right now?' and 'A while back, Eric was telling us about the time when his brother attacked his father with a knife. Has anyone else in the group had a frightening experience like that?'

Choice questions: These questions are useful when processing the outcomes of incidents which arise in a children's group. Examples are: 'What would have been a better choice for you to have made at the time when Hannah snatched your pencil?' and 'If the same situation arises again, what do you think you will do?'

Cheer-leading, accenting and amplifying questions: These questions recognize and affirm that desirable behavioural change has occurred. They make the change newsworthy so that the child receives reinforcement for the changed behaviour. These questions are particularly useful following exception-oriented questions. Examples are: 'How did you do that?', 'How did you manage to carry through that decision?', 'That's fantastic!' and 'That must have been difficult to do. How did you do it?'

Scaling questions: These questions are useful in helping children to set goals and recognize change in themselves which may occur within the group or away from the group. When using scaling questions, the whole group can be used to support the goal-setting of an individual member. Examples of scaling questions are: 'On a scale of one to ten, one being as quiet as a mouse and ten being as noisy as a ferocious dinosaur, where do you think that you would fit right now?', 'Where would you like to be on the scale today?', 'What can you do to reach this point on the scale?' and 'What can the group do to help you reach this point on the scale?'

Confrontation

At times it is necessary for leaders to be confronting. They may wish to draw a child's, or the group's attention, to incongruities between what is being said and what is being done or being expressed non-verbally. They may also need to confront a child or the group with regard to unacceptable behaviour.

A rule of thumb when confronting is that, before confronting a child, a leader tries to ensure that the confrontation is done as a conscious deliberate act rather than as a knee-jerk response to unconscious triggers (Spitz, 1987). It is important that confrontation be designed to achieve a specific result, usually in the 'here and now'. Appropriate confrontation is simultaneously tough and tender, in an empathic atmosphere of genuine concern and caring (Rachman and Raubolt, 1985).

Giving instructions

When children join a group they are naturally uncertain about their leaders' expectations of them. In order to feel safe, they need to be confident that someone is in charge, and that the person in charge will take control and give directions and instructions when necessary. It is also important for children to be clear about group rules and responsibilities and issues related to confidentiality.

Processing skills

We think that processing interactions and activities is an essential part of group work. You may be wondering what we mean by processing, so we will explain. Processing an activity, or an interaction or discussion between members of a group, involves verbally exploring what each child, and the group as a whole, experienced while engaged in the activity, interaction or discussion. Processing is an intervention that is deliberately used by a leader in order to bring into focus what has occurred in the group, and to raise the children's awareness of their emotional feelings, thoughts, opinions and beliefs with regard to what has occurred.

There are considerable advantages to be gained if leaders repeatedly, but not excessively, interrupt the normal flow of group work in order to process activities and interactions. Processing may be carried out after the completion of an activity or interaction, or sometimes an activity or interaction may be interrupted to allow for immediate processing.

Processing usually involves the use of counselling skills. What the leader does, to process an activity or interaction, is to ask questions and use feedback of observations to discover what emotional feelings, perceptions, thoughts, opinions and beliefs, each child experienced while engaged in the activity or interaction.

Additionally, processing may bring into the open factual information about behaviours or group and/or individual processes. Through processing, children learn to take notice of their feelings and thoughts and to recognize the influence of these on their beliefs, attitudes, cognitive processes and behaviours. With this increased awareness, changes in beliefs, attitudes, cognitive processes and behaviours may occur. Importantly, children may recognize the influence of behaviours, thoughts and feelings on themselves and others. This, in turn, may influence the ways they communicate and their relationships with others. Processing not only offers the means for group members to learn about themselves as individuals but also to learn about themselves as members of a group (Ehly and Dustin, 1989).

KEY POINTS

- It is useful to have two leaders in a counselling group for children, one to act as the primary leader and the other as the 'sweeper'.
- The sweeper's main role is to support the leader and to attend to the problems of individual children if these cannot be met in the whole group setting.
- It is helpful if a pre-arranged programme is planned for each session as this will promote the achievement of particular goals.
- Facilitation involves the use of counselling skills, giving directions and instructions, introducing and organizing activities, facilitating discussion, giving support, teaching, modelling appropriate behaviour, dealing with any issues that arise, and processing interactions and activities.
- Processing involves the use of counselling skills, including asking questions and giving feedback of observations to discover what emotional feelings, perceptions, thoughts, and opinions and beliefs the children experienced while engaged in an activity or interaction.

Part 4

Play Therapy – Use of Media and Activities

19

The Play Therapy Room

We have found that counselling children is easier and more effective when we work in a room which has been specifically set up for the use of media and for play therapy. Whenever possible, it is helpful for counsellors who work with children to work in a room which is specifically designed for the purpose. This is not always possible, and useful therapeutic work can take place in less suitable places and with limited equipment. For example, effective and useful counselling of children occurs in schools, hospitals and in government offices, where special facilities for counselling are usually not available. However, in this chapter we will describe what we believe to be the requirements for a well-designed play therapy room.

Ideally, a play therapy room is soundproof, so that extraneous noises do not distract the child. This also helps the child to believe that what they are saying is not being overheard by others. However, it is desirable that the room has a window: internal rooms can be troubling for children who feel trapped and claustrophobic.

It is important that the room has a warm and comfortable feel about it, as distinct from the ambience of most clinical rooms, and also has sufficient space for active, constructive and dramatic play. The sketch in Figure 19.1 shows a typical play therapy room.

The play therapy room ideally has a sink in a wet area for messy play. This enables children to use water and to clean up after using media such as clay and paint. The wet area has a vinyl floor covering, whereas the remainder of the room is preferably carpeted so that sitting on the floor is comfortable.

In Figure 19.1 you will notice that the room has a one-way mirror and a video camera. The mirror allows an observer in a viewing room to see what is happening in the play therapy room without intruding on the process of counselling or causing a distraction. When a one-way mirror is installed, a sound system is also required so that the observer can hear what is being said as well as observe what is happening. In some situations the sound system is linked in with the video system.

A one-way mirror can be used for the following purposes:

• To enable the counsellor to observe the child's play without distracting the child. This is particularly useful when a parent or siblings are in the room with the child. The counsellor can then observe the child's play, and also observe parental and/or family interactions.

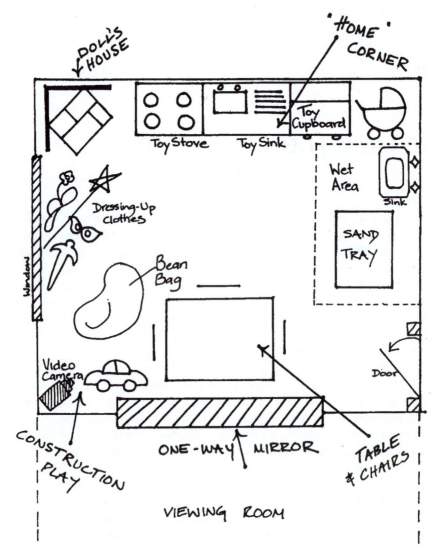

FIGURE 19.1   *The play therapy room*

- To work with a co-therapist in the observation room. By using the mirror the co-therapist does not intrude on the counselling process and does not distract the child.
- To enable a supervisor to directly observe a counselling session.

We recommend that the one-way mirror is curtained so that the curtains can be drawn when the viewing room is not in use. Thus, the child can be sure that no one is watching and that their privacy is assured.

A video camera is another very useful tool to assist in the practice of counselling children. It can be used for the following purposes:

- To help a child to learn and practise new behaviours. For example, when teaching a child to be assertive, the child can role-play and see for themselves whether their behaviour is assertive or not.
- To help parents to discover new and more effective ways of parenting their children. By watching video-taped interactions with their children, parents are enabled to recognize both helpful and unhelpful parenting behaviours.
- To improve counselling skills through supervision. By watching video-tapes of our own counselling sessions we have often been able to recognize ways in which we could have been more effective. The process is even more helpful when peers or a supervisor are involved in the tape review.

Before a one-way mirror and video camera are used, it is essential that the child and parents be informed and their consent obtained. We generally find that parents realize the advantages and are happy to give their consent. Our practice is to ask for written consent, with the parents having a choice of three levels of consent:

- Level one consent: the video-tape is only to be used for the purposes of counselling, and will then be erased.
- Level two consent: the video-tape is to be used for counselling purposes and for counsellor supervision purposes, and will then be erased.
- Level three consent: the counsellor can use the tape for educational and training purposes, as well as for level one and level two purposes.

It is important for parents to have the right to withdraw their consent at any time.

Furniture, equipment, toys and materials

It is desirable for the play therapy room to be equipped with a variety of toys, play materials and media, because different toys, materials and media tend to elicit different forms of play. Materials such as wooden blocks, LEGO® and cardboard boxes inspire constructional play. By comparison, dress-up clothes and housekeeping effects encourage make-believe, imaginative play.

The following is a list of the furniture and other items which we have included in our own play therapy room.

Furniture and associated items

Toy stove

Toy kitchen cupboard

Toy washbasin

(the above items are large enough for a small child to use when engaged in family role plays)

Child's table and chairs

Bean bags

Toys

Doll's house and doll's house family

Doll's bed

Doll's pram

Pillow and sheets for pram, etc.

Rag doll

Baby doll

Teddy bear

Dolls' clothes

Plastic crockery and cutlery

Feeding bottle

Dolls' nappies

Two toy telephones

Mirror

Toy vehicles

Shopping basket

Empty food packets

Play money

Equipment and materials

Sand tray

Symbols for use in the sand tray

Clay

Play–Doh

Paper

Crayons

Felt pens

Finger paints

Puppets

Cardboard boxes

Spools

Pipe cleaners

Glue

Scissors

Sticky tape

Coloured paper and cardboard

Wool

Wooden spatulas

Glitter

Wooden blocks

Miniature animals and figures

Farm animals

Zoo animals

Assorted dinosaurs of different sizes

Miniature figurines including superheroes and other current characters

Dress-up materials

A variety of clothes and materials for dressing up, including jewellery, wigs, swords and handbags

Doctor's or nurse's set

Assorted masks

Books

Story books

Games

Assorted games such as Connect 4, playing cards and dominoes

An uncluttered play therapy room is preferable; otherwise children will be distracted by seeing a large number of toys and several different types of media. This is particularly important for children who are especially disturbed or who have attention deficit problems or poor impulse control. We prefer to store most of our toys and media in cupboards, with only a selected number of items being available for each counselling session.

The way in which the play therapy room is set out enables the child to move freely between activities so that they do not feel restricted. However, it is an advantage to have a space in the room where the child can retire and sit quietly. In this regard, bean bags are not only useful for sitting on generally, but may also be used by the child during relaxation, or when going on an imaginary journey, or at other times when the child needs to sit in a quiet place.

The play environment is preferably left unaltered from session to session so that the child is immediately at ease and has a sense of belonging when coming to a new session. It is as though the child sees the room as their own. Sometimes it may not be practicable to leave the room unaltered; in this case, it can be useful to put a significant toy, materials or media from the previous session into the room to help the child to re-join easily from where they left off in that session.

Clearly, from our discussion of the play therapy room, the appropriate selection of toys, materials and media is important in counselling children. When making this selection of media or activities, it is important to consider the evidence-base for play therapy. In the next chapter we will provide an overview of the current research into the use of media and activities when counselling children.

KEY POINTS

- Counselling children is easier and more effective in a room that has been specifically set up for the purpose.
- Children can be counselled in settings where special facilities for counselling them are not available.
- It is an advantage if a play therapy room has a sink and wet area for messy play.
- It can be useful for a play therapy room to have a one-way mirror and a video camera.
- It is essential to have written consent before video-taping counselling sessions.
- Ideally a play therapy room will be furnished with toy furniture, toys, a range of media, equipment and materials, including books and games.
- It is usually advantageous if only the media required for a particular counselling session is available in the room so that the child does not become distracted.

20

The Evidence-Base for Play Therapy and Counselling Children

Evidence-based practice is an important consideration when counselling children. You want to make sure that the processes you are using have been shown to be effective! Counselling children has a rich and long history with contributions from a diverse range of theoretical orientations as we outlined in Chapter 5. This theoretical foundation was generally supported in early research by case studies in a descriptive manner. However, more and more experimental studies are now being published that show the effectiveness of play therapy and the use of media and activities when counselling children. While play therapy research has a history of over 45 years (Ray and Bratton, 2010), the aim of this chapter is to focus on the more recent research. As you will see, research into a range of media and activities (which we have outlined in Chapters 22 to 30) is being conducted across a number of settings. The focus of this chapter will be on those settings with the largest research base: hospital settings; children who have experienced trauma; supporting children to express and manage their emotions; and supporting children with their behaviour. For those interested in further reading, a number of comprehensive reviews of research into play therapy have been published recently including Phillips (2010) and Baggerly and Bratton (2010).

The hospital setting

Play therapy has been used extensively within the hospital setting in order to support children in preparing for and coping with the hospital experience and related illnesses. The use of therapeutic media and activities to support children in hospital has a large evidence base (e.g., Baggerly and Bratton, 2010; Phillips, 2010). In particular, an extensive body of research has looked into using play therapy to support children when preparing for hospital. A number of other studies have explored the use of various media and activities to support children with the hospital stay itself or when coping with chronic illness.

Preparing children for the hospital experience

A number of media and activities are used in counselling to support children when preparing for hospital. Play therapy is generally used to supplement the standard information provided by hospital staff and is often used in conjunction with other activities such as a tour of the hospital (e.g., Brewer et al., 2006). A number of media and activities are used within the hospital setting including 'medical play', that is, providing the opportunity for children to play with real or toy medical equipment, including preparing a doll or teddy for surgery (e.g., Hatava et al., 2000; Chapters 28 and 29), videos, for example, of a child and their family's visit to hospital (e.g., Ellerton and Merriam, 1994), books or stories (e.g., Felder-Puig et al., 2003; Chapter 27), puppets (e.g., Zahr, 1998; Chapter 28), and art (e.g., Favara-Scacco et al., 2001; Chapter 25). Most of the research has focused on preparing children for surgery; however, there has also been some investigation into the use of media and activities to prepare children for imaging techniques such as Magnetic Resonance Imaging (MRI).

When used to prepare children for surgery, play therapy has been found to lower anxiety levels (e.g., Brewer et al., 2006; Kain et al., 1998) and emotional distress (e.g., Felder-Puig et al., 2003; Lynch, 1994), decrease negative emotions at the induction of anaesthesia (Hatava et al., 2000; Li and Lopez, 2008; Li et al., 2007a), lower physiological symptoms, such as heart rate and blood pressure (Li, 2007; Zahr, 1998), increase cooperation during the procedure (Favara-Scacco et al., 2001; Lynch, 1994; Zahr, 1998), decrease behavioural changes following surgery (Athanassiadou et al., 2009; Margolis et al., 1998), support children and parents to retain information about their hospital stay (Ellerton and Merriam, 1994; Hatava et al., 2000), increase feelings of preparedness (Goymour et al. 2000), and increase parent satisfaction with the hospital procedure (Hatava et al., 2000; Li et al., 2007b).

Play therapy has also been effective when preparing children for MRI scans. The few studies that have been completed in this area have shown that play therapy reduces the need for anaesthesia during the MRI scan and decreases feelings of stress and anxiety (Hallowell et al., 2008; Pressdee et al., 1997).

Coping with hospital stays and chronic illness

A number of studies have investigated the effectiveness of play therapy to support children throughout their stay in hospital or with chronic illnesses, such as diabetes or asthma. As with preparing for hospital, a number of media and activities have been used including playing with toys (e.g., Macner-Licht et al., 1998; Chapters 28 and 29) and art activities, such as drawing (Chapter 25), painting (Chapter 25), and working with clay (Chapter 24) (e.g., Madden et al., 2010). Much of the research in this area focuses on more long-term outcomes such as self-esteem and quality of life, rather than the point-in-time outcomes, such as decreased anxiety during surgery, measured when using play therapy to prepare children for hospital. More specifically, play therapy has been found to support children in hospital and with chronic illness to develop their self-concept/self-esteem (Beebe et al., 2010; Colwell et al., 2005), develop their emotional management and coping skills (Jones and Landreth, 2002; Macner-Licht et al., 1998), improve mood (Beebe et al., 2010; Madden et al., 2010), improve adaptation to their illness (Jones and Landreth, 2002), and improve quality of life (Beebe et al., 2010; Hamre et al., 2007).

Supporting children who have experienced trauma

Unfortunately, exposure to traumatic events is common, with one study finding that 68 per cent of children had experienced at least one traumatic event by the age of 16. Of these children 13.4 per cent reported symptoms of Post Traumatic Stress Disorder (PTSD) and others were found to have ongoing anxiety (9.8 per cent), depressive (12.1 per cent), and behaviour (19.2 per cent) disorders (Copeland et al., 2007). Play therapy has frequently been used to support children in exploring and working through their experiences in a developmentally appropriate and non-threatening manner (Hanney and Kozlowska, 2002) in order to decrease this impact on emotion and behaviour. There are two main areas which have been explored: using media and activities in counselling to support children who have experienced child abuse and/or neglect and natural disasters.

Child abuse and neglect

A number of studies have explored the use of play therapy in supporting children who have been abused and/or neglected or have witnessed domestic violence. Media and activities used include playing with toys (e.g., Fantuzzo et al., 2005; Chapters 28 and 29), art (Chapter 25), and sand-tray therapy (e.g., Ernst et al., 2008; Chapter 23). Children who participated in play therapy showed higher levels of collaborative and interactive play and interpersonal skills, lower levels of solitary play, increased self-control (Fantuzzo et al., 2005; Fantuzzo et al., 1996), improvements in behaviour (Fantuzzo et al., 2005; Fantuzzo et al., 1996; Kot et al., 1998), improved self-concept (Kot et al., 1998), and greater understanding about domestic violence, including that they are not to blame (Ernst et al., 2008).

Natural disasters

Media and activities in counselling have also been used to support children who have experienced natural disasters such as earthquakes and hurricanes. Techniques such as playing with toys (e.g., Shen, 2002; Chapters 28 and 29), art (e.g., Chemtob et al. 2002; Chapter 25), and storytelling (e.g., Macy et al., 2003; Chapter 27) have been researched. Children participating in play therapy following a natural disaster were found to have lower levels of anxiety and depression (Macy et al., 2003; Shen, 2002), lower suicide risk (Shen, 2002), decreased Post Traumatic Stress Disorder (PTSD) symptoms (Chemtob et al., 2002), and increased self-esteem and ability to manage their feelings (Macy et al., 2003).

Expressing and managing emotions

Understanding, expressing and managing emotions can be difficult! Media and activities can be used to support children to explore and manage their emotions, particularly when verbal expression may be difficult or not developmentally appropriate. For example, children provided with the opportunity to draw, communicated more information about emotional events than children who weren't given the opportunity to draw (Driessnack, 2005). In our own research, we found that children who weren't able to report on their emotional abilities cognitively (via a checklist) were able to explore these abilities through drawing using the metaphorical fruit tree we described in Chapter 15 (Geldard et al., 2009). Research has been completed into the effectiveness of play therapy when supporting children to manage feelings around being homeless, family relationship stressors, and grief and loss. Media and activities used in counselling to support children in expressing and managing their emotions included playing with toys (e.g., Baggerly and Jenkins, 2009; Chapters 28 and 29), games (Burroughs et al., 1997; Chapter 30), and art activities (Nabors et al., 2004; Chapter 25).

Participating in play therapy led to significant decreases in feelings of depression and anxiety (Baggerly, 2004) and improvements in emotional security (Baggerly and Jenkins, 2009) for children who were homeless. Play therapy was also found to have a positive effect on children's self-esteem (Baggerly, 2004) and social behaviours such as responding constructively to others and being more engaged with their peers (Baggerly and Jenkins, 2009).

Children who received play therapy to support family relationships were found to have significantly less stress with respect to the parent–child relationship following play therapy (Dougherty and Ray, 2007). In addition, children participating in play therapy within five years of their parents' divorce were reported to have lower levels of depression and anxiety (Burroughs et al., 1997).

After attending a grief camp, children reported that the art activities helped them to express and release their feelings about their grief and also the worries they had in relation to the death. Both children and their parents reported that the camp had been a positive experience and noted the benefits from being with peers who had also lost family members (Nabors et al., 2004).

Behaviour

A number of studies have also explored the benefits of using media and activities with respect to supporting children with their behaviour. Research has looked at the impact of play therapy on the behaviour of children with developmental disabilities and children presenting with behaviours of concern, in particular aggressive behaviour. Media and activities that have been used to support behaviour include playing with toys (e.g., Legoff and Sherman, 2006; Chapters 28 and 29), games (e.g., Garaigordobil et al., 1996; Chapter 30), books and stories (e.g., Shechtman, 1999; Chapter 27).

Play therapy with children with developmental disabilities has been found to support social interaction (Kaduson and Finnerty, 1995; Legoff and Sherman, 2006; O'Connor and Stagnitti, 2011), decrease social disconnectedness and disruptive behaviour (O'Connor and Stagnitti, 2011), increase adaptive behaviour, particularly in the area of social competence (Legoff and Sherman, 2006), and improve attention-related behaviours (Kaduson and Finnerty, 1995; Ray et al., 2007) and self-control (Kaduson and Finnerty, 1995). Using media and activity in counselling was also found to have a positive impact on children's emotions, with decreases in anxiety and emotional instability (Ray et al., 2007).

Media and activity in counselling has also been shown to support positive social and emotional skills by decreasing aggressive behaviours and increasing constructive behaviours such as cooperation, responsiveness and empathy (Bay-Hinitz et al., 1994; Garaigordobil et al., 1996; Garza and Bratton, 2005; Shechtman, 1999). Play therapy has also been shown to support interpersonal understanding in children presenting with behaviours of concern (Karcher and Shenita, 2002).

The child–counsellor relationship

Before concluding this chapter, we felt it was important to again note the importance of the child–counsellor relationship. As outlined in Chapter 2, the child–counsellor relationship is a critical factor when counselling children. In fact, a growing number of studies are finding that the therapeutic relationship contributes more to therapeutic change than does the particular strategy or approach used both with adult (e.g., Lambert and Ogles, 2004; Wampold, 2001) and child (e.g., Karver et al., 2006; Shirk and Karver, 2003) clients. In our experience, the use of media and activities support the development of the child–counsellor relationship as they lend themselves so well to creating a non-threatening and positive environment for the child (e.g., Kool and Lawver, 2010). As such, not only is the research showing play therapy approaches to be effective agents of change; but they also lend themselves to developing a critical factor in counselling: the child–counsellor relationship. Hence, media and activity are important components when counselling children. In the next chapter we will explore issues relating to the selection of appropriate media or activities.

KEY POINTS

- The use of media and activities in counselling has an extensive research base with studies showing the effectiveness of play therapy when counselling children in hospital and children who have experienced trauma, and also to support children with their emotions and behaviour.
- Play therapy also supports the development of the child–counsellor relationship, which research has shown to be a critical factor when counselling children.

21

Selecting the Appropriate Media or Activity

We use media or an activity as a way of engaging the child and enabling the child to tell their story. In selecting media or activities it is important to remember that each child is different, both as an individual and with regard to the issues and behaviours which need to be addressed. Each of the media or activities available has different and particular properties. Therefore, we can match up the medium or activity with the individual child and with that child's abilities and needs. Factors which are of importance when selecting media or activities include the following:

- the child's developmental age
- whether the child is being counselled individually or in a group
- the current counselling goals for the child.

To assist in the selection of media and activities, we have constructed four tables (Tables 21.1 to 21.4). These tables identify the suitability of media and activities in various domains. In each table, the media or activities which are most suitable are indicated by dark cells, those which are moderately suitable are indicated by lightly shaded cells, and the least suitable are indicated by clear cells.

Suitability of media and activities for various age groups (Table 21.1)

Table 21.1 can be used to assist in the selection of media or activities which are most appropriate developmentally for the child. For example, *imaginative pretend play* is an activity which is highly appropriate for pre-school children between the ages of two and five years. This activity is less likely to appeal to pre-adolescents or adolescents because of their cognitive maturity and ability to engage in abstract thinking. They are likely to find working with miniature animals and symbols more appealing.

TABLE 21.1 *Suitability of media and activities for various age groups*

Media \ Ages	Pre-school 2 to 5 years	Primary school 6 to 10 years	Early adolescence 11 to 13 years	Late adolescence 14 to 17 years
Books/stories				
Clay				
Construction				
Drawing				
Finger-painting				
Games				
Imaginary journey				
Imaginative pretend play				
Miniature animals				
Painting/ collage				
Puppet/soft toys				
Sand tray				
Symbols/ figurines				
Worksheets				

Most suitable	
Suitable	
Least suitable	

We have found that, regardless of age, gender differences rarely influence the selection of media or activities. Both girls and boys join easily with the listed media and activities.

Some children are regressed emotionally, socially and cognitively as a consequence of past traumas and emotional issues. Not surprisingly, these children may be more suited to activities which would normally be appropriate for younger children.

Suitability of media and activities for various situations (Table 21.2)

Most often counsellors work with children individually, but they sometimes work with sibling groups or groups of children who have similar issues or have had similar experiences. At other times, counselling occurs in a family setting (see Chapter 9).

Table 21.2 describes the suitability of media for these differing settings. While all of the media and activities are suitable for use in individual counselling sessions, some are not as suitable for group or family work.

TABLE 21.2 *Suitability of media and activities for various situations*

Media / Situation	Individual counselling	Family counselling	Group work
Books/stories			
Clay			
Construction			
Drawing			
Finger-painting			
Games			
Imaginary journey			
Imaginative pretend play			
Miniature animals			
Painting/collage			
Puppet/soft toys			
Sand tray			
Symbols/figurines			
Worksheets			

Most suitable	
Suitable	
Least suitable	

Suitability of media and activities for achieving goals (Table 21.3)

Table 21.3 shows some broad goals, each of which is relevant for different stages around the Spiral of Therapeutic Change (see Figure 7.1, p. 59). The table indicates which media or activities are most suitable for helping children to achieve the goals.

To gain mastery over issues and events

To gain mastery over past events and current issues, it is desirable for the child to do one of the following:

- To re-experience past events or traumas of concern by re-enacting them, acting them out or re-explaining them. In this process, the child may need to imagine how they could have changed their role in those events so that they would have felt more comfortable. They might also need to engage in an activity, which will enable them to experience, in their imagination, the effect of their changed role. In this way they can experience a sense of mastery over the event or trauma.
- To simulate an event which will allow them to experience the feelings of power and/ or control which they may not have experienced in previous instances.

TABLE 21.3 *Suitability of media and activities for achieving goals*

Media \ Goals	To gain mastery over issues and events	To be powerful through physical expression	To encourage expression of emotions	To develop problem-solving and decision-making skills	To develop social skills	To build self-concept and self-esteem	To improve communication skills	To develop insight
Books/stories	Suitable			Most suitable			Most suitable	
Clay	Suitable	Most suitable	Most suitable					
Construction				Most suitable		Suitable		
Drawing	Most suitable	Suitable		Suitable				Most suitable
Finger-painting	Suitable	Most suitable		Suitable			Suitable	
Games					Most suitable			
Imaginary journey	Most suitable		Suitable			Most suitable		Suitable
Imaginative pretend play	Most suitable	Suitable	Most suitable	Suitable	Most suitable	Most suitable	Most suitable	Suitable
Miniature animals	Most suitable		Suitable		Most suitable		Suitable	Suitable
Painting/collage	Most suitable	Suitable	Most suitable			Most suitable	Most suitable	Most suitable
Puppet/soft toys	Most suitable	Suitable	Most suitable	Suitable	Most suitable	Most suitable	Most suitable	Most suitable
Sand tray	Most suitable		Most suitable	Suitable	Most suitable			Most suitable
Symbols/figurines	Most suitable		Most suitable	Suitable	Most suitable	Most suitable	Most suitable	Most suitable
Worksheets				Most suitable	Most suitable		Suitable	

Most suitable	(dark shading)
Suitable	(medium shading)
Least suitable	(no shading)

It follows that in order to gain mastery over past events, it is important to provide the child with the opportunity to use media which allow for the creation of imaginary environments in which there can be powerful roles. These roles might sometimes be fantasy roles which give the child superhuman abilities for dealing with social and physical situations. Examples of the use of suitable media are:

- Books and stories can encourage the child to alter the story. The child can project outcomes which they would have liked for themselves on to characters within the story.
- Drawing allows the child to make pictures which depict traumatic events. In these pictures the child can depict themselves as powerful or in control.

- In the imaginary journey, the child is invited to revisit significant life situations. They can, in their imagination, introduce new behaviours for themselves in order to achieve some sense of control or mastery in situations where they were previously powerless.
- In imaginative pretend play, dramatic representation of powerful roles can be enacted.
- Painting and collage can be used in a similar way to drawing.
- Puppets and soft toys allow the child to assume powerful roles.
- Sand-tray work allows the child to create fantasy environments in which they can feel in control.
- Symbols and figurines can be used in the same way as puppets and are suitable for older children.

To be powerful through physical expression

Children feel empowered when they witness their ability to powerfully impact on their environment. In counselling this can be achieved by providing activities and media that enable them to control the media and to alter them, or to act out powerful roles. For example:

- A child might punch a lump of clay until it becomes flat.
- When using finger-painting, the child can dramatically alter their drawing or destroy the images in their picture.
- In imaginative pretend play, the young child can attack a bean bag with a toy sword.
- Mock battles can be acted out between 'good' and 'evil' puppets. Similar work can be done with older children using figurines.
- In sand-tray work a child can bury figures or objects in the sand to obliterate or conceal them.

Engaging in these types of activities can be cathartic for the child as they symbolize in a concrete way the child's ability to impact on their environment.

To encourage expression of emotions

We have discussed the importance and benefits of encouraging and helping children to express their emotions. Some media and activities lend themselves to the expression of emotion much more effectively than others. For example:

- Clay tends to promote the expression of anger, sadness, fear and worry.
- Drawing allows the child to get in touch not only with their projected thoughts, but also with their emotional feelings.
- Finger-painting tends to generate the emotions of joy, celebration and happiness.
- In painting and collage, the child may connect the texture of the material with emotional feelings.

To develop problem-solving and decision-making skills

At some point around the Spiral of Therapeutic Change the child will be required to explore options, to make choices, to take risks, and to experiment with challenges and changing behaviours. Appropriate media might include:

- Books and storytelling, where alternative solutions can be explored; for example, Little Red Riding Hood might trap the wolf so that the child can rescue her grandmother before she gets eaten!
- Puppets and soft toys, where the child can make up a dialogue to solve problems between two or more characters.
- Sand-tray work, where a child can rearrange a visual picture to accommodate different needs.
- Symbols and figurines, which can be used similarly to puppets and soft toys and are more suitable for older children.
- Worksheets, which can be used to directly address problem-solving and decision-making skills.

To develop social skills

In order to feel better in the future, many children may need to develop social skills. Often this involves learning different ways of relating to others so that they can make friends, get their needs met, be appropriately assertive, identify and live within sensible boundaries, and cooperate with others.

To develop adaptive social skills it is important for a child to understand and experience the consequences of social behaviour. This can be achieved by the use of:

- An activity, such as playing a game with the child and giving the child feedback.
- Imaginative pretend play, which can help younger children to learn about and practise social skills.
- Puppets and soft toys, which can help children to learn about and practise socially acceptable behaviours.
- Worksheets, to address specific social skills issues.

To build self-concept and self-esteem

We have found that a child's self-concept and self-esteem are almost inevitably affected adversely whenever they experience troubling events or trauma. In order to build self-concept and self-esteem, the counsellor selects activities and media which will promote self-fulfilment and independence in the child, and will enable the child to explore, accept and value their strengths and weaknesses. Suitable media and activities are as follows:

- Drawing, where comic strips can be created to illustrate the development of the child's own strengths. For example, a child might show their progression from infancy to the present, highlighting memorable milestones.
- Finger-painting – this doesn't require skill, so anything the child produces is likely to be an acceptable product.
- Games can be selected which target the child's specific skills and give them an opportunity to perform well.

- Imaginative pretend play allows the child to experience roles such as being a leader or helper, and to discover their unique strengths.
- Painting and collage can be used in a similar way to finger-painting.
- Specifically designed worksheets can be used to address issues related to self-esteem and self-concept.

To improve communication skills

Often when a child tells their story to friends and significant others, the story will sound confusing, incongruent and sometimes difficult to believe. Activities which assist in highlighting the sequence of the story, important themes related to the story, the child's understanding of significant events, and how the child felt at different times, are helpful. For example:

- Storytelling helps the child to develop communication skills.
- The imaginary journey allows the child to get in touch with memories and then to relate their perception of events more easily.
- Imaginative pretend play encourages communication through dramatic role play.
- Miniature animals provide a visual picture, which usually encourages the child to talk about their perceptions of relationships.
- Puppets and soft toys help the child to use words to express the feelings and perceptions of characters, and allow the child to project their perceptions onto the characters.
- Using symbols in the sand tray can help a child to develop a visual picture of events they have experienced and to place these in chronological order. The visual picture then enables the child to tell their story and thus to practise communication skills.

To develop insight

If a child is to develop insight and understanding of themselves and others, they may need to understand how their involvement in significant events occurred and how their experience fits into their wider social system. For example:

- Books and storytelling can be used to develop insight by illustrating the reality of human behaviour and the inevitability of consequences of behaviour.
- Drawing allows the child to gain insight into their own involvement in events. This can be achieved by inviting the child to draw a comic strip showing the sequence of past events.
- The imaginary journey allows the child to retrieve memories of their involvement in events and experiences, and thus to gain insight.
- Imaginative pretend play allows young children to take on the role of others in play. Consequently, they can develop insight into the motives and behaviours of themselves and others.
- The use of miniature animals enables the child to gain insight into relationships as animals are placed near to each other or are distant from each other.

- Puppets and soft toys can be used with younger children, and symbols and figurines with older children, in a similar way to imaginative pretend play.
- Use of the sand tray allows the child to develop insight into events by developing a visual picture of the way in which events may have, or could have, occurred.

Properties of media and activities (Table 21.4)

Each type of medium and activity has its own unique and inherent properties. We have divided these into four major categories as shown in Table 21.4.

TABLE 21.4 *Properties of media and activities*

Properties \ Media	Open-ended and expansive	Functional and contained	Familiar and stable	Educational
Books/stories	Suitable	Least suitable	Suitable	Most suitable
Clay	Most suitable	Least suitable	Least suitable	Least suitable
Construction	Most suitable	Most suitable	Least suitable	Suitable
Drawing	Most suitable	Least suitable	Suitable	Least suitable
Finger-painting	Most suitable	Least suitable	Least suitable	Least suitable
Games	Least suitable	Most suitable	Most suitable	Most suitable
Imaginary journey	Most suitable	Least suitable	Suitable	Least suitable
Imaginative pretend play	Most suitable	Least suitable	Most suitable	Least suitable
Miniature animals	Suitable	Most suitable	Suitable	Suitable
Painting/collage	Most suitable	Most suitable	Suitable	Suitable
Puppet/soft toys	Most suitable	Suitable	Suitable	Suitable
Sand tray	Most suitable	Suitable	Suitable	Suitable
Symbols/figurines	Most suitable	Suitable	Suitable	Suitable
Worksheets	Least suitable	Most suitable	Least suitable	Most suitable

Most suitable	(dark shading)
Suitable	(light shading)
Least suitable	(no shading)

Open-ended and expansive media and activities

Primarily, activities and media which are open-ended and expansive allow freedom of expression with no particular boundaries or restrictions. They are activities which are flexible and movable, and often contain a tactile or kinaesthetic element. For example, children can use their imagination to make any changes they like while on an imaginary journey. In imaginative pretend play an unstructured drama can be created, developed and changed at will. Finger-painting and clay have kinaesthetic and tactile qualities. No special skill is required for any of these media and activities so there is very little experience of failure.

Media and activities which are functional and contained

These activities and media allow the child to experience a sense of containment and challenge. They demand attention to detail and often have an end product or result. For example, if we invite a child to construct a sculpture with LEGO® bricks, the child is focused on a specific task for which they need to think and plan the construction, and we can expect a sculpture as the end product.

Media and activities which are familiar and stable

These provide an opportunity for simple, repetitive and sometimes stereotypic inter-action. Using them provides a sense of stability and predictability. For example, when using imaginative pretend play, familiar and stable themes which are already well known to the child can be continually replayed. This is especially useful for children who come from chaotic and unstable backgrounds.

Media and activities which are educational

These offer an opportunity for learning and for the acceptance and rejection of rules. They are structured, do not require lateral thinking, and are progressive in that they require work towards an objective. For example, when using worksheets the child builds on their knowledge of the content of the worksheet.

In conclusion

In this chapter we have provided an overview of how to select media and activities. In the following chapters we will deal with how to use the various media and activities.

CASE STUDY

You have been working with Rose, a 13-year-old, for a couple of sessions now. During the counselling process Rose has been able to begin moving around the Spiral of Therapeutic Change and has started to share her story of being sexually abused by her step-father who is no longer present. What media or activities might you choose to support Rose in continuing to share her story and get in touch with her emotions? What factors influenced your decision? How would your choice change as Rose continued to move around the Spiral of Therapeutic Change?

KEY POINTS

- The selection of medium and activity will depend on the child's developmental age, whether the child is being counselled individually or in a group, and the immediate goal of the counselling.
- Possible goals for counselling include:

  - To gain mastery over issues and events
  - To be powerful through physical expression
  - To encourage expression of emotions
  - To develop problem-solving and decision-making skills
  - To develop social skills
  - To build self-concept and self-esteem
  - To improve communication skills
  - To develop insight.

22

The Use of Miniature Animals

Miniature animals are extremely useful when joining with a child in Phase 1 of the SPICC process (see Figure 8.1, p. 72), and when trying to discover initial information about how the child sees themselves and their family. We will write about the use of miniature animals under five headings, as follows:

1 Materials needed
2 Goals when using miniature animals
3 How to use miniature animals
4 Counselling skills when using miniature animals
5 Suitability of the medium.

Materials needed

A variety of small toy animals and other creatures is required. Preferably there are a few animals or creatures included from each of the following groups:

- Domestic animals
- Farm animals
- Jungle animals
- Zoo animals
- Dinosaurs
- Reptiles (snakes, crocodiles, lizards)
- Insects (spiders, grasshoppers)
- Sea creatures (turtles, dolphins, whales).

It is preferable that the animals and other creatures are made of plastic and be appropriately coloured so that they look realistic. A variety of sizes and appearances is also useful, for example, some having a benign appearance, some an aggressive appearance, and others seeming friendly. It is desirable to have both male and female animals, and baby animals in some species. The inclusion of dinosaurs is important: children like to make use of them, particularly the very large aggressive-looking ones.

It is important that all the animals are able to stand freely without support; children become frustrated and distracted when animals fall over. We generally limit our animal collection to about 50, because some children find it overwhelming if they are asked to choose from a larger set.

A large, flat work space is required when working with miniatures. This can either be a table or floor. Generally we prefer to sit and work on the carpeted floor of our play therapy room.

Goals when using miniature animals

The main goal is to enable the child to tell their story about their perceptions of their personal relationships and their perceptions of other relationships within their family. Working with miniature animals enables the child to do the following:

- explore past, present and future relationships with others;
- gain a fuller understanding of their place in the family;
- explore fears related to their own future relationships;
- fantasize about possible future relationships;
- explore fears with regard to future relationships between others;
- explore possible solutions to relationship problems.

Miniature animals can also be used to explore the child's relationships in other systems and situations; for example, in school, in foster placement, during access visits and during visits to hospital for medical procedures.

Miniature animals can also be used in conjunction with sand-tray work (see Chapter 23).

How to use miniature animals

The counsellor's task, when using miniature animals, is to encourage the child to focus on the important relationships in their life and to tell their story with regard to these. From this storytelling the counsellor can help the child to identify important themes and issues, and can allow the child to experience any emotions which emerge.

The counsellor begins by introducing the child to the animals. The counsellor might say something like, 'I thought that we might play with my toy animals today. We are going to play with them in a special way. First of all, I would like you to choose an animal which is most like you.'

In making this request, it is important for the child to understand that they are being asked to choose the animal which is most like them, as they are at the present time, rather than choosing an animal which represents how they would like to be. For example, a child might believe that they are submissive and compliant, but might have fantasies about being more powerful. If such a child chose a lamb to represent themselves, that would be appropriate, but it certainly would not be appropriate if they chose a Tyrannosaurus Rex. In a similar way, it would not be useful for a child to choose an animal on the grounds of physical similarity alone (for example, a tall thin child might choose a giraffe). The intention is to invite the child to choose an animal which they believe is most similar to them in personality, and in behavioural and emotional characteristics. We find that by making the above request we generally get the required response from the child.

Once the child has chosen their animal, the counsellor can invite the child to tell them what the selected animal is like, by asking 'Tell me about that lion [or whatever animal is chosen]', or 'What is that lion like?'

Some children respond by making obvious and concrete statements about the size and physical attributes of the selected animal. This is not useful, so in order to encourage the child to describe personality traits of the animal, the counsellor might say, 'I wonder what this animal is like inside', or 'Tell me more.'

Notice that the counsellor refers to 'the animal' or uses its name (for example, 'the lion'). The counsellor does not call the animal by the child's name, and does not imply that the animal is the child even though the animal has been chosen as being *most like* the child and will be used to represent the child. Referring to it as 'the animal' or by its name allows the child to distance themselves from the chosen animal, so that although it represents them in some ways, it is not the same as them. They can then project qualities, characteristics and behaviours on to the animal with safety. The animal – not the child – becomes the owner of negative, positive and unacceptable attributes. This enables the child to feel freer in attributing negative and undesirable behaviours, which they may recognize in themselves, but may not be ready to own.

Sometimes a child might choose an animal which the counsellor thinks has particular qualities. For example, the child might choose a panther, which the counsellor sees as aggressive. However, the child might see the panther as powerful but friendly, and not aggressive. Therefore, it is important for the counsellor to be careful not to project their own ideas on to the child's chosen animals.

Occasionally a child will want to choose more than one animal to represent themselves. This can be useful because the two animals might represent different aspects of the same child. For example, a child with a secret might choose a hen for the part of themselves which wants to keep the secret, and a bull for the part of themselves which wants to tell others about the secret.

Once the child has selected the animal which is most like them, the counsellor encourages the child to select other animals to represent each member of their family. Additionally, the child is invited to select animals to represent absent or deceased members of their family. The same procedure is used as before, with the counsellor making requests such as, 'Now choose the animal which is most like your Mum'. As each animal is chosen, the counsellor asks the child 'What is that animal like?'

As each animal is selected, the child is encouraged to place it in front of them. Eventually the child will have a group of animals to represent their family. When the group is complete, the counsellor can note the placement of the selected animals and make a statement about how they have been arranged. For example, the counsellor might say, 'Your animals are all in a straight line', or 'Your animals are all in a circle with the zebra in the centre.' Often, when a counsellor makes such an observation, the child will spontaneously talk about the meaning that is associated with the arrangement of the animals. For example, the child might say, 'All the other animals are watching the zebra because she likes to play tricks on them.'

Sometimes a child will not respond to the counsellor's feedback statement about the arrangement of the group of animals. In this case, the counsellor might say to the child, 'Arrange the animals so that they make a picture.'

Perhaps 'make a sculpture' would be more accurate, but many children don't know what the word 'sculpture' means. Once the child has arranged the animals, the counsellor can comment on the arrangement.

At this point, the counsellor can begin to explore the relationships between the animals in the group. For example, the counsellor may begin to explore the relationship between the dog (representing the child) and the dinosaur (representing the child's father). The counsellor might ask questions such as, 'I wonder what it is like for the dog to be next to the dinosaur?'

Later the counsellor might ask 'What is it like for the dinosaur to have the dog next to him?' and 'How does the horse [representing the child's mother] feel about the dog and dinosaur being together?' It could also be useful for the counsellor to ask the child how they think the other animals in the group feel about this arrangement. The process can be extended by asking the child to move the dog (if that is the animal the child chose to represent themselves) to a new position near another animal. Similarly, the child can be asked to move other animals into different positions in the group. In this way, the various relationships within the group can be explored.

Notice that the counsellor does not move the animals, but asks the child to move them. We believe that by doing this the child develops a greater sense of ownership of the story which they are telling, and is more likely to feel in control of the process and be more in touch with their perceptions.

Sometimes a counsellor may notice that a child is reluctant to move an animal into a particular position. The counsellor might then use reflection to feed this observation back to the child by saying, 'You seem to be unhappy about moving the duck next to the snake.' By feeding back this information to the child, the counsellor is able to raise the child's awareness of important feelings. After each animal is moved, the child is again asked questions about the feelings of various other animals with regard to the altered position. Thus, the child, in an indirect way, shares their picture of their family, and of their family's relationships, with the counsellor. However, remember that the whole process of using miniature animals is primarily projective.

The projective nature of working with miniature animals

Throughout the process involved in working with miniature animals, the counsellor never refers to the group of animals selected as 'the child's family' and never uses the names of members of the child's family. This might inhibit the child in the allocation of attributes, behaviours, thoughts and feelings to the animals, and might block the child's ability to freely explore the relationships between the animals. The whole process is projective, with the child projecting ideas from his family on to the animals, but having the freedom to exaggerate or modify those projections. By using this projective technique, the child is likely to access ideas and beliefs which may have been suppressed into their unconscious because of fears about the consequences of recognizing those ideas and beliefs.

Because the process is projective, the child will make connections between relationships and behaviours in the animal group, and relationships and behaviours in their own family. In so doing, they are likely to make important discoveries about relationships within their family, and to want to talk about these. When this occurs, it is appropriate for the counsellor to use the counselling skills described in Part 3 to enable the child to continue telling their story. At this stage of the process the child may experience strong emotions (as indicated on the Spiral of Therapeutic Change, Figure 7.1, p. 59).

Further discussion on the use of the medium

As well as exploring current relationships, the counsellor can explore how the child might feel about absences of family members. For example, the counsellor might say to the child, 'I would like you to move the dinosaur and put him behind your back.' The visual picture that appears for the child is now one where there is an absent dinosaur (father).

The miniature animals can be used to help the child to explore their ideas about what would make relationships within the family more comfortable. This can be done by inviting the child to put their animal in a place where the animal will feel most comfortable in relation to other members of their family.

It can be useful to invite the child to place their own animal close to an animal which has already been identified as worrying for them. Thus, the child can fully experience the resulting feelings and deal with them.

When the counselling session is drawing to an end, we find that it is useful to invite the child to arrange the animals in a way that will enable all the animals to feel most comfortable. The counsellor might say, 'I'd like you to rearrange your animals into a new picture so that all of the animals will feel happy and comfortable.' This enables the child to leave the session feeling comfortable about their work and with a sense of closure around the issues of relationships within their family.

Generally, when using miniature animals, the counsellor avoids advising, interpreting or congratulating the child while they are telling their story. Similarly, expressions of surprise, approval or disapproval would intrude on the storytelling and might influence it so that it would cease to be authentically the child's. It is important for the counsellor to take the child's story seriously and to communicate respect for it. This is true even when it is clear that factual information in the child's story is completely wrong. It is only by having the opportunity to tell their story, in their own way, that the child can later move forward to test their perception of reality. It is interesting to note that when we have used miniature animals with different children in the same family, we have often heard quite different and unique stories from each child, even though some important elements of these stories were the same.

Counselling skills when using miniature animals

All of the counselling skills covered in Part 3 are required when using miniature animals. The following skills are particularly useful:

1 Observation
2 Reflection of content and feelings
3 Use of statements (for feedback of observations)
4 Open questions.

Here are some examples to demonstrate the common use of the above skills.

Use of observation and reflection of feeling

The counsellor might say, 'I noticed that you looked happy when you put the monkey and the goat together.'

Use of observation and a statement

The counsellor might use a statement to feed back to the child an observation of significance by saying, 'I notice that the chicken is the furthest one away from the rhinoceros.'

Use of an open question

The counsellor might ask, 'What is it like for this animal when the dinosaur is standing in front of him?'

At times, while working with miniature animals, the counsellor may repeat word for word phrases used by the child, to encourage the child to tell more of their story. Consider an example where, after moving a cat next to a hen, a child says, 'The elephant doesn't like that.' If the counsellor repeats, 'The elephant doesn't like that', then the child is likely to think about what they have said and to explore their ideas and feelings more thoroughly.

It is important to remember that the goals of counselling do not include investigating. If a counsellor starts to ask unnecessary questions to satisfy their own agenda, then the authenticity of the child's story will almost certainly be compromised. Therefore, it is good practice for the counsellor to continually remind themselves not to intrude, but instead to gently provide opportunities for the child to continue telling their story. Any questions the counsellor asks are designed to seek further information about the child's story rather than to move the story in a particular direction. Therefore, it is important that questions are carefully phrased to encourage the child to talk about events and the meanings the child ascribes to those events.

'Why' questions aren't useful when working with miniature animals because they invite interpretative answers, which tend to deflect the child away from their internal processes. 'What' and 'how' questions are useful because they invite the child to share information which is not contaminated by contrived explanations. Explanations distract the child from the true essence of the story and allow them to deflect away from painful experiences.

Suitability of the medium

Miniature animals are most successfully used in the way which we have described with children from about seven years of age and onwards. With younger children, their use tends to produce concrete responses and the child is not likely to project their ideas about various family members on to the animals. Instead, the child is likely to talk directly about the selected animals and their characteristics. Further, children under the age of seven have limited ability to abstract and predict. They have little understanding of motive or intent and therefore find it difficult to project other people's behaviours on to the animals.

Miniature animals are more suitable for use in individual counselling than group counselling because use of this medium targets an individual's perceptions about others and relationships between others.

Working with miniature animals requires some direction or guidance by the counsellor. Miniature animals encourage behaviours in the child which are introspective and sometimes private, because the child is required to project thoughts and feelings on to the animals. However, this medium can, in some instances, be used to expand the child's exploration of options and alternatives.

Where a child is regressed and/or emotionally blocked, a warm-up period may be required during which the child is encouraged to play freely with the miniature animals.

> ### CASE STUDY
> You have received a new referral for nine-year-old Daisy whose parents have recently separated. How might you make use of miniature animals to support Daisy with this change in family dynamics? At what stage of the counselling relationship would you consider introducing miniature animals?

KEY POINTS
- Miniature animals are particularly useful for joining with the child and for finding out about the child's perception of their family.
- A variety of small plastic animals and other creatures is required.

- Miniature animals are particularly useful for exploring relationships, fears about relationships, possibilities about future relationships and possible solutions to relationship problems.
- During the process the counsellor refers to the animals/creatures by their animal/creature names and asks the child to move the animals but does not touch the animals.
- The method is projective in nature.
- Most useful counselling skills when using miniature animals are observation, reflection, and the use of statements and open questions.
- The medium is most suitable for children from age seven years. It is generally not suitable for younger children as they do not have the cognitive development to use projective techniques.

23

Sand-Tray Work

Sand-tray work can be very useful in helping a child to tell their story in Phases 1 and 2 of the SPICC process (see Figure 8.1, p. 72). We will discuss sand-tray work under the following headings:

- Equipment and materials needed
- Goals of sand-tray work
- How to use the sand tray
- Counselling skills when using the sand tray
- Suitability of sand-tray work.

Equipment and materials needed

The only equipment required is the sand tray itself. Materials required are symbols, figurines and miniature animals.

The sand tray

The sand tray may be made of wood or plastic. Ideally, it is square with sides of about 1 metre in length and about 150 mm high. Wooden sand trays require a waterproof lining.

It is best if the sand is clean, washed sand. We have discovered from our own practical experience that it is a mistake to use very light fine sand. It can create a miniature sand-storm in the room when used by active children. A good depth of sand in the tray is about 75 mm, with a 75-mm space between the surface of the sand and the top edge of the tray. This makes it easy to work in the sand without the sand spilling out of the tray.

Sometimes, access to water is useful, although this is not essential. Wet sand can be used to make caves, tunnels, hills and other shapes. We keep our sand tray on the floor and sit, with the child, on the floor beside it.

Symbols

The symbols used in sand-tray work consist of a variety of small objects which are chosen because they have properties that enable them to easily assume symbolic meaning.

We have collected our symbols over a period of time, so that they include many different types of objects.

The symbols may be used to represent concrete things such as roads, houses, schools, shopping centres and individual people. Additionally, they may be used to represent less tangible concepts such as secrets, thoughts, beliefs, wishes and emotional barriers. Thus, the symbols can be used to represent anything concrete, or intangible, or abstract, which has a place in the child's story.

A useful set of symbols might include the following items:

General items

Rocks, stones and pebbles	Feathers
Shells	Wood
Small boxes with lids	Marbles
Candles	Small paper flags
Old jewellery	A key
Paper	A padlock
Ornaments	A torch battery
A tin of spaghetti	A crystal ball
A small mirror	Buttons
Beads	A horseshoe
A small pyramid	Gold stars
A notebook	A pencil
A chain	A large nail

Small toys

Plastic trees	Toy fences
Planes	Trains
Boats	Cars

Figurines and superheroes

Male and female figurines	Toy soldiers
Medieval knights	Catwoman
Batman	Power Rangers

Toy animals

Dragons	Farm animals
Zoo animals	Jungle animals
Domestic animals	

Objects which have universal symbolic meaning, for example, those which are funny, frightening, endearing, magical or religious, make ideal symbols.

Goals of sand-tray work

Sand-tray work provides the child with an opportunity to use symbols, within a defined space, to tell their story. While telling their story, the child has an opportunity to re-create in the sand tray, and in their imagination, events and situations from their past and present. The child may also explore possibilities for the future or express their fantasies in the sand tray. Consequently the child is enabled to do all, or any, of the following:

- Explore specific events – past, present and future.
- Explore themes and issues relating to these events.
- Act out those things which are not, or were not, acceptable to them.
- Gain a cognitive understanding of the elements of events in their life and thus gain insight into those events.
- Integrate polarities.
- Alter their story, as created in the sand tray, by projecting their fantasies on to it.
- Experience a sense of power through physical expression.
- Gain mastery over past and current issues and events.
- Think of what might happen next.
- Find resolution of issues through the development of insight.

How to use the sand tray

Because of the tactile and kinaesthetic experience of working in the sand tray, most children seem to engage readily in the task. We usually start by inviting the child to use any of the symbols they wish to make a scene or picture in the sand. In inviting the child to make their picture, we take into account goals for the counselling session. Here are several different examples of instructions which might be useful when starting sand-tray work.

Example one

Sometimes we leave the child with freedom to make whatever picture they choose without any specific direction. This non-directive approach can be useful because it allows the counsellor to observe the way in which the child engages in the task and constructs the picture. The counsellor can then look for any themes and issues that emerge during the creation of the picture so that these can be discussed with the child. Using this approach, the counsellor might start the sand-tray work by saying, 'I'd like you to use these things [symbols] to make a picture in the sand.'

Example two

In some cases, the counsellor may suspect that the child's issues concern relationships with others. The counsellor can then be more specific and might say, 'Make a picture about all the people that you know.'

As the picture develops, the counsellor can notice the qualities of the various relationships, taking particular notice of strengths, weaknesses, distances, closeness and boundaries. Additionally, the counsellor can note any absences of significant others from the picture. The use of feedback statements by the counsellor will then help to raise the child's awareness of their situation so that they can deal with related issues.

Example three

Some children present with a very high level of anxiety. With these children it can be useful to give them the following instruction: 'Make a picture about the things that frighten you most.'

Later, as the picture develops, the counsellor might say, 'Find something that reminds you of ... [ghosts, spiders, or whatever is relevant].'

These instructions can be useful for the child because by concretizing the fear itself, the child can then deal with it symbolically. For example, the child might bury it or put it outside the sand tray.

Example four

Some children who have been emotionally deprived when younger present with issues related to rejection and abandonment. It is important for these children to explore their perceptions of the way in which they were nurtured. In such cases the counsellor might say, 'Make a picture about what it was like when you were a baby.'

Through constructing the picture, the child may be enabled to recognize and experience the pain associated with not having had closeness and nurturing as a young child. By owning and experiencing this pain, the child may, with help from the counsellor, be enabled to discover ways to nurture themselves. Sometimes, in cases where a mother has been absent or neglectful, the child may recognize that another person did provide some nurturing. After dealing with the pain related to their mother's behaviour, the child may be able to gain positive feelings as a consequence of recognizing the nurturing they received from the other person.

As a result of the counsellor's instructions, the child is likely to begin to create a miniature picture, in the sand tray, of their perception of part of their present, or past or future world. While this is happening, the counsellor stays quietly alongside the child, without interrupting the child's story unnecessarily. As a counsellor, be aware of the developing story and support its evolution. Try not to interpret, but instead try to recognize the symbolic representation in the way that the child understands it.

Sand-tray work is powerful because it provides a visual structure in the form of a sand-tray picture, together with feedback from an observer (the counsellor). Hence, the child is able to gain an understanding of their world by directly viewing the scene they have created in the sand tray, and also through the feedback statements made to them by the counsellor.

As the sand-tray picture develops, there may be several stages of construction. For example, a child may create a picture in which they put a fence around the house. As the child develops their story, they might put a barrier of trees around the fence. Later, as the story continues, the child may sculpt the sand beyond the trees into hills and gullies. As the child's story has developed, their picture in the sand tray has undergone three different stages, each one seeming to increase the barriers around the house. Clearly, it is likely that issues of safety are emerging. However, as counsellors, we keep in mind not to make that interpretation because it could be wrong. Instead, we can give the child accurate feedback of what has been observed by saying, 'I notice that you have put a fence, and some trees, and also some hills and gullies around the house.' Through progressively constructing their picture in the sand tray, and with their awareness raised by the feedback from the counsellor, the child is now likely to recognize their issue (be it safety or something else) and may then go on to address it.

It is important for the counsellor to allow the developing process to occur without interpretation or intrusion. Equally, it is important for the counsellor not to make assumptions about the meanings of symbols or objects in the sand-tray story. It is better to explore the meaning which the child gives the symbol. For example, the counsellor might ask 'Can you tell me about this rock?' In response, the child might say, 'That's the church, where we get lots to eat.' In this way, the child's awareness of issues and developments in their story is raised.

We have already introduced some examples of counselling skills while describing how to use the media. However, we would now like to look more specifically at the types of skills which are most important when doing sand-tray work.

Counselling skills when using the sand tray

When intervention is necessary while the child is telling their story, the counsellor can make use of the counselling skills described in Part 3. The skills detailed below are most useful and relevant to sand-tray work:

1   Observation
2   Use of statements
3   Use of questions
4   Giving instructions
5   Termination skills when using the sand tray.

Observation

A counsellor can learn a great deal about a child, the child's life and the child's issues by observing the child as they tell their story while working in the sand tray.

The counsellor can use the observed information by making feedback statements to the child so that the child is able to get more fully in touch with troubling issues and developments in their life. You might find it useful to bear in mind the following, while making your observations:

1 Notice which symbols the child chooses.
2 Identify the special qualities and meanings which the child attributes to the symbols.
3 Be aware of any commonly used or collective meanings of some symbols and consider whether these are relevant.
4 Observe the placement of symbols in the sand tray: which are in the middle and which are at the edges of the sand tray. Notice which symbols are separated from others and which symbols are close to others. Take note of any symbols which are buried and of any symbols which are in dominating positions.
5 Notice any vacant spaces in the sand tray because these may be significant.
6 Observe how the child works. Do they work spontaneously, hesitantly, lethargically, aggressively or forcefully?
7 Observe the way in which the symbols are chosen. Are they chosen thoughtfully and carefully or are they snatched and carelessly placed?
8 Identify emerging themes such as nurturing, secrecy, disintegration, victimization and power.
9 Observe inconsistencies in the child's story.

Use of statements

Sometimes, while a child is working on their picture, they will talk about it spontaneously. Generally, the counsellor observes quietly as the child creates their picture. However, if the child does not talk about what they are doing, after observing for a while it is appropriate for the counsellor to indirectly invite the child to talk about their story by using a statement to feed back what the counsellor has observed. For example, the counsellor might say, 'You've been very careful when making your picture', or 'Your picture looks very crowded', or 'Your picture is very busy'.

These statements are non-intrusive and are likely to encourage the child to talk about the picture, without directing them to one particular part of the picture. Sometimes, however, statements like the above are not sufficient and a question may be needed.

Feedback statements not only allow the child to talk about the picture, but also raise the child's awareness of their internal processes as they construct the picture.

Their awareness of issues, thoughts and feelings is intensified and consequently they are able to bring these into focus so that they may be addressed.

Use of questions

Before asking questions, it is important for the counsellor to remember to sit quietly and to observe, rather than to interrupt the natural flow of the child's process. However, at appropriate times, during pauses, questions can be used to help the child to explore more fully or in more depth certain parts of their picture or story.

Here are some examples of the use of questions:

- When using the sand tray it can be helpful to ask a general question such as, 'Can you tell me about your picture?'
- If there are empty spaces in the sand tray, the counsellor could draw attention to this by pointing to an empty space and making a comment such as, 'I wonder what's happening over here?'
- If the sand-tray picture contains symbols and figures which are big and strong, the counsellor might say to the child, 'These things look big and strong. Do you ever feel big and strong?'

Giving instructions

Earlier in this chapter we gave examples of instructions which may be used to invite the child to start to create a picture or to tell their story by using the symbols in the sand tray. During the process, other instructions may be required. Consider the following examples.

Example one

A child might develop their story by making verbal suggestions about what might happen next. However, they may not move the symbols in the sand tray to illustrate the change. For example, the child may have set up a scene where children are playing in the park. Later, they may talk about the children going home. However, the child may have left the symbols set up the way they were when the children were playing in the park. In this case the counsellor might say, 'Show me what happens when they go home.' In response, the child is likely to rearrange the symbols and to continue telling their story. As a consequence, new and important issues might emerge which otherwise could have been missed.

Example two

If a child were to show more interest in, or to concentrate on, a particular part of their picture, the counsellor might ask 'Tell me about what is happening here', or 'Tell me about this shell [where the shell is in the relevant part of the picture]'.

Termination skills when using the sand tray

The counsellor judges when the time is appropriate for ending a piece of work in the sand tray. Good indications of this are if:

- the child stops work spontaneously;
- the child is unable to develop the story any further; or
- the time allocated for the counselling session is drawing to an end.

At the appropriate time, the counsellor can summarize what has emerged from the work and check what the child needs to do to finish working. The counsellor can then affirm the child for completing the current piece of work and to give the child an opportunity to dismantle the picture themselves or to leave the picture for the counsellor to dismantle after they have left. It would be inappropriate for the counsellor to dismantle the picture in the child's presence because it is the child's story. To do so would be intrusive and might lead to undesirable symbolic interpretations by the child. However, it is important for the child to know that the picture will not be there when they return for another counselling session.

If the counsellor takes a photograph of the arrangement of the symbols in the sand tray, they can easily identify recurring themes and changes by comparing photographs from session to session.

Suitability of sand-tray work

Children from about the age of five years and upwards enjoy sand-tray work. Even adolescents and adults can find it useful. Younger children enjoy playing in the sand but are not developmentally able to engage in the symbolic use of the media.

As when working with miniature animals, sand-tray work is ideally suited to individual counselling. It is an open-ended and expansive activity because it allows the child to explore any possibilities within the limits of their own fantasies. The size and edges of the sand tray provide a sense of limitation and boundary without inhibiting the internal explorations of the child. Sand-tray work encourages the child to focus on internal processes. It can also invite the child to be adventurous and interactive, with the counsellor's encouragement.

Further information about sand-tray work can be found in Lowenfeld (1967), Ryce-Menuhin (1992) and Pearson and Wilson (2001).

CASE STUDY

One area in which sand-tray work has been used is supporting children who have experienced trauma. Ernst et al. (2008) used sand-tray work as part of an intervention to support children who had witnessed domestic violence (see Chapter 20 for more information about the evidence-base for play therapy techniques). Imagine you have received a new referral for 10-year-old Mark. Mark has recently been placed with a foster family following domestic violence at home during which he was sometimes physically abused. How might you use sand-tray work in the course of counselling to support Mark in exploring his experiences?

KEY POINTS

- Sand-tray work is particularly useful for helping the child to tell their story.
- Symbols required in a sand tray include general items, small toys, figurines, and toy animals.
- By giving suitable instructions the counsellor can invite the child to create a miniature picture in the sand tray of their perceptions of their present, past or possible future world.
- Counsellors can learn a great deal about the child through observation while the child is involved in sand-tray work.
- Statements can be used to feed back to the child what the counsellor notices about the child and about the placement of symbols in the sand tray.
- Most of the time it is best for the counsellor to sit quietly and observe, but at appropriate times questions can elicit useful information.
- Instructions can be useful in helping the child to enlarge on their story.

24

Working with Clay

Clay can be used for a variety of purposes when counselling children but is particularly useful in Phase 2 of the SPICC process (see Figure 8.1, p. 72) when helping the child to get in touch with and release strong emotions. Additionally, clay is an excellent material to use when working with children because its physical properties are both inviting and useful therapeutically. Most children find that the texture of clay makes it pleasant to touch and manipulate. It is easy to make shapes with clay and to change these shapes in size and appearance. Many children engage readily with clay and become absorbed in feeling, stroking, pressing, punching, squashing and shaping it. They find the tactile and kinaesthetic experience pleasant and satisfying. In some ways, the clay can almost become like an extension of these children, as though it were a part of them.

Clay enables a child to be creative. During this creative activity, emotions within the child are likely to emerge and to be expressed through the activity. Clay allows a child to express a very wide range of emotions: a child may serenely stroke the clay, or aggressively punch it or pull it apart in frustration. Thus emotions which the child is holding in are likely to be expressed outwardly, and with cathartic effect.

Because shapes made in clay are easy to change into new shapes, this medium invites the child to continue working by developing existing themes and exploring new themes.

Clay is a three-dimensional medium. This allows the child to have more creative freedom than when working in two dimensions with paint or when drawing. Using clay, the child is free to create shapes which can be realistic, imaginary or symbolic. For example, a child could create a shape in clay to represent a monster. This shape, representing the monster, could be realistic and look like an animal, or it could look like a fantasy figure, or it might have a particular symbolic shape, or it might just be a roughly shaped piece of clay.

Working with clay can be particularly rewarding for children who feel inadequate about their creative skills because it is a medium which can be used with very little skill – there is little chance of failure. Additionally, the counsellor does not need to impose any expectations or rules, so the child can feel free to express themselves confidently by responding to their inner experiences without unnecessary restraint.

Because clay stimulates tactile and kinaesthetic senses, it allows children who have shut down or blocked their sensory and emotional experiences to get in touch with them again. As these children become fully engaged in working with clay, their increased sensitivity to kinaesthetic sensation is likely to result in the useful expression of emotion. The counsellor can expect to see behaviours which are likely to reflect the child's inner processes. Therefore, the counsellor can observe the child's non-verbal and verbal responses, and respond to these by using appropriate counselling skills.

Materials required when using clay

Soft, pliable clay is required. It is important that the clay is not too wet or sticky, because, if it is, working with it will be unpleasant. Additionally, if the clay is too coarse and gritty it will be rough on the skin. Clay can be bought in blocks of about 30 cm × 20 cm × 10 cm in size from a craft shop.

We prefer to work with clay on the floor, rather than on a bench, so that the child can more easily join with the clay, work right beside it and move between clay sculptures. Children can work with clay on a vinyl floor, but the floor needs to be washed afterwards and this is time-consuming. Usually we work on a groundsheet, which can be folded up after use and washed at our convenience. The groundsheet is large enough to provide an adequate work space and to have room for both the child and the counsellor to sit on it comfortably.

A piece of thin wire or nylon finishing line of about 40 cm in length, with wooden handles on each end, is useful for cutting the clay into pieces. If this is used like a cheese cutter, the clay can easily be separated into pieces. It can sometimes be useful to have tools for sculpting the clay, including wooden spatulas, stiff paintbrushes, and plastic knives and forks. A garlic press to extrude the clay can also be of value.

Clay dries out during use, especially in rooms where there is heating, air-conditioning or fans. If clay has partly dried out it can be reconditioned. This can easily be done by shaping it into a large block, making deep holes with your fingers in the top of the block, and then filling these holes with water. The holes can then be sealed by moulding the clay over their entrances. Next, the block can be stored inside a sealed plastic bag. By the following day the water will have distributed itself through the clay, making the clay soft and pliable again.

Some children become anxious because clay is messy. To deal with this, we provide plastic aprons and easy access to a sink and running water.

In summary, the materials required when using clay are as follows:

- A large block of clay
- A groundsheet
- A plastic apron
- A wire for cutting the clay
- Sculpting tools
- Access to water for cleaning up.

Goals when using clay

Asking the child to make clay shapes to symbolize or represent important people, objects, feelings or issues in their life, provides the child with an inviting opportunity to tell their story. As the child does this, the counsellor can use counselling techniques to assist them in exploring relationships, in understanding their past and in developing insight.

Because clay allows the child to give an outward expression to internal processes which occur as they tell their story, it provides a connection or bridge linking the inner processes of the child and the counsellor and allowing the counsellor to share the intimate detail of the child's story. Thus, the counsellor has an opportunity to encourage the child to express emotions and to address issues.

Clay is particularly useful in helping a child to project feelings, rather than leaving them bottled up. This projection occurs as the child acts out emotions physically. For example, a child may pound or punch the clay, or may smooth or roll the clay. As this happens, the counsellor can assist the child to recognize and own the inner feelings associated with the physical expression.

Clay can allow the child to experience satisfaction and success by making a finished product.

Clay is very useful when working with children in groups. In a group setting, children can be encouraged to interact with each other as they work with the clay and gain insight and understanding of other children in the group through sharing. This sharing can enhance the children's individual sense of belonging to the group. Additionally, clay work can be used to help children discover the consequences of their behaviour when in a group.

In summary, goals of importance when using clay include those listed below.

Goals when working with clay individually and in groups

- To help the child to tell and share their story by using the clay to illustrate elements of that story.
- To enable the child to project inwardly contained feelings onto the clay so that they can be recognized and owned.
- To help the child to recognize and deal with underlying issues.
- To help the child to explore relationships and to develop insight into those relationships.
- To enable a child to experience success and satisfaction in completing a creative task.

Additional goals when working with clay in a group

- To help the children gain insight and understanding of others.
- To increase a child's sense of belonging to a group.
- To help children discover the consequences of their behaviour when in a group.

How to work with clay

In discussing how to work with clay we will use the following headings:

- Starting work with clay
- Using the clay to address specific issues

- Creating a dialogue between two sculptures
- Terminating work with clay
- Using clay in a group.

Starting work with clay

We have found that a good way to start work is to invite the child to make friends with the clay. This technique is one suggested by Violet Oaklander. Making friends allows the child to relate to the clay in a personal way. We say to the child, 'Pick up a piece of clay', and then, 'Hold the clay in your hands, and close your eyes.'

Some children may not want to close their eyes, and that's OK. The child is next given the following instructions, with time being allowed between each instruction for the child to complete the task:

Roll the clay.

Flatten it.

Pinch it.

Pull it to pieces.

Gather it all up together, and roll it again.

Poke a hole in it with one finger.

Tear a piece off and make a snake.

Wrap the snake around one finger.

The child is then invited to get in touch with the immediate experience of using the clay. The counsellor might offer this invitation by asking, 'What was it like to make friends with your clay?' and then, 'What did you like doing most?'

The child may say that they enjoyed the experience of flattening the clay. The counsellor might then ask the child, 'What was it like when you were flattening your clay?'

The counsellor can then invite the child to repeat the most pleasurable part of the 'making friends with your clay' exercise.

Using the clay to address specific issues

After the child has made friends with the clay, the counsellor can encourage the child to create a sculpture. This sculpture will be targeted toward particular goals, so it is important for the counsellor's instructions to be specific with regard to these goals. Here are some examples of possible instructions:

'Make a sculpture which will let me know how you feel right now.'
'Make a sculpture with your clay which is like you when you were a baby.'
'Make a sculpture with your clay which is like you when you were living in your foster placement.'
'Make a sculpture with your clay which is like you when you visited Dad on access.'

Sometimes a child might say, 'I'm no good at doing this' or 'I can't make anything'. In this case, the counsellor can encourage the child by saying, 'Just make any shape to be like you when you were … [see suggestions above].'

Sometimes it is useful for the counsellor to model for the child by shaping another piece of clay themselves and talking about what they are doing. For example, the counsellor might make a sculpture with a lot of spikes, bumps and holes in it to represent busyness, and might say 'I'm feeling very busy right now, because I have a lot of work to do, and this is how my clay looks.'

Once the child has made a sculpture, the counsellor may be tempted to invite the child to talk about it. However, before this happens, it is important to check out the child's current experience by asking a question such as 'What was it like to make a sculpture of you when you were a baby?' (or whatever the sculpture was about). Exploring the child's current experience in this way will enable the child to get in touch with their 'here and now' experience. They have an opportunity to tap into current feelings and thoughts and to talk about these. There may then be emotional release and exploration of issues.

The counsellor might make a statement to feed back one or more of their observations. For example, the counsellor might say, 'I noticed that you took a long time to make your sculpture', or 'I noticed that you were very careful when you were making your sculpture of the baby.' The counsellor might then invite the child to be the sculpture by saying, 'I want you to pretend that you are that baby', or 'I want you to pretend that you are that shape.'

Then, while the child is imagining that they are the shape, the counsellor might explore the feelings, which are symbolically represented by the shape and texture of the clay sculpture by asking 'Tell me how it feels to have these bumps around here?' or 'What is it like to have these spikes sticking out of here?'

Next, the counsellor might invite the child to move the sculpture or walk around the sculpture and view it from a different perspective. The counsellor might invite the child to express their experience. For example, the counsellor might say, 'When you look at your sculpture from over here, is it the same, or is it different from when you were over there?' and 'Tell me more.'

Creating a dialogue between two sculptures

After the child has created a shape to represent themselves, the counsellor might ask them to make a second shape to represent either a significant other person in their life or an emotion which is troubling them. The counsellor can then invite the child to alternately imagine that they are each of the shapes, and to engage in a dialogue between them. For example, a child called Jane might make a shape to represent her foster mother. The counsellor might then say, 'Imagine that you are your foster mother' (pointing to the clay representation of the foster mother). 'What would you like to say to Jane?' (pointing to the clay which represents the child).

This process is then continued, with the child swapping between imagining that she is Jane and imagining that she is her foster mother, and thus developing a dialogue between the two.

In all of the work described above, an important goal for the counsellor is to invite the child to continue sharing more information about the sculptures and about themselves. This sharing enables the child to recognize, own and deal with emotional feelings, and to recognize and work through issues. During this process, it is important for the counsellor to remember not to be interrogative or intrusive.

Terminating work with clay

When the child and counsellor recognize that there is no more to be said, the counsellor can invite the child to make a decision about what to do with the sculpture. The child may wish to leave the sculpture intact, where it is, with the understanding that the counsellor will break it up and add it to the rest of the clay after they have left. Another option is for the child to move the sculpture to a safe place so that, although dried out, it will be available in the future. Alternatively, the child may want to pound the sculpture into one lump and add it to the rest of the clay. This closing activity is important for the child because the clay represents a part of themselves. A child's choice and action during closure can give the counsellor additional information about the child and their perceptions of the sculpture.

Using clay in a group

When working with a group it is useful to adopt the counselling and facilitation skills described in Chapter 18. If you personally are intending to run counselling groups for children you may find it helpful to read our book *Working with Children in Groups* (Geldard and Geldard, 2001), as that book provides more extensive information about group work with children.

When starting to work with clay in a group it is usually helpful to begin by using the exercise described earlier in this chapter to enable the children to make friends with the clay. After this the counsellor might say, 'Make a shape which will let the other children in the group know how you are feeling right now.'

When all the children have finished making their sculptures, the counsellor can invite members of the group to look at one child's sculpture and to guess how that child might be feeling. Interaction between the children in the group is encouraged as the children try to guess what each sculpture suggests.

Next, the counsellor might say to the group, 'Make a shape to represent yourself.' When all the children in the group have finished making their new sculpture, the counsellor can ask each member of the group the question 'What can you tell me about your shape?'

Once again, interactive discussion is encouraged. It is important to refrain from pressuring a child to talk about their shape if they don't want to do this. Sometimes the counsellor might ask a child, 'Would it be OK if Johnny said something about your sculpture?' Assuming that the child says 'Yes', the counsellor can invite Johnny to comment by saying, 'What would you like to say about Jane's shape?' This also encourages interactive discussion.

We have found that at the end of a group session using clay, most children will participate with interest in making a group sculpture by combining their individual sculptures. This can help the children to look at their relationships within the group. To do this, the counsellor might say, 'Look around the group and find someone else's sculpture which might fit with yours.'

If a child called Joanne says, 'I think that my sculpture would look good beside Millie's', then the counsellor might ask 'Millie, would it be OK for you if Joanne put her sculpture next to yours?'

If Millie says 'Yes', then Joanne can be invited to move her sculpture. After this the counsellor can check out how Millie feels about the change: 'Millie, what is it like having Joanne's sculpture next to yours?' Millie might say that it is too close or not close enough, in which case she might be asked, 'Would you like to move your sculpture further away [or closer]?' She can then be invited to move her own sculpture to a more comfortable position and Joanne can be encouraged to express her feelings now that Millie has moved her sculpture.

This process can be repeated with other group members until a group sculpture is created involving all of the individual sculptures. By using this approach, members of the group are able to come to an understanding of the relationships in the group, and an understanding of their own and others' needs with regard to these relationships. This can be achieved without the children needing to verbalize all of their thoughts and feelings.

It is interesting to note that usually in a group there will be some children who prefer to leave their sculptures standing independently at a distance from other sculptures. This preference can be respected and valued, and seen as a preferred level of inclusion rather than as exclusion.

During group work, it is important that choices be offered and respected at all times with regard to moving sculptures, the closeness of sculptures, and the impact of closeness or distance on the owners of the individual sculptures.

When the group sculpture has been completed, the counsellor might ask the group, 'How did you feel when you were putting the sculptures together?' and 'Is there anything that you would like to do with the sculpture now?' It is important that the group be given choices about what to do with the completed group sculpture.

Suitability of the medium

To use clay as a therapeutic medium requires the child to have the ability to abstract and symbolize. For this reason, the medium is most suitable for children from the age of six and upwards. Younger children enjoy playing with the clay and constructing representational forms. However, because of their developmental level, they are not able to benefit from the processes described in this section.

Clay is a medium that can be used in individual, family and group counselling. It is open-ended and expansive, allowing the user to manipulate, change and control it at will.

Because clay stimulates the senses, it allows the child to come into contact with feelings and emotions, so is most useful when working with children who are blocked emotionally: it enables them to access and express their emotions in acceptable and appropriate ways (for example, children who are angry can pound and bash the clay). Further, it allows introspective private processing of issues to occur.

CASE STUDY

Supporting children during extended hospital stays or repeated hospital visits is one area in which clay has been found to be an effective medium (e.g. Madden et al., 2010; see Chapter 20 for more details). As part of your role in the hospital you support children during their hospital stay. You have received a referral for Maddie, a seven-year-old who has recently been diagnosed with leukaemia and admitted for her first hospital stay. As you work with Maddie, how might clay be useful in supporting her during her hospital stay? Perhaps you feel Maddie would benefit from participation in a group with other children who have leukaemia. How might you use clay in this group setting?

KEY POINTS

- Clay is particularly useful for helping children to get in touch with and release strong emotions in Phase 2 of the SPICC process.
- Because clay shapes are easy to change, the child is encouraged to continue working by developing existing themes and exploring new themes.
- Clay has an advantage over most other media because of its three-dimensional nature.
- Clay stimulates tactile and kinaesthetic senses, making it easier for children to get in touch with emotional experiences.
- It can be useful to start working with clay by inviting the child to use the exercise 'making friends with the clay'.
- Specific issues can be addressed by inviting the child to make sculptures related to those issues.
- Clay is very suitable for group work.

25

Drawing, Painting, Collage and Construction

In this section we will be discussing four different types of media. These media fit into a group because they can be used in similar ways and, if desired, they can be used together. The media to be discussed are:

1 drawing
2 painting
3 collage
4 construction.

While these media are useful in various stages of the counselling process, they are particularly useful in Phase 2 of the SPICC model (see Figure 8.1, p. 72) where the child continues to tell their story and get in touch with strong emotions, and in Phase 3 where the emphasis is on helping the child to change their self-perception. When using any of these media the focus is on creativity. All of them invite the child to explore, experiment and play. The child can use the media to make pictures or symbolic representations of issues, feelings and themes, related to their story or to a part of their story. Hence, the child can visually develop a picture of their environment and recognize their position in that environment. They can also use the media to explore any changes that have occurred in the environment or changes which they may have made over a period of time.

Children can use the media to create sequences to express the chronological development of their personal stories, as in a comic strip. They can create different and more satisfactory endings for experiences which have had unpleasant outcomes for them.

The media allow a child to make strong statements in acceptable forms. For example, aggressive or socially unacceptable behaviour can be expressed in a painting. In this way, the behaviour is contained instead of being acted out. This enables the child to experiment with, and experience, negative emotions.

The media also allow the child to be constructive – and destructive – but in a useful way. For example, a child may destroy a picture they have created by scribbling over part of it which symbolizes something that angers them. If they wish, they can totally destroy the picture by tearing it up and throwing it away.

Children who are not able to talk about their wishes and needs in connection with past, present and future situations may be able to do so by using the symbolic language of drawing, painting or constructive artistic creation. We have found that by using a visual metaphor (as described in Chapter 15 and later in this chapter), children who found it challenging to talk about themselves were able to do so through drawing (Geldard et al., 2009).

All of these media are powerful because they allow children to express and communicate internal thoughts, feelings and experiences by using their own individual imagery and symbolism. Using the symbolic language of art, children can experience and deal with their emotional feelings and make changes in related behaviours.

When selecting drawing or painting, it is important to remember that children will perform with various levels of skill depending on their developmental age. It is desirable for a counsellor to have some understanding of developmentally appropriate skill levels so that the child's performance is not incorrectly interpreted as abnormal and maximum benefit is obtained therapeutically when using the media.

Firstly, consider very young children below the age of four. It is normal and appropriate for these children to scribble and to experiment by trying out new ways of drawing. They do not relate the colours used in their paintings to the actual colours of objects, but mostly use colour in response to their emotional feelings. Although the counsellor may not be able to understand the meaning of the child's drawing or scribble, the child knows what it represents. Usually children in this age group won't tell a counsellor what they have drawn, unless asked. Also, the child may sometimes change the meaning of the drawing, first calling it a man, then a dog and then Mummy going shopping. This can be confusing for a counsellor.

As the child develops, from four to six years, they will see their drawing or painting as something of value which they have created. They may want to keep the drawing or to give it to someone.

From the age of five to seven years, proportions in drawings of the human figure tend to be unrealistic. A child may draw a person with hands which are large and out of proportion to the figure. This could be wrongly interpreted, with the counsellor making inappropriate assumptions about the size of the hands in an individual drawing.

At the age of seven or eight, a child may begin to draw figures on the bottom edge of the page, and to draw other things around those figures, such as the sky, birds, the sun or clouds. Colour is used more realistically. However, the child may draw 'X-ray' pictures – for example, a picture of a house showing both the outside of the house and a view of the rooms inside. Similarly, a child might draw a picture of their pregnant mother and include in the picture the baby inside the mother's 'stomach'. The child may also draw several different events, occurring at various stages in time, in the one drawing.

From the age of eight onwards, symbols become more complex in their meaning and drawings begin to reflect individual differences according to the child's needs and issues. There tends to be a fascination with detail and patterns at this stage. For example, girls may decorate dresses elaborately and boys may draw elaborate designs on aeroplanes or rockets.

As the child moves into early adolescence, motivation when drawing becomes less focused on what the child sees and more on the child's emotional or subjective experience.

A younger child will draw or paint as though they were a spectator at a scene, and will try to represent their drawing in a three-dimensional way by using perspective. By contrast, the early adolescent is more likely to draw or paint as if they were directly involved in the action and to use colour in response to their emotions.

While there are noticeable age-related developmental stages in drawing and painting, there are some common ways in which children generally reflect their feelings by their use of line, shape and colour. A line has a quality of movement or action: it might suggest direction, orientation, motion or energy. A vertical line is upright and obvious. A horizontal line is calm and might be associated with the absence of motion or with sleep. A diagonal line has a dynamic quality and could suggest instability or loss of balance. Circular or curved lines are fluid and could suggest a calm, easy motion.

Similarly, colours have symbolic meanings which are generally accepted. These meanings can be helpful in enabling children to express their feelings. For example, if we asked you to think of any symbolism associated with green and red colours, what would you say? Many people would say that green colours are more often used to symbolize 'a relaxed state' and red colours are more often used to symbolize 'anger' or 'danger'.

Notice any rhythm which occurs in a drawing or painting. A child may express rhythm in the form of repetition of the same shape, or line, or colour, or direction. Rhythms within a child's drawing or painting are often related to the emotions the child is expressing through the work.

Materials needed

Materials for drawing

- Sheets of white and coloured drawing paper of various sizes
- Pencils
- Coloured felt pens
- Pastels
- Crayons
- A selection of brightly coloured highlighters.

Primary school children can work comfortably on A4 paper. Younger children usually find this size restricting and prefer larger sheets. Although generally children prefer to work on white paper, sheets of coloured paper sometimes appeal to children, especially those who lack confidence in their drawing abilities. We rarely provide erasers, but instead encourage children to try again if they are unhappy with their drawings.

Materials and equipment for painting with brushes

- Large sheets of butcher's or art paper
- Acrylic or poster paints
- Large hair brushes
- A plastic apron to protect clothing
- A horizontal working surface
- Access to water.

Paper suitable for painting is more absorbent than that used for drawing. Painting is best done on a horizontal surface because running paint may cause frustration.

Materials for finger-painting

- Large sheets of poster or art paper
- A polythene sheet
- Acrylic or poster paints
- Paint containers for holding and squirting paint
- Spray containers of shaving cream
- Vegetable dyes
- A plastic apron to protect clothing
- A horizontal working surface
- Access to water.

For finger-painting, squeezable containers with lids suitable for squirting paint are useful. Alternatively, bowls of paint can be used. Shaving cream, used in conjunction with vegetable dyes, can add texture to the work. For obvious reasons easy access to water is essential!

Materials for collage

Essential materials include the following:

- Large sheets of white or coloured paper or card
- Craft glue or another fast-setting adhesive
- Scissors
- A stapler
- Masking tape
- Sticky tape
- String.

The collage is created by gluing, stapling or tying materials to a backing sheet of white or coloured paper or card. Sometimes we use cardboard, as this provides a stronger backing for firmer materials. A range of materials suitable for sticking to the backing sheet is required. These might include any of the following:

Magazine pictures	Glitter (various colours)
Newspapers	Coloured stars
Feathers	Sequins
Fabrics	Leaves
Yarns	Cottonwool
Wood shavings	Sand

Sandpaper	Sawdust
Small pieces of foam	Highly textured wallpaper
Coloured wool	

Good collage work can be done using pictures and words cut from magazines and newspapers. This approach appeals to many adolescents.

Materials for construction work

In construction work we can make use of any objects or materials which lend themselves to creating three-dimensional sculptures. Expensive materials aren't needed: creative construction work can be done using any clean items of household junk which do not present a safety hazard but would normally be thrown in the rubbish bin. Here are some examples:

Plastic containers	Lids
Old tins	Wire
Styrofoam packing	Bubble wrap
Unused cake cases	Pipe-cleaners
Ice-lolly sticks	Matchsticks
Coloured paper	Coloured card
Boxes such as plasters and toothpaste boxes	Cardboard tubes from paper towel rolls

Clearly, sculptures made from such materials involve fixing things together. Although glue is sometimes useful, most children become frustrated when waiting for it to dry. Hence, it can be advantageous to use alternative ways of holding pieces of a sculpture together. For example, Styrofoam shapes can be connected with toothpicks, Velcro tape or double-sided tape. Many other materials can be tied together with picture-hanging wire, fishing line or string. Paperclips, staplers, masking tape and packaging tape can also be used.

Goals when using drawing and painting

Goals when using drawing and painting include the following:

To enable the child to tell their story

By drawing and painting, a child who finds it challenging to tell their story verbally can describe and disclose information about themselves, their family and their environment. They can do this either by direct representation of people and events, or indirectly in a projective way through symbolic representation.

To enable the child to express repressed or intense emotional feelings

These can be expressed through the creative activity itself, or concretized in the symbols used in the drawing and painting.

To help the child to gain a sense of mastery over events which they have experienced or are experiencing

By drawing or painting, a child can serialize the events in their life through the use of comic book representation and storytelling. They can then, by combining the creative elements of art and fantasy, experiment with changes to their story and thus gain a sense of mastery.

How to use drawing and painting

Some children find it difficult to get started when they are invited to draw or paint. This may be for a number of reasons, such as the following:

1 The child may have a poor self-image.
2 The child may have been conditioned into copying rather than creating.
3 The child may have had negative messages about their ability to draw.
4 The child may be being oppositional.

To deal with a child's difficulty in getting started we can use warm–up exercises.

Initial warm-up exercises

We often start by using the warm–up exercises described below. The first two of these are known as 'Chasey' and 'Mr Squiggle'.

Chasey
With a large sheet of paper, the counsellor uses a coloured felt pen to run around the paper, continually changing direction, while the child, using another pen of a different colour, tries to follow and catch up with the counsellor. After a while the counsellor stops, holds the drawing up and says, 'Oh, I wonder what we've made? Can you see anything in this picture?' and 'Does it look like anything to you?' If the child has no suggestions, the counsellor might make a suggestion of their own.

Mr Squiggle
The child is invited to draw lines, or scribble on the page, and the counsellor then uses these lines to make a picture. For example, a counsellor might add eyes and whiskers to a scribble to create a cat.

Warm-up exercises to help a child to get in touch with feelings

When a child says, 'I can't draw' or 'I don't want to draw', it is helpful for the counsellor to focus on the child's feelings. The first step is to help the child to get in touch with their bodily experience. We might say to the child, 'Close your eyes', and then 'Notice what your body is feeling.'

Additionally, the counsellor might say something like, 'Notice that your elbows are resting on the table', and 'What does that feel like?' A question might then be asked about the child's feet resting on the ground. The child can be invited to draw their feet. The counsellor might say, 'Can you feel your feet on the ground?' and 'Draw me a picture of your feet on the ground.'

To provide some contrast, we can say to the child, 'Stand up, close your eyes, and reach for the ceiling', and then 'Draw the feeling of standing up straight and reaching for the ceiling'. The child could also be invited to curl up in a tight ball on the floor, and then to draw what that felt like.

After doing these exercises, we might then ask the child about a recent experience. For example, 'What did you do just before you came to this session?' The answer might be 'I rode my bike down the street.' The counsellor can then ask questions such as the following:

• 'What did it feel like to ride your bike down the street?'
• 'What did it feel like having your feet on the pedals?'
• 'What did it feel like having your hands on the handlebars?'

Once the child is in touch with how their body feels, the counsellor can invite them to draw the feeling by saying, 'Draw me a picture which will tell me how you are feeling right now.'

The purpose of the warm-up exercises is to get the child in touch with their feelings and to help them to start using the media.

Making use of drawing and painting

For children from the age of eight or nine years and upwards, drawing or painting which involves fantasy is invaluable. It allows them to release socially unacceptable emotions, such as hate and anger, and to express secrets and desires.

The counsellor might start by asking the child to create their own world on paper, using shapes, lines and colours, and might say, 'Think about your world as lines, shapes and colours. Use the whole page to show me where the people, places and things are in your world.'

When the drawing or painting has been completed, the counsellor might explore the relationships between shapes by noticing the closeness of some shapes to others, or the distance between some shapes and others. The counsellor might then use a feedback statement to encourage the child to talk about the significance of these relative positions. For example, the counsellor might point to some shapes and say, 'I notice that this shape here is a long way away from this shape here.'

The technique of using shapes, lines and colours can also be used effectively to help children to draw their families. For example, the counsellor might say, 'Think of each member of your family and draw them as if they were a shape, a line or a colour on the page.'

Sometimes the counsellor might want to help the child to find out more about themselves as an individual. A good way of doing this can be to invite the child to imagine that they are a tree. The counsellor might say, 'Imagine that you are a tree and draw a picture of yourself as the tree.'

Sometimes children may need prompting and help to get started after being given the above instruction. In this case, the counsellor can ask questions to help the child to get in touch with their creativity. For instance, we might ask:

- What kind of tree are you?
- Do you have fruit?
- Are you large?
- Are you tall?
- Do you have flowers?
- Do you have many flowers, or just a few?
- What do you look like in the winter?
- Do you have thorns on your branches?
- Do you have large leaves or small leaves?
- Do you grow next to other trees, or are you on your own?

Following this, we might invite the child to describe their drawing by saying, 'Pretend to be the tree and tell me what it is like to be in this drawing.'

We often find that children identify strongly with the tree they have drawn. This is very useful in helping a child to start working on personal issues.

Useful topics for drawing or painting

Suitable topics can be addressed by using the following instructions:

- Draw a picture of when you were a baby.
- Draw a picture of your headache.
- Draw a picture of your anger.
- Draw a picture of your worry.
- Draw a picture of where you would like to be if you were magic.
- Draw a picture of your dream.
- Draw a picture of your nightmare.

With any of the above drawings or paintings, it might be useful to explore how the child feels if they have included themselves in the drawing. For example, if the child has drawn themselves as a baby, the counsellor might ask, 'I wonder how that baby feels?'

If there were other people or objects in the drawing, then the counsellor might point to one of them and say, 'Pretend to be this person [or object]', and 'I wonder how you feel?'

Painting has additional value because of its texture and the flowing quality of paint, so it is more powerful in allowing the child to connect with their emotions. When using painting we might sometimes say to a child, 'Paint a picture of how you feel right now', or 'Paint a picture of how you are when you are sad [or happy].'

Children seem to be able to represent feelings more easily with paint than with drawing. When drawing, they tend to be more representational.

Finger-painting

Some children are frightened of making mistakes. A good way to desensitize them is to get them to experiment with shaving cream or finger paint. Let the child squirt shaving cream onto a polythene sheet, then colour the shaving cream by dripping food colouring on to it and mixing it in.

Finger-painting is best done on a large sheet of butcher's paper using plastic containers of acrylic paint which can be squirted or splashed onto the paper. The child can then be encouraged to move the paint around with their fingers. Plastic aprons are strongly recommended! Once the process has started, the counsellor can say to the child, 'Let's see if you can show me how you're feeling by making a picture out of the paint.'

Finger-painting involves tactile and kinaesthetic experiences. It can be soothing and flowing or it can encourage expansive and less controlled expression. Finger-painting allows the child to make pictures and to change them quickly, or to cover them up or erase them with more paint. The size of the paper is the only restraint or boundary, so the child can feel free and be expressive. Finger-painting is sometimes best used as a warm-up exercise for children before they begin creating more representational images with the use of brushes.

Collages

Collages add yet another dimension to the creative expression of children. Similar instructions can be given to the child to those used for drawing or painting. Additionally, collage allows the child to make connections between the texture of objects (such as cottonwool, sawdust, feathers, and so on) and emotional feelings. To help a child to make such a connection, the counsellor might say, 'How does this sandpaper feel?' The child might reply 'Scratchy'. The counsellor might then ask, 'If you were that piece of scratchy sandpaper, how would you feel?'

Collage is a good medium to use when asking a child to make a self-portrait. A self-portrait in collage can help the child to become more fully aware of their perception of themselves and can give them the opportunity to move from superficial descriptions to greater self-disclosure. We might begin by inviting a child to choose any of the materials provided to create a picture of themselves, then make statements like 'I notice that you have chosen the crunchy sawdust for your hair. What is it like to have hair that is crunchy like sawdust?' or 'I notice that you have chosen feathers for your arms and legs. What would it be like to walk around on feathers?'

Collage can be used with older children to explore their perceptions of issues and events in their lives. Older children will often use pictures and words of varying type sizes to make statements about current or past issues which are of concern to them. Depending on the materials available, collage can sometimes move into the activity of construction.

Construction or sculpture

Many of the suggestions given for drawing, painting and collage can be adapted for construction work or sculpture. For example, the counsellor might say, 'Make a tree to represent you.'

Construction and sculpture are often useful for children who are clumsy or awkward, or who have experienced little success in their lives. As the child creates the sculpture, the counsellor can observe the child's responses to failure, success, decision making, problem solving and completing tasks. In instances where the construction may take time to complete, the counsellor can observe the way in which the child deals with delayed gratification and can then make statements of observation about the child's behaviour, like 'I notice that you are hard on yourself when you make mistakes', or 'When things don't work out right, you seem to give up easily'. The child's awareness of their behaviour is raised, so that relevant issues can be addressed.

Suitability of drawing, painting, collage and construction

All of these media are very suitable for use in individual counselling. Drawing can also be used effectively in groups and in family counselling. Similarly, finger-painting can be used effectively in group work.

Construction, collage and painting are most effectively used with pre-school and primary school children. From early adolescence to late adolescence, drawing and sometimes painting are the most useful of these media.

Finger-painting is the medium most likely to elicit open, expansive and expressive behaviours in the child. Drawing, and to some extent painting, lends itself to more representational and introspective behaviour. Construction, and to some extent collage, promotes the expression of more functional and less emotionally expressive experiences. Construction and collage also promote the exploration of insight and understanding of the child's own behaviour.

CASE STUDY

Use of art activities, such as drawing, painting, collage and construction, when counselling children has an extensive evidence base (see Chapter 20 for more details). For example, Nabors and her colleagues (2004) explored the use of art activities to support children who had recently experienced the death of a loved one. The children reported that the art activities helped them to express and release their grief and related feelings. You are planning a group programme for children who have recently lost a loved one. How might you make use of art activities to support the children in the group to explore their experiences? At what stage of the group would you consider using art? How would you introduce and go on to use the art activity?

KEY POINTS

- Drawing, painting, collage and construction, invite the child to make pictures or symbolic representations of issues, feelings and themes, related to their story.
- The media allow the child to tell their story, express and release strong emotions in an acceptable way, and gain a sense of mastery over events.
- As some children find it difficult to get started when drawing or painting, warm-up exercises are useful.
- Finger-painting can be soothing and flowing or it can encourage expansive and less controlled expression.
- Collage encourages creative expression and is useful for older children in helping them to explore their perceptions of issues and events.

26

The Imaginary Journey

The imaginary journey can be helpful in several of the phases of the SPICC process (see Figure 8.1, p. 72). It can be particularly useful in Phase 2 in raising the child's awareness of troubling issues and enabling the child to get in touch with emotions and gain mastery over past events, and in Phases 3 and 4 in helping the child to change their self-perception and to explore alternative ways of thinking and behaving.

The imaginary journey is a very powerful technique and as such needs to be used with care and only in situations where it will be helpful to the counselling process and to the child, and where there is confidence that it will not have any detrimental effects on the child. We strongly recommend that the imaginary journey is only used by fully trained and experienced counsellors who are able to judge when its use is appropriate, or by new counsellors under the close direction of a competent supervisor who is able to judge that its use is appropriate. Having said this, we believe that this technique can help many children.

Most people, in their daily lives, go on imaginary journeys from time to time. They allow themselves to daydream or to fantasize about what has happened or might have happened in their lives, about what is currently happening or might be happening, and about the future. In a similar way, guiding a child on an imaginary journey allows the child to freely explore, in their imagination, real and imaginary scenarios from the past and present and to fantasize about possible scenarios for the future.

Taking a child on an imaginary journey involves telling the child the outline of a story and allowing them to fill in the details from their own imagination and experiences. Thus, when the counsellor guides the child on the journey, they create the scenes along the journey, but leave the child to create in their imagination the people, the objects and the activities within the scene. Consequently, the child is provided with an opportunity to create scenarios, which are projections of their own inner world, in total privacy, and to explore the most personal themes and ideas, which emerge spontaneously from within themselves. As the child moves through the journey, memories, emotions and fantasies may be triggered so that they may become aware of them and can work through them with the help of the counsellor.

During the imaginary journey, the child becomes deeply involved in the processes occurring within themselves as they find, enter and explore the scenarios which are their own creation. It is as though they establish an intimate personal relationship with themselves through which they gain in self-knowledge.

In this chapter we will describe two different imaginary journeys which we have found to be useful. Imaginary journeys are carefully designed so that the child and not the counsellor is in control during the journey. It is important to word instructions so that the child has choice about what they do and don't do. The child must also be able to leave the journey whenever they want.

Goals when using the imaginary journey

The imaginary journey can be used to help a child to get in touch with experiences which may have been very painful for them and may have been repressed. Equally, it may be used as a way of helping a child to renew contact with happy or pleasant experiences from the past.

By sharing their experience of their journey with the counsellor, the child can deal constructively with memories that have been brought into focus by the journey. The child can work through emotional feelings which those memories have triggered and address troubling thoughts and beliefs. The imaginary journey enables the child to get in touch with their inner pain and then to deal with that pain through the counselling process.

An imaginary journey can provide a child with an opportunity to gain mastery over past issues and events so that they can feel as though they had an active role in those events and were not just a passive and helpless observer. Consider the case of a child who had witnessed and been troubled by the bullying of one of their friends in the playground. They might feel guilty because they ran away and deserted their friend. In the imaginary journey the child might reconstruct the scene, but instead of running away they might do something different, such as punching the bully on the nose or telling a teacher about the bully. Although these alternatives are not necessarily appropriate or acceptable for the child, they allow him to experience some sense of power and control. The counsellor can then help the child to look at the alternative behaviours and their consequences, and as a result to feel better.

During the journey, the child can, in their imagination, change something they have done or said in the past. They can say or do things which might give them a sense of completion or satisfaction with regard to past events in their life. Consider the case of a child whose father has died. The child might, in some way, feel responsible for their father's death. In the imaginary journey they might visualize their father and might say something to him which they need to say in order to make them feel better.

Most importantly, the imaginary journey encourages the child to tell their story and helps them to develop insight into their own behaviour, the behaviours of others and the possible reasons for the occurrence of events in the past. The journey provides an opportunity for the resolution of issues and for the exploration of alternative behaviours or options.

In summary, goals when using the imaginary journey include the following:

- To enable the child to tell their story.
- To help a child to get in touch with, and work through, painful experiences that have been repressed.

- To help a child to re-experience happy or successful events.
- To help the child experience imaginary completion of unfinished scenarios or events, with resolution of related issues.
- To help a child to gain mastery over past issues or events.
- To help a child to discover alternative behaviours or options which might have more satisfactory outcomes for them.
- To help the child to gain insight into their own behaviour and the behaviour of others.
- To help the child to understand the reasons why past events occurred.

Materials needed when using the imaginary journey

It is important for the child to be relaxed when going on an imaginary journey. A quiet room with no intruding noises from outside is required. Preferably, the lighting is pleasantly subdued rather than bright and glaring. In the room, a comfortable place to sit or to lie is made available for the child. We usually provide an adult-size bean bag for this purpose because it gives children a choice of sitting or lying. Allowing for this choice is important because some children feel vulnerable when lying down. This is particularly true for children who have been sexually abused.

On completion of the imaginary journey, we provide the child with paper and felt pens to draw a picture related to the journey. In summary, materials needed are:

- A quiet room
- A large bean bag
- Drawing paper
- Coloured felt pens.

How to guide a child on an imaginary journey

We begin the imaginary journey by encouraging the child to sit or lie comfortably on a large bean bag. We then say to the child something like, 'In a minute, I'd like you to imagine that you are going on a journey. I will help you to go on the journey by telling you about some of the things that you might see on the journey. The things I will tell you about are only my suggestions, so you can ignore them if you like.'

Before proceeding further, it is important to tell the child that during the journey they may stop at any time they like. We might say, 'If you don't like the journey, stop going on it, and let me know. Do you think that you could do that?' and 'If you do want to stop going on the journey what will you do? Will you say something? What do you think you would say?' or 'Would you signal that you wanted to stop?' and 'How would you do that?'

It is important to give the child permission to ignore any directions which the counsellor might give, but which the child might not like. To give this permission, the counsellor might say, 'During the journey, I may suggest that you imagine that you are doing some things. If you don't want to do these things, don't do them. Instead just imagine that you are doing something that you would like to do, or stop going on the journey altogether.'

We then invite the child to sit comfortably on the bean bag by saying, 'Firstly, though, move around on the bean bag until you are comfortable.'

When guiding the child along the journey, we use a quiet tone of voice and talk slowly so that we do not intrude on the child's relaxed mood and attention to the journey. As we guide the child along, we leave pauses between each instruction to allow the child to fill in details of the story by using their imagination and to allow them to fully experience the journey in their imagination.

We will now describe two examples of imaginary journeys. We call the first of these examples 'My secret place', and the second 'The country house journey'.

My secret place

We start the journey by saying, 'You are going to go on an imaginary journey – if you want, you can imagine that I am going on the journey with you, or you can imagine that you are on your own if that is what you would like to do. If you want to, you can close your eyes.' We then say the following sentences, leaving pauses between them:

Imagine that you are walking down a hallway. Notice whether it is light and airy or dark and dismal. Notice the colours of the walls, the floor and the ceiling. Notice how it smells. Imagine that as you walk slowly down the hallway you are looking around. There are doors all along the hall. Have a closer look at one of the doors. Notice what it looks like, how big it is, and what the door handle looks like. Imagine that you touch the door handle. When you are ready, you can open the door if you want to. If you open the door you will find yourself looking at a scene which you remember. Look at the scene from the doorway – look around. Notice anyone who is there. Maybe you can see yourself in the scene. If you wish you can imagine that you are yourself in the scene. If you want to you can look around – you can look at any people who are there – you can look at them one at a time. [Time needed.] You may want to say something to someone and they may say something to you. [Time needed.] Now imagine yourself standing in the doorway ready to leave. Is there anything that you want to do or say before you leave? If there is do it now. [Time needed.] Imagine yourself going back through the door into the hallway – closing the door – and walking back down the hallway. Now leave your imaginary journey and notice that you are sitting on the bean bag. When you are ready, open your eyes and without talking look around this room.

After this, we ask the child to draw a picture of the journey because by doing this the child will reconnect with important parts of the journey and will concretize these in the drawing. By giving some permanent expression to the experience of the journey, the child is more easily able to explore, and to share, the emotional and cognitive experiences related to the journey. We ask the child to draw the picture by saying, 'Stay silent. Now take a piece of paper and some felt pens and draw a picture of your journey.'

Next, the counsellor supports the child to process their experience of the journey. Before discussing this we will give our second example of an imaginary journey.

The country house journey

We begin by saying, 'You are going to go on an imaginary journey – if you want you can imagine that I am going with you on the journey, or you can imagine that you are going on the journey by yourself, if you would prefer to do that. If you would like to close your eyes, close them.'

Then, talking slowly and softly with a pause between each sentence or phrase as appropriate, we say:

Picture yourself walking down a long dirt road. On either side there are tall trees. It is sunny and warm. In the distance you can see a house. Imagine that as you get closer to the house you can see the garden around the house. Imagine yourself walking through the garden to the front door which is partly open [pause], pushing the door open [pause] and walking inside. It's cool and dark after being out in the sun. It takes you time to get used to the light and when you do you may be surprised by what you see. There may be people there or it may be empty. Imagine that you look around the room and the house, touch things you want to touch, and talk to people you want to talk to [pause]. When you are ready to leave, imagine yourself going back out of the front door [pause], walking through the garden to the road [pause] and walking back down the road. Now leave your imaginary journey [pause] and notice that you are sitting on the bean bag. When you are ready, open your eyes and look around [pause]. Now I would like you to draw a picture of your journey. You can draw any part of it or all of it.

Before processing the child's picture it is important to allow the child to take as much time as they need to finish drawing whatever seems relevant to them.

Processing the child's picture and journey

When the child has finished their picture, the counsellor can help the child to process the drawing by asking one or two questions about the drawing and the journey. For example:

- What can you tell me about your picture?
- What was it like to go on the journey?
- What was it like to walk down the road?
- What was it like being in the house (or hallway)?
- What was it like opening the door?
- Did you want to stay or did you want to leave?
- Would you have liked to have done anything different on your journey?
- Did this journey remind you of something which has happened to you before?

By asking these questions, information may emerge connecting the journey, or part of it, to an authentic experience from the child's life. This might give the child an opportunity to tell important parts of their personal story. Thus the counsellor will make use of the full range of counselling skills (see Part 3) in helping the child to deal with painful emotions, troubling thoughts and issues of concern. During this process, the counsellor can help the child to redefine distorted memories in a more emotionally comfortable way and to challenge self-destructive beliefs.

Some children may not be able to draw a picture, or may not want to draw one. In this case, the counsellor can directly process the imaginary journey by using some of the questions listed above which do not relate to a picture, but relate directly to the imaginary journey itself.

After the journey, a child may be able to share a great deal of useful information and this will enable them to make progress therapeutically. However, some children will be unable to share anything: they may not feel safe about sharing private information which emerged in the journey, and it is important to respect their right to say nothing. When a child is unable to share, it is still possible that therapeutic processing will occur privately within the child.

Suitability of the imaginary journey

Please note the caution at the start of this chapter with regard to the use of the imaginary journey. The imaginary journey should never be used with children who have known psychotic tendencies, or seem to be out of touch with reality, or who are disoriented with respect to time, place or person. The imaginary journey is also not recommended for children with low ego-strength because the activity might be too challenging for them. Nor is it recommended for children who are dissociative following trauma.

The imaginary journey is most suitable for children from early adolescence onwards. Some primary school children can also benefit from the use of this technique. It is suitable for individual counselling, but not for group work. The imaginary journey is open and expansive because it provides an opportunity for the child to make changes to the way that they remember things. It encourages introspective and private thoughts in the child, which they can usually share with the counsellor.

CASE STUDY

Under the heading 'Goals when using the imaginary journey' we provided two examples of experiences in which the imaginary journey might be beneficial: responding to a bully and the death of a loved one. Rather than providing a case study this time, we would like to invite you to come up with your own case study. What is another experience which could be suited to the use of the imaginary journey? What other aspects would you need to consider when planning your case study? While developing your case study remember to keep in mind the examples of children for whom this technique is not recommended.

KEY POINTS

- When using the imaginary journey the child is given the outline of the story and allowed to fill in the details from their own imagination and experiences.
- It is important to give the child permission to ignore the counsellor's directions whenever they wish and to stop going on the imaginary journey at any time.
- After going on the journey the child can be invited to draw a picture of the journey or any part of it.
- The usefulness of the imaginary journey depends on the way it is processed in order to help the child gain from the experience.

27

Books and Stories

In this chapter we will consider the following:

- The use of story books in counselling children.
- Helping children to create therapeutically useful stories.
- The use of books for educational purposes within the counselling process.

Books and stories are useful for achieving a variety of goals as will be explained in this chapter and can be used in any of the phases of SPICC process (see Figure 8.1, p. 72).

However, they are particularly helpful in Phases 3, 4, and 5, when the child is changing self-perception and beliefs, looking at options and choices and experimenting with new behaviours.

The use of story books in counselling children

We invite you, the reader, to think for a moment about the nature of children's stories. Do stories have special qualities which make them suitable tools for use in counselling children? We think that they do. Children's stories involve people, animals, fantasy figures and all kinds of inanimate objects such as trains, rocks, clocks and flowerpots. The people, animals, fantasy figures and objects are given personalities, beliefs, thoughts, emotions and behaviours. Most importantly, as a story unfolds, themes develop, issues emerge, and the characters and objects in the story respond with particular thoughts, emotions and behaviours. When a child listens to a story, they may identify with a character, or a theme or an event within the story. If they do this, then they are almost certain to reflect on their own life situation. Their interest in the thoughts, emotions and behaviours of the characters in the story allow them to, at some level, share the experience of the story book characters and to project onto these characters beliefs, thoughts and emotional experiences of their own. Thus, they can projectively work through their own emotional turmoil. Additionally, a child will often recognize the relationship between events and themes within a story and events and themes in their own life. When this occurs they have an opportunity to work directly on their own issues.

Creating stories

An alternative to reading a story from a book is to encourage the child to create their own story: the child is certain to project ideas from their own life onto the characters and themes in the story. The child may even include themselves as a character in the story, or may describe events which have occurred in their own life in the story. Once again, as when reading a story book, the child is provided with an opportunity to explore their own issues, thoughts, emotions and behaviours, either projectively or directly.

Books for educational purposes

Sometimes, as counsellors, we may need to teach children new behaviours which are more appropriate than the ones they have previously learnt. Consider, for example, children who have been sexually abused. Often, such children have learnt to be trusting and to have open boundaries. Additionally, they may have been taught to be polite to adults and to be compliant. Through books or stories such children can learn about appropriate boundaries and to realize that it is appropriate and necessary to say 'No' when their boundaries are at risk. Books can be used in an educational way with regard to a number of other issues and/or areas of knowledge, including abuse, violence, social skills, anger management, sex education, separation, divorce and death.

Goals when using books and stories

There are a number of goals that can be achieved by using books and stories. These include general goals, goals specific to the use of story books, goals specific to creating stories, and goals when using books for educational purposes.

General goals when using story books or when creating stories

- To help the child to recognize their own anxiety or distress by identifying with characters or situations in a story.
- To help a child to discover themes and related emotions which recur in their life from time to time. For example, the child may discover that they have a fear of being left alone, a fear of betrayal or excessive feelings of responsibility for others. By becoming aware of such feelings, the child can deal with them and move towards a resolution of related issues.
- To help a child to think about and explore alternative solutions to problems. This goal can be achieved by changing stories so that they have different outcomes.

Goals specific to the use of story books

- To help a child to normalize events in their life by letting them know that others have had similar experiences. This goal can be achieved by reading stories which have themes similar to their own experiences.

- To help reduce stigma related to socially unacceptable experiences. Children who have experienced sexual abuse or domestic violence feel better about themselves when they know that other children have been through similar experiences and have had similar feelings. They can discover this by reading stories about other children having similar experiences.
- To help the child to recognize that some events are unavoidable. For example, a child who has become ill and has to go to hospital may be helped by reading a book about another child going to hospital and may thus identify with some of that child's fears and hopes.

Goal specific to creating stories

- To help a child to express wishes, hopes and fantasies. This is particularly useful for children who are experiencing painful life situations and are telling untrue stories to avoid the pain of facing reality. For example, a child who has no parents might be ashamed of being different from their friends and might find it too painful to tell them the truth. Consequently, they might tell their friends that their parents are famous people who are working overseas. By using storytelling, the counsellor is able to help the child to recognize that their stories are not true, but may be expressions of wishes.

Goal when using books for educational purposes

- To help educate children in appropriate beliefs and behaviours. Books commonly used in this way are those related to protective behaviours, anger management and social skills.

Materials needed when working with books and stories

We make use of a variety of story books which cover different themes and situations, including the following:

- Making friends
- Families
- Rejection
- Magic
- Monsters
- Fairytales
- Fables.

We also have story books which are useful for helping children to identify and own their feelings. For example, we have books on cheating, bullying and temper tantrums.

Additionally, we have a collection of books which we use for educational purposes on topics such as:

- The development of skills which reflect self-esteem issues
- Sexual abuse
- Protective behaviours

- Domestic violence
- Sexual development.

For creating stories, we use the following materials:

- Large sheets of white paper
- Felt pens of assorted colours
- An exercise book with widely spaced lines
- A voice recorder.

How to use books and stories

Storytelling is an interactive process between the child and the counsellor. Usually, children don't like writing in counselling sessions. Many of the children who come to see us have previously had unsuccessful experiences when attempting to be creative by writing stories. Because of this, we try to make story writing an easy, enjoyable and positive creative experience. Usually, as a child develops a story, we write the story down using a felt pen and a large sheet of paper. Sometimes we also use a tape recorder to record the story.

Children generally need some modelling by the counsellor before they fully understand the process of story making. We usually begin by saying to the child, 'Today we are going to be telling stories to each other', and 'I will begin, and sometimes I might stop, and when I stop, I would like you to fill in the gaps.' This allows the counsellor to choose a theme and to encourage the child to explore pertinent issues for themselves.

The counsellor can then continue by saying, 'The story will have a beginning, a middle, and an end', and 'I will begin. Once upon a time there was a prince and this prince liked ...'

The counsellor can then stop in mid-sentence and invite the child to say what it was that the prince liked. The child might respond by saying 'to ride his horse in the country'. The counsellor could then continue 'As he rode around the countryside, he realized that ...'

Once again the counsellor can stop in mid-sentence so that the child fills in the next part of the story. The storytelling can continue in this way until there is an outcome or an end.

When the story is complete (it has usually been taped) we like to play it back and to ask the child to identify with any character in the story by asking, 'Who would you like to be the most in this story?'

The child can be further encouraged to explore their own behaviour if we ask, 'If you were a prince, would you have done the same as him or something different?' and 'What would you have done?'

Finally, the counsellor can then thank the child for the story they have told.

An alternative is to encourage a child to tell stories about a picture they see. The counsellor might present the child with a picture from a magazine, or a photograph, and ask the child to tell a story about the people, animals or objects in it. It is useful, once again, to remind the child that stories have a beginning, a middle and an end. However, these stories can be short and brief.

For children who find it difficult to make up stories, it is better to use story books, fairytales or fables initially. This can help to familiarize the child with the way in which stories develop and can help them to recognize the way in which stories can relate to their own personal experiences.

The classic fairytales and fables such as *Little Red Riding Hood*, *The Three Little Pigs* and *Hansel and Gretel,* although very dated, can sometimes be useful. Caution is needed though in using such stories as they may be troubling for some children. However, when they are deemed suitable they encourage the child to work projectively in the first instance and then to talk directly about themselves, their family and significant others.

The tale of *Little Red Riding Hood* can be very useful when used with some children because it raises issues of disempowerment, fleeing, helplessness and rescue. We might read the story to the child and then invite them to identify with one of the characters. After this, we might invite the child to think of alternative solutions to different situations in the story. For example, after reading *Little Red Riding Hood*, if the child identified with Grandma we might ask, 'How could Grandma have been more powerful so she could have outwitted the wolf and not have been pushed into the cupboard?'

We might then encourage the child to think of several different alternatives by asking, 'What else could Grandma have done when the wolf tried to push her into the cupboard?' and 'If you had been Grandma, what would you have done?' We might then be able to affirm the child's bravery, courage and resourcefulness.

Story books written around topics such as domestic violence or sexual abuse can be used to help a child to understand that other children have similar experiences. This enables a child to feel the same as some other children and to feel less of a victim. Such stories allow the child to identify with, or to reject, similarities between themselves and characters in the story. They may also invite the child to disclose more information about their own experiences.

We often use books as a way of educating children with regard to important beliefs and behaviours. Books can be used to address a wide range of issues such as protective behaviours, stranger danger, secrets and inappropriate touching. They can be used by the counsellor to help the child to explore choices and options about future behaviour. For example, a book might encourage a child to say 'No' to a stranger. The counsellor can then check out whether the child believes that they have the ability to say 'No', and can help the child to practise saying 'No' in a loud voice. The child and the counsellor can then engage in role plays that teach appropriate behaviours.

When using books for educational purposes, we like to give the child a copy of the book to take home and to share with family members or care-givers.

Suitability of books and stories

Books and stories can be used with children of pre-school age through to late adolescence. They are particularly suitable for young children, who are used to listening to stories and find them comforting.

Books and stories are most suitable for use in individual counselling or in parent–child counselling. They enable children to be expansive in their thinking. However, work can be focused by the selection of specific topics or subject matter.

Helping children to make up their own stories is very useful when working with children who are naturally creative and have good language skills. This approach will not appeal to children who are less gifted.

CASE STUDY

Macy and his colleagues (2003) made use of storytelling as part of a program to support children who had experienced a natural disaster (two severe earthquakes). They found that following the program, children reported lower levels of anxiety and depression and increased self-esteem and ability to manage their feelings (for more information about the evidence-base for play therapy techniques see Chapter 20). Imagine you have received a referral for nine-year-old Brent whose North Queensland town was hit by a cyclone. Brent and his family weren't physically injured during the cyclone; however, their home was destroyed and is currently being rebuilt. How might you make use of storytelling to support Brent in processing his experience? At what stage during the SPICC process would you considering introducing books or stories?

KEY POINTS

- Children will often identify with a character, theme, or event in a story and by doing so they are almost certain to reflect on their own life situation.
- When a child creates a story, the ideas from the story are likely to come from the child's own life experiences, enabling the counsellor to draw parallels and help the child to address their own issues.
- Educational books can be used to deal with specific problems such as self-esteem, sexual abuse, protective behaviours, domestic violence and social development.

28

Puppets and Soft Toys

When working with young children, puppets and soft toys can be useful at any phase within the SPICC process (see Figure 8.1, p. 72). The way we use puppets and soft toys is to invite the child to create and direct a drama in which the puppets and soft toys are the characters. In the drama, the child projects their own ideas onto the puppets and soft toys, gives them their personalities, chooses their behaviours and puts words into their mouths.

Children enjoy using puppets and soft toys because they are easy to manipulate. They require very little preparation and are familiar toys for most children.

It is important for a new counsellor to understand the difference between the drama created when using puppets and soft toys and the drama involved in imaginative pretend play. In imaginative pretend play (see Chapter 29), the child role-plays, identifies with, and effectively becomes a character, or some characters, in the drama. By contrast, when using puppets and soft toys, the child uses stories and other dramatic events and projects ideas from these onto the puppets and soft toys. The child sees them as separate from, and external to themselves, and can, without restraint, attribute to the puppets and soft toys, beliefs, behaviours and personalities which they believe are quite different from their own.

There are also differences between the use of puppets and soft toys and the use of stories. Stories give the child an opportunity to express fantasies and to explore conflict situations. They also enable the child to deal with important issues and feelings even when it is too difficult for the child to talk about these directly. Puppets and soft toys are similarly useful and also add an extra dimension to storytelling. Through puppets and soft toys, the child becomes directly involved in creating and speaking the dialogue of the story and in manipulating the puppets and soft toys to act out the story. By doing this the child becomes involved in and personally connected with the story. This enables them to more easily make the link between their own emotional feelings and those of characters in the story.

The dramatic sequences created when using puppets and soft toys provide children with a way of dealing indirectly with issues which might be difficult for them to own as personally theirs. The indirect approach of puppetry protects the child's inner pain from direct exposure; instead it is disguised as belonging to the puppets or soft toys. At the same time, the child can gain confidence in talking about relevant issues and has the opportunity to develop the courage to directly own and confront those issues when ready to do so.

The drama allows the child to project their beliefs, behaviours and personality characteristics, and those of significant others, onto the puppets and soft toys. For example, as
the child creates the dialogue of the drama, they can replicate the personality and behaviours of a hated person or of a loving friend from whom they may have been separated.
Consequently, puppets and soft toys provide a safe outlet for the expression of fantasies
with regard to the interactions of others and the child's own interactions with them.

During the drama the counsellor can intervene to help the child to express, understand and work through their issues, thus bringing about change.

Some individual puppets and soft toys have inherent symbolic attributes. For
example, wolves can be dangerous, monkeys can be entertaining and mischievous,
and policemen may be helpful or authoritarian. Teddy bears are soft, cuddly and
nurturing, or may need to be nurtured.

Goals when using puppets and soft toys

Puppets and soft toys can be used to achieve the following goals:

- To gain mastery over issues and events.
- To be powerful through physical expression.
- To develop problem-solving and decision-making skills.
- To develop social skills.
- To improve communication skills.
- To develop insight.

To gain mastery over issues and events

When using puppets and soft toys, the child has an opportunity to re-enact unpleasant
experiences. Through doing this the child can gain mastery over the experience. For
example, in the actual life experience the child may have been passive and disempowered. In the re-enactment, the puppet or soft toy onto which the child projects their
experience may behave in a more powerful and active way. The drama can be repeated
several times, with the puppet becoming progressively more successful in dealing with
the situation, until the child becomes satisfied.

By using puppets and soft toys in combination with familiar fables, fairytales and
stories, the child can restructure past events so that victims are empowered, consequences are just and opportunities are given for issues and feelings to be expressed.
This process is useful to the child psychologically: it moves them from a psychological space where they feel helpless and powerless into a new space where they
have a sense of their own inner power and a sense of an improved ability to control
their own actions and responses. Thus the child moves from being disempowered
towards empowerment.

To be powerful through physical expression

An ideal way for the child to express feelings of power and strength is through the use
of selected characters or puppets. Similarly, emotions which may be unacceptable can

be expressed and exaggerated without fear of reprimand. Clearly, these processes are useful for children who have become submissive as a consequence of past experiences or who have low ego-strength.

To develop problem-solving and decision-making skills

Often, children find it difficult to explore a range of solutions to their problems because they are inhibited by their expectations of the likely demands and restraints, which they think will be imposed on them by others. However, by creating a drama with the puppets or soft toys they can safely explore a range of alternative solutions. The counsellor can then relate these to the child's own life situation.

To develop social skills

To help the child to develop social skills, the counsellor becomes involved in the child's puppet play. The counsellor then creates situations which require the child to respond by using their own puppets or soft toys. These responses can then be received negatively or positively by the counsellor's puppet. In this way the child can indirectly explore the appropriateness or inappropriateness of their own social behaviour.

To improve communication skills

Using puppets and soft toys in a drama demands both verbal and non-verbal activity by the child. Consequently, communication about imagined or real events or issues is encouraged. This enables the child to develop insight into the effect of various communication styles and thus to develop improved communication skills. Also the child can identify with the characteristics and behaviours of the puppets and soft toys. By doing this they have a way of indirectly experimenting with alternative relationships and can, if they wish, explore issues such as separation and closeness and communicate these needs openly.

To develop insight

When a child creates the dialogue between puppets, they have to consider the various and sometimes conflicting points of view of the individual puppets in their drama. Consequently, the child will develop insight, which will hopefully enable them to recognize and understand other people's points of view in their own life situation. This might be useful in helping them to develop a more meaningful understanding of past events in their life.

Materials needed when using puppets and soft toys

We like to use both puppets and soft toys. Our puppets are glove puppets; the type where a child puts their hand into the puppet and uses their fingers and thumb to move the mouth and ears and to change the facial expression.

Unlike with puppets, we can't change the facial expressions of soft toys. However, they do have the advantage that it is easy to use several of them at the same time.

It's useful to have a variety of puppets and soft toys so that different types of characters and personalities can be represented. We suggest that a suitable range includes the following:

- family figures suitable for representing a mother, father, grandmother, sibling, baby, uncles, and so on;
- fantasy figures, including a devil, a ghost, witches, fairies and a magician;
- wild animals, farm animals and domestic animals; for example, wolves, sharks, bears, elephants, horses and rabbits; and
- some soft toys which have a degree of disguise. These might include a masked person, a clown and a faceless person.

How to use puppets and soft toys

Because we use puppets and soft toys similarly, we will only refer to puppets in the following discussion, although this discussion applies equally to soft toys. There are four ways of using puppets:

1 Allowing the child to use the puppets spontaneously.
2 Inviting the child to create and direct a puppet show.
3 Combining the use of puppets with well-known fairy stories or fables.
4 Using puppets in dialogue with the counsellor.

Allowing the child to use the puppets spontaneously

We usually begin by letting the child know that we are going to play with the puppets. We invite the child to select whatever puppets appeal to them. This can give valuable information. For example, children tend to pick up most of the puppets and then to discard them after checking out their shape, size and other features. When the child has selected some puppets, they will usually spontaneously start up a dialogue between some of them. If they don't, we model this by selecting a puppet and talking through the puppet to the child. For example, when counselling a child called Samantha, we might select the puppet bear, speak as though the bear were talking and say, 'Hello, Samantha. Have you come to play with me today?' We can then invite the child to begin their puppet show by introducing the characters. We might ask, 'Why don't you show me all of the characters in your play and introduce them to me one by one?'

As the child introduces the characters, the counsellor can engage in conversation as each character is presented. For example, the counsellor might say, 'Hello Teddy, I'm looking forward to this show. Are you?' or 'Hello Teddy, nice to meet you. I like your big red bow tie.' This participation by the counsellor helps the child to feel more comfortable about the activity, sets the scene and allows the child to project themselves onto the characters.

Some children find it easy to make up a story and to act it out. Others find it more difficult. With these children we usually suggest themes for them to use, which are likely to address issues or events relevant for the child. For example, we might suggest themes concerned with being moved from the family home into care, or regarding access visits with an absent parent, or themes which reflect helplessness, fear or abandonment.

With some children we use a more formalized puppet show approach as discussed in the following paragraphs.

Inviting the child to create and direct a puppet show

We start to create a puppet drama by saying to the child, 'Together, we are going to make up a play using these puppets and soft toys. You can choose the characters in the play. One of the characters is very lonely, frightened and uncertain about what is going to happen to him. Another character is strong and powerful and the boss. There are three other characters in this play. Would you like to choose the characters now?'

After the child has introduced the characters (as discussed previously), the counsellor can then help the child devise a theme and to start the puppet show. The content of the story that emerges will give clues about the child's preoccupations and their ways of dealing with these.

We usually invite the child to act out their puppet 'show', or puppet 'play', on a table with the child sitting on the floor behind the table, which serves as a miniature stage. Some children like to use props in their drama such as sticks, balls, pillows and blankets. However, too many props can lead the child into dramatic imaginative pretend play (see Chapter 29) instead of helping the child to focus on projecting ideas onto the puppets or soft toys.

Generally, we sit opposite the table like an audience watching the child's dramatic play. Naturally, we intervene to ask questions, make comments and to assist with the creation of the drama, when appropriate.

At different times during the drama, the counsellor might intervene and talk directly to one of the characters in an attempt to discover more about that character's behaviour within the play. For example, the counsellor might ask the bear, 'What does it feel like to be left outside the house while the others are having a party?'

Children will inevitably project different aspects of themselves onto the various characters. For example, a child may project the mischievous part of himself onto the monkey who causes trouble between others, and at the same time project his wish to magically change the situation onto the wizard. During the process the counsellor might encourage the characters to persevere with particular behaviours so that the child becomes aware of the way in which other characters respond. For example, the counsellor might say, 'Wizard, do that again because I think it might work this time.' This gives the child an opportunity to evaluate the consequences of particular behaviours and to make decisions with regard to suitable responses for other characters in the play.

An alternative to the above idea is for the counsellor to suggest a change in the behaviour of one of the characters. For example, the counsellor might say to the wizard, 'Wizard, I don't think that what you are doing is working. I wonder what else you could do?'

Some children resent intrusions from the counsellor and with these children the counsellor may need to watch a puppet show without interrupting. However, following completion of the show, the counsellor might discuss with the child various parts of the drama, or aspects of the drama. A discussion such as this could be started by the counsellor asking questions such as, 'Who, of all the people or things in the story, would you most like to be?' or 'Who in the story would you not want to be?' It would not be helpful to ask a child 'Who are you in this story?' Such a question could be confusing because clearly a child will project parts of themselves on to all of the characters. Sometimes, asking a child what happens to the characters in the story after the play has finished can be useful in helping a child to look at outcomes.

Combining the use of puppets with well-known fairy stories or fables

With some children, when using puppets, we make use of well-known fairy stories or fables to directly address specific issues. When doing this, the child is invited to use the puppets to act the story out. We then help the child to restructure the story so that more satisfactory outcomes are achieved. For example, a victim may become empowered, or alternative solutions to a problem situation may be discovered. A counsellor might get a child to act out the story of *Little Red Riding Hood* using puppets or soft toys. After the drama has finished, the counsellor might ask, 'What else could Grandma have done when the wolf decided he was going to eat her?' The child might suggest that Grandma could have run out of the house to seek help. The counsellor can then encourage the child to act the drama out once again using this alternative idea.

Using puppets in dialogue with the counsellor

Sometimes, by using a technique of dialogue between a puppet and the counsellor, a child may be enabled to discover solutions to their own problems.

Soft toys and puppets can also be used in direct one-to-one interaction with a child. We sometimes use a particular teddy bear, which we describe as being wise, experienced, knowledgeable and magical. This soft toy can be helpful to a child who is having difficulty discussing certain issues. For example, a child may be frightened about going to school for fear of being bullied, but not feel comfortable enough to talk about this. We can suggest to the child that Teddy is often pretty good at knowing what children are thinking. We might say, 'Teddy sometimes knows what children are thinking. If he sits on your lap, he might be able to tell me about the things that are troubling you.'

We can then ask the child to hold the bear on their lap and direct the following comments to it: 'Teddy, Jenny is having some problems. I wonder if you know what they are?' The child is then invited to respond on behalf of the bear: 'Jenny, can you tell me what Teddy is saying?'

Some children may not feel comfortable doing this. In this case, the counsellor can hold the bear so that its mouth is close to their own ear and pretend to be listening to the bear. The counsellor can then repeat what the bear is supposed to have said and might say, 'Teddy says that he thinks that your problem might be about going to school. I wonder if he's right or if he's wrong?'

The child can then be encouraged to engage in ongoing dialogue between the counsellor, the bear and themselves. The child can be asked to listen to the bear and to repeat what he 'tells' them. Thus they become the voice of the bear and are enabled to say what they would like through the bear.

Suitability of puppets and soft toys

Puppets and soft toys are useful when working with pre-school and primary school children. Interestingly, some early adolescents find them appealing; however, they are generally more suitable for the younger age group.

Puppets and soft toys are ideal to use in individual counselling sessions, but can also be used in groups where each child selects and characterizes a particular puppet or soft toy.

Using puppets and soft toys allows the child to explore and expand their thinking and encourages them to be interactive and sometimes adventurous. Puppets and soft toys can also be used to convey moral messages and to educate: for example, concepts of protective behaviours can be explored.

CASE STUDY

Puppets (Zahr, 1998) and soft toys, particularly teddy bears (Hatava et al., 2000), have been used extensively when counselling children in preparation for hospital. The use of puppets and soft toys has been found to decrease anxiety, physiological responses (heart rate and blood pressure), and behavioural responses during the child's hospital stay. For more information about the use of media and activities in preparing children for hospital please refer to Chapter 20. You have received a new referral for five-year-old Mary. Her parents shared that they are concerned about Mary who has been very anxious after finding out that she needs to go to hospital for an operation. It is her first hospital visit. How might you use puppets and/or soft toys to support Mary in preparing for her hospital visit? What other media or activities might you consider?

KEY POINTS

- Puppets and soft toys are used to allow the child to create a drama which provides the child with an indirect way of dealing with issues which might be difficult for them to own as personally theirs.
- In the drama the child can project beliefs, behaviours, and personality characteristics of significant others in their lives onto the puppets and soft toys.
- Change can be initiated if the counsellor intervenes in the drama to help the child to express, understand and work through their issues.
- Puppets and soft toys provide a safe outlet for the expression of fantasies with regard to interactions with others.

29

Imaginative Pretend Play

Imaginative pretend play is the naturally occurring play of young children. It can be used in any of the phases of the SPICC model (see Figure 8.1, p. 72), when appropriate, in order to achieve the goals required by a particular phase.

Young children enjoy pretending to be someone else, such as a doctor examining a patient or a mother feeding her children. In their play, they dress up and make use of props, for example empty food packets when they are pretending to be shopping. Thus, they combine the use of objects, actions, words and interactions with imagined people to produce a drama.

Although very young children between the ages of two and three can mimic the roles of familiar adults in their lives, they need to use real objects, or toy replicas of them, in their representational play.

Older children from the age of four and upwards rely less on real objects in their imaginative pretend play. In this age range, they are generally able to use unrelated objects to symbolize, or take the place of, objects which are involved in their play. For example, a wooden block might be used as a telephone. These older children are also capable of substituting actions for objects in their imaginative pretend play. For example, a child may raise a clenched fist to their mouth as a substitute for a cup when pretending to drink. Because older children are able to engage in abstract thinking, they can easily play the roles of fantasy characters like superheroes, monsters and fairies.

In imaginative pretend play the whole child becomes totally involved in acting out a character within an imagined situation. The child becomes an actor in the fullest sense.

Imaginative pretend play sometimes, but not always, includes the use of social skills. When social skills are involved, we refer to the play as socio-dramatic play. The use of social skills occurs when using imaginative pretend play in the form of verbal and non-verbal interaction between the counsellor and the child while the child is role-playing.

Imaginative pretend play involves the child's use of objects and replica objects. Some children can't use objects in this way and are unable to engage in imaginative pretend play. Such children fondle, stack, pound or manipulate objects in much the same way as a baby would. This immature play might be due to any of the following:

- The child may have language difficulties or cognitive delays.
- The child may have been deprived of a stimulating play environment and consequently lacks the experience needed to engage in imaginative pretend play.

- The child may be inhibited as a result of previous emotional traumas, abuse or neglect.
- The child may be shy or cautious about taking risks in play.

Because children between the ages of three and five normally engage in imaginative pretend play as a natural part of their development, the absence of such play is significant. A child with little ability to engage in imaginative pretend play may have limited personal resources for working through emotional issues.

By using imaginative pretend play, a child can act out significant observations with regard to their life and the people in their life and they can achieve a number of useful goals.

Goals of imaginative pretend play

Imaginative pretend play can be used for the following purposes:

1 To enable a child to externalize and articulate ideas, wishes, fears and fantasies, both verbally and non-verbally.
2 To enable a child to express underlying thoughts or thought processes.
3 To achieve cathartic relief from emotional pain.
4 To enable a child to experience being powerful through the physical expression of emotion.
5 To allow a child to gain mastery over past issues and events.
6 To provide an opportunity for a child to develop insight into current and past events.
7 To help a child to take risks in developing new behaviours.
8 To help a child to practise new behaviours and to prepare for particular life situations.
9 To give a child the opportunity to build self-concept and self-esteem.
10 To help a child to improve communication skills.

Materials and equipment needed for imaginative pretend play

The materials used in imaginative pretend play can evoke strong responses in children. They often stimulate fantasies and sometimes trigger specific issues. For example, a magic wand may have strong appeal to a child who would like to have more control over their environment and relationships.

It is important to have a wide variety of props so that we can prompt children to enter into specific imaginative pretend play scenarios which are individually relevant and which might achieve the goals listed above. Some props are directly representational and realistic so that younger children can use them easily; others can be less representational, for use by the older age group.

We have in our play room the following equipment and materials to encourage imaginative pretend play (some of these are also listed in Chapter 19):

Furniture and associated items

Toy stove

Toy kitchen cupboard

Toy washbasin

Child's table and chairs

Doll's bed

Doll's pram

Baby doll's bath (the above items are large enough for a small child to use when engaged in family role plays)

Plastic crockery, cutlery, pots and pans

Play-Doh (useful for making pretend food)

Dolls, soft toys and associated items

Rag dolls to represent adults and children of both genders

Baby doll

A variety of soft toys including a teddy bear and a monkey

Dolls' clothes

Feeding bottle

Dolls' nappies

Pillow and sheets for pram

Dress-up materials

Dress-up clothes

Hats

Ties

Belts

Adult shoes

Sunglasses

Wigs

Make-up (non-allergenic and which can be washed off easily)

Jewellery

Swords

Badges

Assorted masks

Doctor's or nurse's set

Old camera

Crowns

Magic wands

Old watches

Handbags

Wallets

Purses

Shopping baskets

Lengths of coloured material

Blanket

Sheets (to make a Wendy house)

Telescope

Hand mirrors

Wall mirror

Hairbrush and comb

Toothbrush

Toy telephone

Toy vehicles

Empty food packets

Play money

Cardboard boxes

Wooden blocks

How to use imaginative pretend play

Imaginative pretend play is play which starts to occur at the point along the child's developmental continuum where the child is ready to move from playing directly with objects to using objects in symbolic representation. From that point onwards the child can engage in make-believe. Whenever a child uses imaginative pretend play to experience a make-believe world, they can experiment by using an unlimited variety of roles and behaviours. Additionally, they can transform their original perceptions about life issues and situations into new and different perceptions.

It is the counsellor's responsibility to provide an environment in which the child can create and enter an imaginary world, and then use the experience therapeutically. In providing the necessary environment it is important for the counsellor to do the following:

1   Provide a physical place, including materials and equipment, to help the child to enter a make-believe world.
2   Use the relationship between the child and the counsellor to help the child to participate in, and benefit from, imaginative pretend play.

With regard to item 1, we have already discussed the requirements for a play therapy room (see Chapter 19), and have listed equipment and materials required for imaginative pretend play earlier in this section.

With regard to item 2, it is important to recognize that the counsellor has a choice of roles and that appropriate choice will significantly influence the therapeutic effectiveness of the play. Additionally, most young children don't need an adult to be present as a play partner. However, they do need someone to provide time, space, props and sometimes themes and experiences. They benefit from someone to act as a facilitator to help them to start playing, sustain their play, modify and extend it. Children who have limited play skills may need not only a resource person and facilitator, but also an adult who will join in their play to help them to improve their play skills.

So when working with most children, a counsellor generally adopts the role of facilitator. For the child with limited play skills there are three alternative roles which the counsellor can assume. These roles involve parallel play, co-playing and play tutoring.

Parallel play

When parallel playing, the counsellor sits next to the child and copies the child's play. For example, if the child is sitting near the doll's house and rearranging furniture, the counsellor will sit beside the child and also rearrange furniture. The counsellor may then make comments about what they are doing. For example, they might say, 'I am going to put this chair against this wall so that the mother and father can watch television more easily.'

By making this statement, the counsellor does not intrude on the child's play by commenting on that, but does provide a model of imaginative pretend play which includes verbal communication about what is happening. Because the counsellor has initially copied the child's play, the child is likely to see their own play as important and valued. Thus, parallel play gives the counsellor the opportunity to model new ways of using available materials and can encourage the child to play longer.

Co-playing

In co-playing, the counsellor joins in with the child's play and can influence the child's play by responding to the child's actions and comments and asking the child for instructions. For example, if a child is already engaged in play as a mother looking after and feeding a young baby (doll), the counsellor might ask, 'What should I do now? Dolly hasn't eaten her cereal and I'm her big sister.' This gives the child an opportunity to join with the counsellor in the imaginative pretend play. However, the child might reject the counsellor's involvement by saying something like, 'She doesn't have a big sister.' Alternatively, the child might respond by attempting to feed the doll with the pretend cereal or by instructing the counsellor (big sister) to feed the doll.

The aim of co-playing is to influence the play and to enrich it by adding new elements. In the example given, the new element introduced was the non-compliance of the baby doll.

Play tutoring

Play tutoring, although similar to co-playing, does differ. In play tutoring, the counsellor can begin the play theme rather than join in on a theme which the child has already started. Secondly, the counsellor assumes more control and direction over the play. In play tutoring, the counsellor uses questions, statements and reflection of content to help the child in their play. For example, the counsellor might ask, 'Are you the doctor, or the Mum?' and 'Are you in the house or in your car?'

The counsellor might also make statements such as, 'Here's a car, you can use this to go to the shops [as they offer the child a toy car].'

Alternatively, the counsellor can reflect content and might say, 'You've put out five plates. I think there must be five people in this family.'

Such statements, questions and reflection of content help the child to use more imaginative pretend play skills by drawing the child's attention to new uses of materials. The counsellor can also model new role-playing behaviours by becoming an active participant and taking on a role themselves. For example, if the child were to assume the role of a doctor treating a sick child, the counsellor could assume the role of the mother of the child. Such role-playing and modelling can help the child to gain new play skills.

Although play tutoring can be helpful, it can also be intrusive. It is desirable for counsellors to limit the amount of play tutoring and to move back into the role of an observer as soon as the child's play is developing and being maintained.

In summary, it is important for a counsellor to be able to act as a facilitator and to use co-playing, parallel play and play tutoring at appropriate times when working with children who are involved in imaginative pretend play.

Starting the imaginative pretend play session

Before starting the session, we make sure that the play therapy room is set up with the equipment and materials which will be needed to stimulate imaginative pretend play. Sometimes, we select particular props and equipment because we wish to explore specific themes in a certain way. However, generally we provide the full range of equipment and materials so that the child can freely choose what they want to use. When the child enters the room, we usually begin by saying something like 'Today, we are going to spend some time playing with the things in this room.'

Because the equipment and props are appealing to most children, the child will generally begin to explore what is available. The child will usually select some of the props, and begin to dress up and to imitate particular characters. Younger children usually move straight to the 'home' corner where we have the kitchen furniture (see Figure 19.1, p. 164), and begin to play roles that are familiar to them. For example, they may pretend to cook a meal as a mother or start to look after a baby doll. When the child begins to engage in this kind of play, the counsellor can engage in play with the child, if appropriate, or simply observe the child, the themes and the sequences of the play. The counsellor can then choose opportunities as the play progresses to make statements, ask questions and provide feedback about what the child is doing.

Having started the session, the counsellor can take opportunities, as they arise, to help the child to achieve specific goals.

How to use imaginative pretend play to achieve specific goals

We will now discuss ways to use imaginative pretend play to achieve each of the ten goals which we listed previously.

How to use imaginative pretend play to enable a child to externalize and articulate ideas, wishes, fears and fantasies, both verbally and non-verbally

This goal will occur naturally as a consequence of imaginative pretend play. Such play allows the child to re-create their world in a symbolic and dramatic way. This is done spontaneously as the child creates a script and directs the 'players', both animate and inanimate. These players include themselves, the dolls and soft toys, and perhaps even the counsellor. In the drama some children will spontaneously express their wishes, fantasies and fears, and the counsellor can retain the role of observer. However, for other children the counsellor can enrich the fantasies, wishes and ideas of the child through co-play. The counsellor might do this by exaggerating the role assigned to them, or by behaving in a paradoxical way and thus encouraging the child to become more forceful in expressing the ideas, fears, wishes or fantasies being acted out. However, it is important for the counsellor to stay strictly with the role assigned to them by the child, otherwise they will intrude on and inhibit the child's personal expression.

How to use imaginative pretend play to enable a child to express underlying thoughts or thought processes

To do this, it is important for the counsellor to spend time observing the child's play without interference. The child is then allowed, through free association, to use the imaginative pretend play time to explore unconscious wishes or desires. During this process, it is useful for the counsellor to reflect thoughts, feelings and content back to the child. For example, the counsellor might say, 'When Dolly is naughty she gets locked in her room. I wonder what it would be like for her to be locked in her room?' This enables the child to explore their own issues related to being trapped.

How to use imaginative pretend play to achieve cathartic relief from emotional pain

Imaginative pretend play is a way of giving a child an opportunity to act out feelings and problems, and thus to achieve emotional release or catharsis. When this happens, the imaginative pretend play is in itself the therapeutic intervention because the process of play is healing in itself. When seeking to achieve this goal, the therapist is totally non-directive and provides a safe environment and an empathic relationship with the child.

How to use imaginative pretend play to enable a child to experience being powerful through the physical expression of emotion

By using play tutoring, the counsellor can model powerful fantasy roles for the child. The child can then be encouraged to act out powerful roles not previously experienced as applicable to themselves, and can experiment with these roles with the aid of suitable props. The roles of rescuer, adventurer, nurturer or healer can be modelled by the counsellor and can then be encouraged in the child. Once a child has assumed a powerful role, the counsellor can move back into a position of co-playing to support that role.

How to use imaginative pretend play to allow a child to gain mastery over past issues and events

The counsellor can invite the child to use imaginative pretend play to re-create an unpleasant or painful experience where the child felt helpless and disempowered. As this is acted out in the form of a mini-drama, the child can be encouraged to be more actively involved in events that may previously have been experienced passively. This can be achieved by inviting the child to repeat the mini-drama several times. With each repetition, the child is encouraged to experiment with new behaviours which are more powerful and involve taking more control. Thus, the child moves from a victim position and gains a sense of mastery over events that had been threatening. The counsellor can help by highlighting the process that the child uses. For example, the counsellor might say, 'You didn't just tell that burglar to go away, you pushed him out of the door as well. I think you must be feeling very brave.' This helps the child to understand that they are becoming more in control of the situation.

How to use imaginative pretend play to provide an opportunity for a child to develop insight into current and past events

Imaginative pretend play gives an opportunity for the child to learn about themselves, develop insight into current and past events, and provides them with an opportunity to change in a safe environment without judgement or pressure.

To help to achieve this goal, the counsellor can invite the child to create a drama which includes events similar to those experienced by the child. During the drama, the counsellor can invite the child to successively change roles so that they are first one character, then another, and then the first character again. By repeating this process a number of times, the child becomes involved in playing the parts of two different characters, and a dialogue, of the child's making, emerges between these two characters. Consequently, the child experiences what it is like to be both characters and will gain insight into the behaviours, beliefs and perceptions of others, and into current and past events.

How to use imaginative pretend play to help a child to take risks in developing new behaviours

In imaginative pretend play the child can experiment with new behaviours, which they might initially believe are too risky to use in real life. During imaginative pretend play, they can try out new behaviours which would otherwise never be tried, in order to check out their likely consequences. The counsellor can help the child to take risks by reminding them that what is happening in the imaginative pretend play is make-believe and will not have real consequences. The counsellor might say, 'Let's pretend that you are magic and you can change things whenever they go wrong.'

With this assurance of an 'escape' the child is encouraged to enter into simulated risk-taking scenarios with safety.

How to use imaginative pretend play to help a child to practise new behaviours and to prepare for particular life situations

Consider a child who needs to be more assertive. In imaginative pretend play, the child could be invited to assume the role of a figure of authority such as a teacher. The counsellor can then co-play by pretending to be a child subjected to the behaviours of the authority figure (the teacher). In order to help strengthen the child's authoritarian role, the counsellor might become provocative by pretending to be non-compliant. For example, if the 'teacher' asks them to go to the 'time-out room', the counsellor might say, 'I don't really feel like doing that. I'm just going to sit here in my seat.'

This provocative response challenges the child's role. Whether the child becomes more authoritative or not can then be discussed. The counsellor might say, 'I noticed that you didn't make me go to the time-out room. I wonder how you could have persuaded me to do what you wanted?'

How to use imaginative pretend play to give a child the opportunity to build self-concept and self-esteem

Experimenting with various roles can help the child to discover dormant and undiscovered parts of their self. The counsellor can encourage the child to expand on qualities which are emerging by co-playing with the child in roles which will support the emergence of behaviours such as leadership, friendship, helpfulness, problem solving, cooperation and collaboration. The counsellor might assume the role of helpless victim, chaotic friend or forgetful adult to highlight the contrast in the behaviour of the child and of the co-playing counsellor. The counsellor can then affirm the qualities the child is exhibiting. For example, if the child had been helpful in the role play, then the counsellor could say, 'You are really good at being helpful. I wouldn't have been able to do that if I hadn't had your help.' This affirms the child's ability to be helpful.

How to use imaginative pretend play to help a child to improve communication skills

Dramatic scenarios in imaginative pretend play depend on both verbal and non-verbal communication. Thus, through the dialogue of play, a child can experience success or lack of success in verbal and non-verbal communication.

Unfortunately, some children do not make a verbal commentary on their non-verbal activity during role play and do not spontaneously engage in dialogue. To encourage the child to do this, the counsellor might reflect back to the child what the child is doing and invite them to share their thoughts with the counsellor. For instance, the counsellor might say, 'I notice that you are putting Dolly back to bed. What would you like to say to Dolly while you are putting her to bed?' This encourages the child to communicate rather than just to engage in non-verbal behaviour.

Suitability of imaginative pretend play

Imaginative pretend play is the play of children between the ages of two-and-a-half to five years. It is a time developmentally when skills are rehearsed in preparation for later life. When children reach school age, pretending becomes more covert and, rather than act things out, older children engage in fantasizing. Children from the age of six to twelve turn towards reality and their play becomes more realistic because they realize that overt pretend play is not socially acceptable. The use of imaginative pretend play is therefore more appropriate for younger children.

Imaginative pretend play can be open-ended and expansive, allowing the child to explore options and possibilities without boundaries and to express feelings, issues and concerns with safety. It encourages the child to be interactive and adventurous. However, it does allow them to stay within boundaries if they wish by using simple repetitive themes.

CASE STUDY

Non-directive play therapy, which includes imaginative pretend play, has been found to support children who are homeless develop a sense of emotional security and decrease feelings of depression and anxiety (Baggerly, 2004; Baggerly and Jenkins, 2009). For more information on the evidence-base of using media and activities to support children's emotional expression and management skills please refer to Chapter 20. How might you use imaginative pretend play to support three-year-old Molly who has been referred by her parents due to concerns about her emotional outbursts? What other information might be helpful for you to know when working with Molly?

KEY POINTS

- Young children from the age of about two-and-a-half to five years naturally engage in and enjoy imaginative pretend play.
- Generally, children aged two to three years need to use real objects or toy replicas of them in their representational play, whereas older children are able to use unrelated objects to symbolize the article they are pretending to use.
- A range of toy furniture and household equipment, dolls, soft toys and dress-up materials are required for imaginative pretend play.
- During parallel play the counsellor copies the child's play and may comment on what they are doing.
- When play tutoring the counsellor initiates the play theme and assumes more control and direction over the play.
- Imaginative pretend play can be used with young children in achieving a number of goals which are useful in various phases of the SPICC model.

30

Games

Games are particularly useful in the later stages of the SPICC process (see Figure 8.1, p. 72), that is during Phases 3, 4 and 5, where the child is looking at their view of self and making decisions about their choices and behaviours.

Games, some formal and others informal, are played by young children across all cultures. They are enjoyable and also help children to develop physically, cognitively, emotionally and socially. Games require specific skills and these vary in complexity. Some games, such as Snap and Memory, have rules which are simple and easy to understand and remember. These games are suitable for young children between the ages of four and seven. Many games require a more complicated set of rules and are therefore more suitable for older children between the ages of seven and eleven.

From a counselling perspective, games can be a useful way of engaging children who are shy or, for other reasons, reluctant to enter the counselling relationship.

Playing a game with a child can create a relationship that may be a precursor to meaningful counselling. Games can also be used as the central focus of a counselling intervention to achieve goals such as those listed later in this chapter. These goals generally relate to the later stages in the Spiral of Therapeutic Change (see Figure 7.1, p. 59) and are particularly relevant to the stage where the child rehearses and experiments with new behaviours.

Games contrast directly with free play. In free play there are no rules, whereas a child's behaviour is restricted by the rules of a game. From these rules a child learns what the goals of the game are, learns how to play the game, and learns what limits and consequences there are in the game.

The use of games can be a good way to challenge and develop a child's ego-strengths. In games a child has to face issues such as losing, cheating, taking turns, missing turns, sticking to rules, failure, fairness, unfairness and being left out. Additionally, the use of games allows the child to experience, experiment with and practise responses to tasks involving communication, social interaction and the solving of problems.

While some games challenge the child's own abilities, most involve the interaction of two or more players and a comparison between their performances. In many games, the behaviours of participants are interdependent, with the outcome depending on each player's behaviour. Consequently, these games involve a high level of social activity.

Developmentally, it is normal for children between the ages of seven and eleven to assess their own levels of competence by comparing their performance with that of others. The element of competition in games therefore provides a useful opportunity for a child to make an assessment of their abilities. In doing this they will become aware that they are good at some things and not so good at others. However, it is important to recognize that children with low ego-strength may feel threatened by the use of games if the competitive element is over-emphasized. Therefore, high levels of friendliness, cooperation and collaboration are desirable when using games in counselling. The emphasis is on the personal skills required within the game-playing exercise rather than on winning or losing.

The personal skills a child draws on when playing a game include impulse control, dealing with frustration and the ability to accept the limits on behaviour which the rules of the game demand. The child also needs to attend, to concentrate and to persevere so that a game is followed through to its conclusion. Playing a game also requires the child to have a certain level of cognitive ability because most games involve the use of numbers, counting and a level of logical problem-solving ability.

Historically, many games have mirrored or paralleled events in our culture and have, as it were, acted as practice grounds in which children could rehearse skills and behaviours used by adults in our society. A good example of such a game is Monopoly, which allows the child to experience the successes and failures of free enterprise trading through the 'buying', 'selling' and 'renting' of property. In this new millennium there is an increasing range of video and computer games, and many of these games can be played by individuals on their own. Unless these games can be played with two handsets, the nature of the social interaction is limited.

As counsellors, we try to keep ourselves informed about games which appeal to children of various ages and abilities. Understanding what each game offers enables us to make sensible decisions about which game to use in a particular counselling situation.

Materials needed when using games

Games can be classified into three categories according to what determines who wins:

1 Games involving physical or motor skill
2 Games involving strategy
3 Games of chance.

Games involving physical or motor skills include Fiddlesticks, tiddlywinks, Operation, some simple board games like Hungry Hippo and Mouse Trap, and games where small bags of beans are thrown at targets. Additionally, there are games such as basketball and handball that require a higher level of physical activity and help children to work off energy or dissipate anger.

In games involving strategy, cognitive skill determines the outcome. These include noughts and crosses, Connect 4, Chinese chequers, chess, Cluedo and many card games.

In games of chance, the outcome of the game is clearly accidental. Games of chance include bingo, snakes and ladders, card games and many games which use a die or a numbered wheel.

We have included games from each of the three categories in our own collection. We usually select games which are suitable for two people, or very small groups, and which are suitable for the space available. We choose games where the pieces or parts of the game are unlikely to cause injury to participants or damage to property. For example, soft sponge balls or Velcro-covered balls are selected in preference to harder alternatives.

It is also important to consider the time it takes to play a game. It would obviously be inappropriate to expect a young child to continue to concentrate throughout a very long game. Moreover, a game used in a counselling session needs to be completed within the time allocated for the session. Generally, we prefer to use short games which can be repeated several times in a session. Such games give a child opportunities to become aware of their current behaviours and then to experiment with new behaviours.

Goals when using games

Games can be used by counsellors to:

- build a counselling relationship with a resistant or reluctant child;
- help a child to explore their responses to restrictions, limitations and the expectations of others;
- provide an opportunity for a child to discover their strengths and weaknesses with regard to fine and gross motor skills and/or visual-perceptual skills;
- provide a child with an opportunity to explore their ability to attend, to concentrate and persevere with tasks;
- help a child to practise social skills such as cooperation and collaboration, and to practise appropriate responses to disappointment, discouragement, failure and success;
- help a child to practise skills in problem solving and decision making;
- provide an opportunity for a child to learn about specific issues or life events (domestic violence, sexual abuse, stranger danger).

How to use games

We will now look at how to use games to achieve each of the above-mentioned goals.

The use of games to build a counselling relationship with a resistant or reluctant child

Some children do not engage in the counselling process easily because they are shy or resistant. Games such as chequers, snap, or snakes and ladders can be used to help in the joining process between the child and counsellor. Involvement in the game provides a safe context with easily recognized boundaries for both child and counsellor. Consequently, the child is unlikely to feel threatened and will relax.

Sometimes, using a game in the way described results in direct counselling gains because significant internal processes of the child are revealed during play. For example, when playing a game it might emerge that a resistant child is resistant because they are fearful, or angry, or frightened of making mistakes. They may also be uncertain about the expectations of the counselling process.

If, during a game, a counsellor notices particular issues emerging for a child, then these can be addressed through the use of statements, reflection of feelings and content, and questions. For example, a counsellor might notice that a child is fearful of failure and might make a statement such as, 'Playing this game might be a bit tricky for you. It's tricky for me too sometimes.'

By making this statement, the counsellor acknowledges the child's anxiety about performance. The counsellor might also reflect feelings by saying, 'You seem to be anxious, when you are not able to do as well as you would like.'

The counsellor might also ask: 'What will it be like for you if you lose the game?' and 'What will it be like if you win the game?'

By using counselling skills such as those given in the examples above, the counsellor can help the child to start entering the counselling process during the game by raising the child's awareness of thoughts and feelings that may be relevant to the child's issues.

The use of games to help a child to explore their responses to restrictions, limitations and the expectations of others

Although games can sometimes be useful for helping a child to become aware of troubling unconscious material, they are probably more valuable for helping them to deal with their responses to restrictions, limitations and the expectations of others. Clearly, games depend on rules and these rules provide restrictions and limitations on the child. Also, when playing a game, the child will be subjected to the expectations of others (for example, the counsellor or members of a group) with regard to their behaviour. Thus, they have an opportunity to confront, explore and work through issues that arise because of the rules of the game and the expectations of others.

Consider the example of a passive, dependent child. Such a child may respond to the restrictions of a game by continually asking for help. In order to address the underlying behaviours of passivity and dependence, the counsellor might mirror the child's behaviour by asking the child for help. The child can then be commended for their ability to give advice. The counsellor can thus highlight the child's own capacity to deal with the restrictions and limitations of the game.

Some children will try to cheat when playing games. A child who cheats is attempting to avoid facing the painfulness of failure in an immature and socially maladaptive way. Such behaviour interferes with the child's development of the ability to cope with painful experiences. Instead of coping with painful experiences adaptively, the child creates an unreal or untrue outcome. To address this problem, the counsellor could help the child to confront reality by encouraging them to explore their wish to win and then to contrast this with reality. For example, the counsellor might ask, 'I wonder what it would have been like if you had won?' and 'What was it like for you to lose?'

The child can then express what it would have been like to have been successful and to recognize what it was like to have been unsuccessful. Thus, the child is encouraged to experience rather than to avoid the feelings of failure and to learn how to cope with these feelings. This approach is useful for many, but not all, children. Some require an intermediate step to help them to cope with reality. This is because for young children, around the age of four to six years, creating an unreal or untrue outcome is normal behaviour. 'Cheating' can be seen as an immature behaviour which is developmentally appropriate for this age group. With younger children the counsellor might use the following, different approach.

Consider a dice game. The counsellor might suggest that the child can throw the dice twice, instead of once, each turn and choose the best outcome from the two throws. This gives the child more control over the outcome because they can choose which dice result to use. Consequently, the pressure to cheat is reduced and the child learns to comply with rules. The counsellor might then encourage the child to take risks when deciding which dice score to use. By using this process the counsellor has maximized the child's chance of winning, while at the same time helping the child to confront the reality of the possibility of failure.

The use of games to provide an opportunity for a child to discover their strengths and weaknesses with regard to fine and gross motor skills and/or visual-perceptual skills

Games which involve fine motor skills include Hungry Hippos, Jenga, Barrel of Monkeys, Fiddlesticks and some computer video games. Games which require gross motor skills include quoits, Velcro-darts, basketball, handball, hide-and-seek, hopscotch and Twister. All of these can be played with the counsellor as the second participant.

Games that involve visual-perceptual skills include Connect 4, Guess Who?, some video computer games, memory games, card games and some board games such as Battleship.

The counsellor can assist a child to ascertain strengths and weaknesses by engaging the child in the games described and by giving appropriate feedback. A recognition of strengths and weaknesses is helpful when exploring the child's self-esteem (see Chapter 31) and in enabling a child to deal with self-destructive beliefs concerning themselves.

The use of games to help a child to explore their ability to attend, to concentrate and to persevere with tasks

During a game, a counsellor can address a child's behaviours by making suggestions and providing encouragement, information and positive reinforcement. Children are more willing to experiment with new behaviours and to practise new behaviours in a game-playing situation than in other situations.

The simple act of taking turns can be helpful for a child with impulse-control problems. Thus, a suitable game can be used to teach the child self-control. A child who has difficulty in attending and/or persevering may be encouraged to complete a game by the use of a statement such as, 'When you have won three hands we will stop the game.' By saying this, the counsellor provides the child with an opportunity to visualize an end to the game, and the child is able to practise and experience completion of a task.

The use of games to help a child to practise social skills such as cooperation and collaboration, and to practise appropriate responses to disappointment, discouragement, failure and success

Playing games allows children to evaluate existing social skills and to learn and practise new social skills. Social skills include observing non-verbal communication, matching affect, asking appropriate questions, giving information, cooperating, sharing and collaborating. Games can also help children to change attitudes and values which are socially inappropriate.

Board games which require children to answer questions or to respond to item cards as they move around the board are particularly useful in achieving the above goal because they take advantage of the social and interactive nature of children. These games are best played in a group so that behaviours can be affirmed or challenged within the group.

A popular game called the Ungame is useful when working with early adolescent groups. In a different way, the Talking, Feeling and Doing Game also enables social skills practice and does not rely on a group to be successful. While playing games such as these, a counsellor can explore the issues and thought processes of the child as they are confronted with difficulties or obstacles. For example, the counsellor might say to the child, 'It seems as though you may be having difficulty responding to this particular item card. What is the hardest part about the instruction on this card for you?'

The counsellor may suggest alternative responses and behaviours during the game. Later, the child may want to practise them so that they can be generalized for everyday use.

The use of games to help a child to practise skills in problem solving and decision making

Most board games, and some card games such as Memory, involve the skills of selecting alternatives and taking risks in response to particular situations. Card games which have a high element of chance are a useful way of helping a child to understand that even when care is taken life may not always go according to plan.

Instant Replay is a game which is useful for helping children to learn and use rational problem-solving methods. In this game, the child is invited to tell the counsellor about a difficult event in their life. They are then asked what happened next as a result of the event. They are also invited to say what they were thinking during the event, with particular reference to their own part in the event. The child is next invited to think of other things they could have thought or done when they were in the situation. After these have been explored, the child is invited to speculate about what the consequences might have been for each of the new possibilities, and is invited to choose the best alternatives and to practise them at home and at school.

The use of games as educational tools to provide an opportunity to learn about specific issues or life events (domestic violence, sexual abuse, stranger danger)

Specifically designed games such as Breakthrough are now available to help children to become aware of, and deal with, specific issues such as physical abuse, sexual abuse, divorce, domestic violence, pornography and stranger danger. These are often board games and they invite the child to respond to questions and to give answers which are then evaluated in terms of the myths or realities.

Suitability of games

As mentioned earlier, games can be used either individually or with groups. They are most useful for primary school children and early adolescents. It is important to remember that children up to the age of about eight years old may have difficulty in consistently staying within the rules of a game, and regressed behaviour may occur. Games suitable for young adolescents require a high level of challenge in cognitive, social and problem-solving areas.

CASE STUDY

One goal of using games in counselling is that of supporting the development of social skills such as cooperation and collaboration. Garaigordobil et al. (1996) found an increase in cooperative behaviours within a group following participation in a cooperative game programme they developed (please see Chapter 20 if you would like more information about the evidence base for using games in counselling). Imagine that you are a school counsellor. One of the Year 5 classes is finding it challenging to settle into the new school year. The teacher and you have both noticed a lot of competitive behaviours and a tendency for some children to pick on others in the class. How might you make use of games to support the class's social skills and ability to work as a group?

KEY POINTS

- Playing a game can help create a relationship with a child who is shy or reluctant.
- Games can sometimes help a child to become aware of troubling unconscious material.
- Games can be used to give the child an opportunity to work through issues related to rules, restrictions and limitations.
- Games give the child an opportunity to discover their strengths and weaknesses.
- Games can help a child to learn and practise social skills, and to practise skills in problem solving.
- Games can be educational, providing the child with information related to the issues they may be facing.

Part 5

The Use of Worksheets

Most children are familiar with worksheets because they are commonly used in schools for teaching purposes. Similar activities are often found in weekend magazines and daily newspapers.

Activities involving worksheets have many different forms, including answering questionnaires, working on quizzes, finding words, joining dots, looking for differences between pictures, finding hidden items in pictures and matching similar items. Some worksheets include measuring scales, such as pictures of thermometers, or continuum lines which stretch from one extreme to another, to measure attitude, performance or other criteria. Clearly, well-designed worksheets are inviting for children, who enjoy using them. Most importantly, from the counsellor's point of view, worksheets act as a springboard for discussion because they tend to draw out and focus the child's thoughts about particular issues or behaviours.

Worksheets can be useful at various stages in the counselling process. At the beginning of a counselling session a worksheet can be used to help a child to begin to look at, and then to explore, particular issues. When a counselling session, or series of sessions, is ending, worksheets can be used to reinforce recently acquired ideas, beliefs and behaviours, and to help the child to consolidate problem-solving skills. By using worksheets, the counsellor actively facilitates change (see Chapter 16).

Worksheets can be used to help a child to:

- begin to look at particular issues so that these issues can be explored;
- consider new ways of thinking and behaving;

- explore, understand and develop problem-solving and decision-making skills;
- make choices about how they might respond to a particular social situation or event, and to explore the possible consequences of these responses;
- recognize differences between old and new behaviours;
- affirm and/or reinforce concepts, ideas, beliefs and behaviours which have been explored or discussed during counselling;
- develop a plan so that learnt skills are generalized into the child's environment.

Additionally, worksheets can be used in a group as a way of helping children to share different points of view.

We will focus on the use of worksheets for the following purposes:

1 Building self-esteem (Chapter 31)
2 Social skills training (Chapter 32)
3 Education in protective behaviours (Chapter 33).

For each chapter, we are providing a selection of worksheets that we have designed for specific purposes. The worksheets are to be found at the end of the book on pp. 289–324. You are welcome to photocopy these for your own personal use when working as a counsellor for children. Please remember, however, that they are copyright and must not be used for other purposes. We find that they are easiest to use if they are enlarged to A4 size.

31

Building Self-Esteem

Worksheets can be particularly helpful when used in conjunction with Narrative Therapy in helping the child to change their view of self in Phase 3 of the SPICC process (see Figure 8.1, p. 72).

From a very early age a child begins to form an image, or picture, of themselves. This image or picture is generally referred to as the child's *self-concept* and is largely based on the way in which the child is treated by the significant people in their life. These people, through their responses, give the child information about themselves and about their behaviours. As a consequence, they will develop both positive and negative attitudes towards themselves.

We would like to stress that self-concept is not the same as self-esteem. The image, or picture, that the child has of themselves is their *self-concept*. That is how they see themselves. The value they put on this image is the measure of their *self-esteem*. Self-esteem, therefore, is an indication of the extent to which a child values themselves.

It is important, when counselling children, to recognize the difference between self-concept and self-esteem. Although many children with a generally positive self-concept will have high self-esteem, this is not always the case. Some children see themselves as having many positive attributes: they may be clever academically, good at sport and articulate, and as a result have a positive self-concept. However, they may not value these attributes, so may have low self-esteem and feel bad about themselves. Some very capable children, who have high expectations of themselves, see themselves as unsuccessful and unworthy when their performance doesn't match their personal aspirations. Their fear of failure raises their anxiety and their self-esteem is threatened. The opposite also happens: some children may see themselves as being unintelligent, poor at sport and inarticulate. However, they may like the way they are and have high self-esteem.

The value and judgement a child places on their self-concept, that is, the level of a child's self-esteem, will inevitably have a major influence on their adaptive functioning. Their beliefs, thoughts, attitudes, emotional feelings, behaviours, motivation, interest and participation in events and activities, and expectations for the future, will all be significantly influenced by their level of self-esteem. Additionally, the child's ability to enter into and sustain meaningful relationships will be dependent on their self-esteem.

Children with high self-esteem tend to have the following characteristics:

- They have a greater capacity to be creative.
- They are more likely to assume active roles in social groups.

- They are less likely to be burdened by self-doubt, fear and ambivalence.
- They are more likely to move directly and realistically towards personal goals.
- They find it easier to accept differences between their own levels of competence and that of others in areas such as academic performance, peer relationships and physical pursuits.
- They also tend to worry less about differences in physical appearance. They are able to accept these differences and still to feel positive about themselves.

Many children who come for counselling help do not have the attributes listed above. Instead they feel helpless and inferior, incapable of improving their situation, and believe that they do not have the resources to reduce their anxiety. They have low self-esteem.

Some children with low self-esteem strive for social approval by behaving in ways which are over-compliant, or by pretending to be self-confident when they are not, while continuing to receive negative responses and feedback. They are struggling to feel good about themselves.

Generally, the self-esteem of a child remains fairly constant and stable over a period of several years. However, self-esteem can, with appropriate interventions, be influenced either directly or indirectly. A counsellor can help a child to raise their self-esteem.

Interventions to directly enhance self-esteem usually involve the use of praise and performance feedback to improve both the child's self-concept and self-esteem. However, although useful, this type of direct intervention is not always the most effective way to bring about improvement in self-esteem. Alternatively, or additionally, we can use an indirect method. An indirect approach targets specific areas, such as the child's performance as a student, their relationships with peers or their motor performance. Clearly, a child's self-esteem is likely to improve if they can acquire competence and confidence in these areas.

We believe that, for most children, work in a group provides the best opportunity for self-esteem improvement. Children can realistically and positively evaluate themselves through the process of group interaction. Specific areas of skill development can easily be targeted through exercises and activities.

Although, in our view, group work is generally the most effective way of enhancing self-esteem, some children may not have the ego-strength or behavioural characteristics to enable them to satisfactorily participate in a group process. These children may have come from environments where they have had few experiences of love and success, and where domination, rejection and severe punishment have resulted in a high level of damage to the child's ego. They may have become submissive and withdrawn, or may have responded by becoming extremely aggressive and dominating. Because such children may be unable to fit comfortably into a group, their self-esteem needs are most appropriately met through one-to-one counselling. When working with children such as these, worksheets are useful. Such children are usually adept at avoiding and deflecting away from any discussion which focuses on their incompetencies, limitations and anxieties. Worksheets can be used to help them to focus and to target significant topics.

Some self-esteem programmes focus on helping the child to recognize and accept their own personal attributes, strengths and limitations. This is rather like saying 'This is what you have got. Make the most of it'. Although this approach can be useful, we do not think that it is sufficient, because it limits the child's potential to change.

We like to emphasize not just the child's acceptance, but also the child's *ownership* of all of their qualities, both negative and positive. Imagine that you were given an old paintbox and worn paintbrushes and with them the instruction: 'These are yours to use. Paint a picture and do your best'. Now imagine that instead you were given the same paintbox and brushes and a different instruction: 'These are yours to *keep*. Paint a picture and do your best'. The second instruction implies ownership and subtly changes the user's attitude, responsibility and commitment to the proposed use of the paints. In both cases you might well choose to paint a picture. However, in the second case you might also be interested in *caring for and improving* the paintbox and brushes so that they can be maximally useful for you in the future. Similarly, by stressing the ownership of a child's attributes we believe that we help that child to more fully discover themselves. By doing this they are more likely to develop strategies to deal with and manage those characteristics of themselves which they perceive as negative.

If a child is prepared to accept and own their strengths and limitations, then they are likely to accept responsibility for developing and learning to improve on, and manage, their limitations, believing that they alone are responsible for the changes within themselves.

Self-esteem is heavily influenced by the ability to interact in a socially adaptive way. Social skills are of such major importance that we have devoted a separate chapter (32) to social skills training.

To enhance their self-esteem a child can do the following:

- discover themselves, so that they have a more realistic self-concept;
- recognize and understand their strengths and limitations;
- establish goals for the future and devise and implement a plan to achieve these.

For each of these three areas we have prepared three worksheets. A summary of these worksheets and their uses is given in Table 31.1.

TABLE 31.1   *Self-esteem worksheets*

Topic addressed	Worksheet number	Title	Page number
Discover yourself	1	I can do anything ...	291
	2	Where am I? ...	292
	3	My choice ...	293
Strengths and limitations	4	Inside-out	294
	5	News headlines	295
	6	Jump the hurdle	296
Goals for the future	7	Balance your life	297
	8	These are my wishes ...	298
	9	Picture yourself ...	299

In the following paragraphs we will discuss ways to use the worksheets. Please remember that the worksheets are not intended to be sufficient in themselves: they provide the stimulus for discussion of the relevant issues.

Discover yourself

The worksheets are designed to help children to discover themselves so that they can have a more realistic self-concept. These worksheets give children permission to do the following:

- express various polarities within themselves;
- examine which parts of themselves they expose freely to others and which parts of themselves they hide;
- discover how they can make choices about what they do;
- discover how they can make choices about when to do things by themselves and when to do them with others.

The three worksheets are entitled:

I can do anything ... (Worksheet 1, p. 291)

Where am I? ... (Worksheet 2, p. 292)

My choice ... (Worksheet 3, p. 293)

The worksheet *I can do anything* ... stimulates discussion about which parts of themselves the child feels most comfortable in expressing at different times and in different situations. For example, a child may feel powerful and strong when with their peers, yet submissive with their parents. When using this worksheet we encourage discussion to focus around the belief that it is OK to behave differently in different circumstances, and we explore the need to be adaptive and considerate of others.

The worksheet *Where am I?* ... allows the child to develop a visual picture of those parts of themselves which they can comfortably let others see and those parts of themselves which they prefer to hide. Discussion can then explore the risks which might be involved if they were to expose the hidden parts of themselves to others. By connecting the characters on the page to parts of the tree, the child is encouraged to explore the possibility that hidden parts might grow to become an exposed part of the tree for others to see and appreciate.

The worksheet *My choice* ... encourages the child to begin to view their life in terms of activities which fit into particular categories. It invites them to identify activities within categories and to create a picture about themselves. This picture can help the child to discover how much time they spend in particular activities and to decide whether or not they would like to make changes. During a counselling session a child can be encouraged to make some choices or decisions about whether they would like to change parts of the picture they have of themselves.

Strengths and limitations

In designing worksheets related to strengths and limitations, our goals are to help the child to:

- identify strengths and limitations;
- discover resources within themselves which they can use to enhance their self-esteem;
- identify any thoughts and self-destructive beliefs they have about themselves, which prevent them from changing to becoming stronger;
- discover how to care for themselves;
- recognize mistakes as opportunities for learning and changing.

The three worksheets that deal with strengths and limitations are:

Inside-out (Worksheet 4, p. 294)

News headlines (Worksheet 5, p. 295)

Jump the hurdle (Worksheet 6, p. 296)

The worksheet *Inside-out* allows the child to identify three separate components of themselves: their body, their emotional feelings and their thoughts. The worksheet then provides suggestions to help the child to discover new ways of caring for their body, their emotional feelings and their thoughts. The worksheet also helps the child to recognize and own behaviours that prevent them from developing their strengths.

The worksheet *News headlines* highlights a specific incident in the child's life where they have made a mistake. It gives the child an opportunity to process a negative experience but to focus on the positive outcomes of that experience.

The worksheet *Jump the hurdle* attempts to encourage the child to be flexible in their thinking, to consider taking risks and to discover the issues that prevent them from making new and different choices.

Goals for the future

Following through on plans and goals is an indicator of confidence and belief in oneself. In this section we attempt to encourage the child to combine their wishes and dreams with reality. We have designed three worksheets to address the topic of goals for the future:

Balance your life (Worksheet 7, p. 297)

These are my wishes … (Worksheet 8, p. 298)

Picture yourself … (Worksheet 9, p. 299)

The worksheet *Balance your life* encourages the child to view their daily life in terms of various categories. This worksheet gives the child a picture of how their day is divided. It presents them with information about whether, for instance, they spend most of their time learning and not much time relaxing. The child is then encouraged to think of ways in which they might change their daily life to achieve a more satisfactory balance across each of the categories.

The worksheet *These are my wishes* … allows the child to fantasize about their life and to think about what they would like in the present, in the near future and in the long term. When using the worksheet, we encourage the child to be as imaginative and creative as they can be.

The worksheet *Picture yourself* … allows the child to plan the big picture of their future by examining the past, looking at the present and preparing for the future fulfilment of dreams and wishes. The child is encouraged to identify what they have achieved, and want to achieve, and who or what they need to help them achieve their goal.

KEY POINTS

- Self-concept is the image or picture that the child has of themselves.
- Self-esteem relates to the value the child puts on their self-concept.
- For those children who are suited to group work, this is generally the most effective way of enhancing self-esteem.
- For self-esteem to be enhanced a child can be supported to develop a realistic self-concept, recognize and understand their strengths and limitations, and establish and plan for goals for the future.

32

Social Skills Training

As mentioned in the previous chapter, a child's self-image and self-esteem are dependent on the child's skills in relating to peers and adults. These skills contribute to self-esteem because a child with good social skills is likely to build satisfying relationships and to receive positive feedback from others. A child with poor social skills is likely to have unsatisfactory relationships and to receive negative feedback. Consequently, if we are to help a child to change their view of self in Phase 3 of the SPICC process (see Figure 8.1, p. 72) we may also need to help them improve their social skills. Additionally, in Phase 5 of the SPICC process, where a child is rehearsing and experimenting with new behaviours, it may be important to help the child to learn more adaptive social skills.

Many of the emotionally disturbed children who have come to see us for counselling help have had poor social skills. Consequently, these children have had dysfunctional interpersonal relationships. Often, they have also engaged in socially unacceptable behaviours, which have resulted in painful consequences for them.

Poor social skills can occur as a result of poor modelling by adults. Additionally, children who have experienced trauma often develop socially inappropriate behaviours: they may become aggressive or overly compliant. Other children develop irrational and self-destructive beliefs, which set them up to mistrust others and to misinterpret the behaviours of others.

It is clear that poor social skills lead to problems not only in childhood but also later in life, so it is very important for children with poor social skills to receive appropriate training to help them to improve their skills so that they can enjoy their social interactions and feel good about themselves.

What are the characteristics of children with poor social skills? How are they different from other children?

We believe that the following characteristics are typical of children with poor social skills:

- Often they don't adapt their behaviour to accommodate the needs of others.
- They tend to choose less socially acceptable behaviours.
- They have difficulty in predicting the consequences of their behaviours.
- They misunderstand social cues.

- They are unable to perform the social skills required for particular situations.
- They often have an inability to control impulsive or aggressive behaviour.

There are three components to social skills training that are essential if the training is to be effective and useful, these are to:

1 Help the child to gain clear ideas about what constitutes socially adaptive behaviour.
2 Help the child to discover how to use appropriate social skills.
3 Help the child to generalize the skills learnt so that they can be put into practice in the various social situations of the child's own environment.

In order to meet the requirements of these components, it is preferable to use a combination of group work and individual counselling.

Group work provides an opportunity for children to identify and discuss acceptable and unacceptable social behaviours as these behaviours occur in the group. It also enables the practice of new behaviours.

In individual counselling, we use worksheets to help the child to think about their current behaviours and the consequences, to recognize alternative behaviours and to make choices about how they intend to respond to particular social situations in the future. Working individually gives the child the opportunity to examine their own responses and choices without pressure from others. Clearly, this is an individual task, as each child is different and has their own unique social environment. Once the child has chosen appropriate skills for use in particular situations, we can help them to devise a plan of action. In this plan the child decides on the best time to use the selected skills within the various situations of their environment. Thus they are able to think about ways in which to generalize learnt social skills into the various settings of their own unique and individual environment.

After the child has attempted to carry out their plan of action, they can be invited to evaluate the success of the plan and to modify it, if necessary, for future use. We can also help the child to think about possible responses to any new problems that may arise as a consequence of their use of new social skills.

There are three major areas that are addressed when training children in social skills:

1 Identifying and expressing feelings
2 Communicating with others
3 Self-management.

It is important for a child to be able to identify their own and other people's feelings if they are to relate adaptively. Communicating effectively in ways which validate their own needs and are respectful of others' needs is also important; as is learning to manage their own behaviour effectively so that it is socially acceptable.

In each of the three areas listed above, we have identified three specific issues that can be explored and have prepared two worksheets for each issue. A summary of these worksheets and their uses is given in Table 32.1.

TABLE 32.1 *Social skills worksheets*

Worksheets for **IDENTIFYING AND EXPRESSING FEELINGS**			
Issue addressed	**Worksheet number**	**Title**	**Page number**
Identifying own feelings	10	*Find a feeling*	300
	11	*Artemus is anxious!*	301
Identifying others' feelings	12	*Guess what?*	302
	13	*Your body*	303
Expressing feelings	14	*The volcano*	304
	15	*Fighting fear with Felix*	305

Worksheets about **COMMUNICATING WITH OTHERS**			
Issue addressed	**Worksheet number**	**Title**	**Page number**
Making friends	16	*Conversation starters*	306
	17	*??Questions??*	307
Being left out	18	*Advice for Jim*	308
	19	*Gertrude & Grommet Gumbo – the gossips*	309
Solving conflicts	20	*Fighting!*	310
	21	*Terry, Tyrone and me*	311

Worksheets on **SELF-MANAGEMENT**			
Issue addressed	**Worksheet number**	**Title**	**Page number**
Chilling out	22	*Look before you leap*	312
	23	*Choices & options*	313
Consequences	24	*If – then – but*	314
	25	*Crime & punishment!*	315
Sticking up for yourself	26	*Saying 'No' ... made easy*	316
	27	*Reward yourself*	317

Identifying and expressing feelings

To function adaptively so that they can relate easily with others, it is important for children to be able to identify their own feelings, identify other people's feelings and express their own feelings.

In the following paragraphs we will discuss ways to use the worksheets that we have designed to address the three issues listed above. The worksheets are not intended to be sufficient in themselves; they provide the stimulus for discussion of the relevant issues.

Helping children to identify their own feelings

The following worksheets help children to identify their own feelings:

Find a feeling (Worksheet 10, p. 300)

Artemus is anxious! (Worksheet 11, p. 301)

Quite often we find that children are unable to label the feelings that they are experiencing. For some children, this may be because they have had confusing information about feelings. For example, a child might have been told by their mother that she was 'just tired' when she was actually behaving in an angry way. Other children may have difficulty in recognizing the differences between feelings which are fairly similar: for example, feeling disappointed might be confused with feeling sad, and feeling embarrassed might be confused with feeling shy.

Find a feeling helps the child to identify particular feelings by relating them to events and situations.

Artemus is anxious! presents the child with a list of situations they might find anxiety provoking. The worksheet also invites the child to consider situations and events, specifically relevant to themselves, which might make them anxious.

Helping children to identify other people's feelings

The following worksheets help children to identify other people's feelings:

Guess what? (Worksheet 12, p. 302)

Your body (Worksheet 13, p. 303)

Once a child has learnt to identify their own feelings and to match them with situations and events, they are more likely to be able to predict or guess how other people might feel in particular situations.

Guess what? invites the child to guess how other people, shown in the picture on the worksheet, might be feeling. By using this worksheet, the child might also, in their imagination, project themselves into situations similar to those depicted, and discussion about specific events and issues might ensue.

Your body encourages the child to use observational skills. The child is asked to consider how people use their bodies, and the expressions on their faces, to indicate how they are feeling. Following on from this exercise, the child might be invited to think about their own body language and how they use this to express their emotions.

Helping children to express their own feelings

The following worksheets help children to express their feelings:

The volcano (Worksheet 14, p. 304)

Fighting fear with Felix (Worksheet 15, p. 305)

Once a child can identify their own feelings and recognize the feelings which other people are expressing, it is important that they learn how to express their own feelings clearly and appropriately. This means expressing feelings in ways that are comfortable for both the child and the other party involved.

The volcano is specifically targeted at the expression of anger. When using this sheet, each point on the volcano is discussed. For example, once the child has identified what kinds of things make them angry, they may look at the bottom of the volcano where sitting on angry feelings can be imagined. The child might be encouraged to talk about what it would be like to sit on angry feelings, what might happen if they did, and what that might be like for other people. They could then be asked whether they could identify other children or people who sit on their anger. Moving up the volcano to the level where anger is allowed to ooze out provides an opportunity for the child to explore a different way of expressing anger. Once again, the kinds of behaviours that they might see in others, when they let their anger ooze out, can be identified. At the top of the volcano is the explosive angry reaction. Here the child is encouraged to examine the appropriateness and inappropriateness of this kind of expression of anger. Remember that worksheets are a springboard for further discussion.

Fighting fear with Felix encourages the child to explore possible reactions to fear and to look at their own reactions to fear. The situations listed might not be relevant for a particular child, so when using this worksheet we usually invite the child to tell us of their own experiences of fear. They can then explore their reactions during such experiences. *Fighting fear with Felix* also allows the counsellor to normalize the feeling of fear. This is very important because some children believe that feeling frightened is abnormal and is not OK.

Communicating with others

Once children can identify feelings in themselves and in others and can begin to express their feelings appropriately, they are more likely to be successful in communicating with others. Social communication involves an exchange between two (or more) people. Usually, one individual initiates the communication and the other responds. In early childhood, this peer interaction is based on shared play activities. However, as children grow older, the interaction becomes more focused on peer acceptance and intimacy. Friendships tend to move from being physical with a focus on actions, towards relationships with an increased awareness of the feelings and emotions of others. In middle childhood, between the ages of about seven and eleven, children have more social contacts and are able to identify 'best friends'. With the establishment of best friends they begin to demonstrate commitment to each other. Aggressive interactions tend to decrease and friendships tend to involve more verbal interaction. At this stage it is important for children to be able to communicate adaptively, otherwise they will not be able to establish satisfying social relationships. Additionally, they also learn to deal with the emotional consequences of situations which inevitably occur in childhood, such as being left out, being ignored, being in demand as a popular child, or being ridiculed.

In order to help children to learn appropriate communication techniques, we have devised worksheets to address the following issues:

- Making friends
- Being left out
- Solving conflicts.

Making friends

The following worksheets help children learn how to make friends:

   Conversation starters (Worksheet 16, p. 306)

   ??Questions?? (Worksheet 17, p. 307)

Conversation starters suggests several different ways in which a child could start a conversation during their first day at a new school. The child is asked to identify those conversation starters that would be OK to use. They are also invited to think about the responses they might get if they were to use one of the other starters that they hadn't chosen. This worksheet helps the child to think about suitable conversation starters when in new situations and helps them to explore the anxiety related to going into new social situations.

??Questions?? teaches children how to use questions and answers to start up and maintain a conversation. The worksheet invites the child to ask questions beginning with 'what', 'where', 'how', 'when', 'why' and 'who' in order to discover information about a picture. Each time the child asks a question about the picture, the counsellor responds creatively so that a story develops. For example, the child might ask, 'What caused that puddle on the floor?' In response the counsellor might reply, 'There is a hole in the roof and the house was built right under a giant waterfall.' As the child asks more questions, the counsellor can develop the story, using humour if they wish. Similarly, the counsellor can use questions to encourage the child to tell a different story about the picture. Later, the child and counsellor might take turns in asking questions and developing a story together.

By doing this exercise the child learns to use questions and answers to initiate conversations. They also learn to listen and to take turns. The child can then practise these skills in their social situation when sharing interesting or exciting information with peers.

Being left out

The following worksheets are useful for addressing the issue of being left out:

   Advice for Jim (Worksheet 18, p. 308)

   Gertrude & Grommet Gumbo – the Gossips (Worksheet 19, p. 309)

Being left out is something that children experience from time to time both at school and at home. *Advice for Jim* helps the child to explore their reactions to being left out. It also allows the counsellor to invite the child to talk about times in the past when they felt left out and to discuss the ways in which they reacted. The counsellor can then validate the child's feelings and encourage the child to explore alternative ways of responding.

Gertrude & Grommet Gumbo – the Gossips looks at the way in which gossiping damages social relationships, with the consequence that children get left out. This worksheet helps the child to learn suitable responses to use when another child is inviting them to join in gossiping. Additionally, it allows the child to explore the reactions that they experience when they are left out as a result of gossiping.

Solving conflicts

The following worksheets help children to learn how to solve conflicts:

Fighting! (Worksheet 20, p. 310)

Terry, Tyrone and me (Worksheet 21, p. 311)

Resolving conflicts in interpersonal relationships requires understanding, skill and practice. It is important for a child to identify the reasons why conflict occurs and to understand their own responses to conflict. *Fighting!* invites the child to think about possible reasons why fights occur. The child is also encouraged to talk about conflict situations, which have occurred at home and school, and to think about how these happened.

Terry, Tyrone and me explores a number of different ways of responding to conflict. When the dots have been joined, Terry can be seen to be a tortoise whose responses might be timid, fearful and unassertive, coming from a position of helplessness and victimization. In contrast, Tyrone is a troll whose responses might be aggressive, bullying, controlling and powerful. The counsellor can encourage the child to explore assertive ways of dealing with conflict when they think about their own responses in the 'me' section of the worksheet. The counsellor can also validate the child's emotional feelings, whether they be fear or anger, in a conflict situation.

Self-management

To be socially competent it is important for a child to be able to identify and express feelings, develop skills to communicate successfully with others, and at the same time be aware of, and manage, their own behaviour. Being aware of their own behaviour helps them to be sensitive to feedback cues from others and to be aware of the timing and pace of their own behaviour during interactions. In managing their own behaviour it is important that they be able to understand and recognize consequences, to recover after social errors, to present themselves in a way which is socially acceptable, and to reinforce their own social behaviours in a positive way.

In order to help children to learn self-management skills we have devised worksheets to deal with the following topics:

- Chilling out
- Consequences
- Sticking up for yourself.

Chilling out

Chilling out is the opposite to being impulsively reactive. The following worksheets help children to learn how to chill out:

Look before you leap (Worksheet 22, p. 312)

Choices & options (Worksheet 23, p. 313)

Look before you leap uses the stop–think–do plan as described in detail in Chapter 16. This plan is widely used by students in schools when experiencing difficulties with self-management. After a provocative or annoying event has occurred, chilling out involves:

1 **STOP:** Don't respond reactively, instead withhold action.
2 **THINK:** Take time to think about and to assess the event. Work out what seems to be the best way of behaving.
3 **DO:** Practise the way you wish to behave and then do it.

The worksheet encourages the child to identify behaviours that they might sometimes use, but which could lead to unsatisfactory consequences. When using this worksheet, the counsellor might work with the child to identify a particular situation which recurs in the child's life. A plan, using new behaviours, can then be developed by the child. After the child has carried out the plan, its effectiveness, in terms of outcome, can be evaluated. If the child believes that the plan was unsuccessful, then alternative solutions can be explored, a new plan devised, and the child can practise once again.

Choices & options allows a child to explore the consequences of alternative actions which can be taken at different points in time. It can be useful for the counsellor to invite the child to think about how they feel emotionally while they are making a choice at one of the decision boxes on the sheet. Thus, though the task is cognitive, the importance of recognizing emotional feelings when making decisions is highlighted. This is important because choices can be heavily influenced by emotional responses.

Consequences

The following worksheets address the issue of consequences:

If – then – but (Worksheet 24, p. 314)

Crime & punishment! (Worksheet 25, p. 315)

Having a clear understanding of the nature and appropriateness of the consequences of behaviour is important if a child is to be able to self-manage their behaviour.

If – then – but is unique in that it invites children to explore both the positive and negative consequences of particular behaviours. The worksheet also helps the child to realize that by making some adaptive behavioural decisions, there may be some loss of immediate gratification. This worksheet can be used as a starting point to help the child to consider new choices and options, and to plan to use new and different behaviours. If the child then experiments with these new behaviours in their own environment between counselling sessions, the positive and negative outcomes can be subsequently evaluated. If necessary, a new plan can then be developed.

Crime & punishment! allows the child to examine their concept of the seriousness of particular unacceptable behaviours. It also allows the child to explore the appropriateness of consequences and punishments for certain behaviours.

Sticking up for yourself

The following worksheets help children to learn to stick up for themselves:

Saying 'No' … made easy (Worksheet 26, p. 316)

Reward yourself (Worksheet 27, p. 317)

While the main thrust of exploring self-management is about restraining or restricting outbursts of aggressive or other inappropriate behaviour, it is important to emphasize that self-management also means the child rewarding themselves for their own positive achievements and valuing themselves as a unique individual.

There are many situations where children feel pressured into behaving in ways which may compromise their own beliefs, values and ambitions. Good self-management includes the ability to say 'No' when it is appropriate to do so. However, saying 'No' to peers is not generally easy for children to do. It can result in the child being ostracized, being unpopular, being criticized, or being ridiculed by peers. *Saying 'No' … made easy* gives the child some practical ways of responding to pressuring situations by peers. The worksheet allows the counsellor to explore with the child the ease with which they might be able to use some of the suggested statements. This worksheet can also be used to help the child to invent their own ways of saying 'No'.

Reward yourself allows the child to reinforce their own positive social accomplishments. In the shields the child can write or draw something they have done that they feel proud of. The worksheet also provides an opportunity for the child to practise telling somebody about their accomplishments in a way which is appropriate, acceptable and likely to encourage further affirmation or reinforcement of positive behaviour.

Summary

In designing the worksheets in this chapter we chose the areas that we believe are the most significant in helping children to develop social skills. It is clear to us that there are many more behaviours, feelings and situations which could be usefully explored by using worksheets. Perhaps you would like to design some worksheets of your own. We have found that doing this can be both useful and satisfying.

KEY POINTS

- Social skills training involves helping the child to have a clear idea about socially adaptive behaviour, to learn to use appropriate social skills, and to generalize the skills learnt.
- Working in a group provides an opportunity to identify and discuss acceptable and unacceptable social behaviour.
- Worksheets enable the child to think about their current behaviours, the consequences of these, and to recognize alternative behaviours.
- Adaptive social skills involve being able to identify and express feelings, communicate appropriately with others, and exercise self-management.
- In learning social skills it is important for a child to become aware of their own feelings and the feelings and emotions of others.
- Important conversational skills related to creating good relationships involve the use of conversation starters and appropriate questions.
- To effectively self-manage their behaviour it is important that children become aware of their own behaviour and its effect on others.
- To avoid reacting impulsively it is important that a child learns how to chill out.
- A plan of action can be used to help the child to generalize learnt social skills.

33

Education in Protective Behaviours

Protective behaviours education involves giving children the message 'Look after yourself and keep yourself safe from harm and potential danger.' If children are to respond appropriately to this message, then it is important that they be able to:

1 Understand appropriate boundaries.
2 Protect themselves from physical harm.
3 Protect themselves from emotional harm.

Most often, protective behaviour education will occur in Phases 4 and 5 of the SPICC model (see Figure 8.1, p. 72), where the child's beliefs are changing, they look at their options and choices, and rehearse and experiment with new behaviours. However, there are sometimes situations where it is important to help the child to learn to use protective behaviours earlier in the process in order to ensure the safety of the child. As explained in Chapter 2, where a child is at risk it is essential that appropriate action is taken to protect the child.

Helping children to understand appropriate boundaries

Having a clear understanding of what boundaries are normal, desirable and acceptable in our society helps children to be safe, and to feel safe. It is also important for children to understand the limits, expectations and behaviours relevant to those boundaries. Once children have this understanding, they are more likely to be able to make decisions and to take action to live within and to protect those boundaries.

When helping children we consider developmental, family, social and cultural boundaries.

Developmental boundaries

As a child grows older and moves through the normal developmental stages, their social, emotional and physical boundaries change. When a child is an infant many people may be actively involved in physically caring for them: they may feed them, bath them and change their nappy. People from outside the family circle may, at times, play with them. Sometimes admiring strangers may touch them or hold them. As the child grows older they will become more discriminating and will start to set boundaries of their own. They will start to express their wishes about who should meet their physical, emotional and social needs. As the child begins to set their own boundaries, others are likely to become more respectful and less intrusive, particularly with regard to intimate needs. Certainly, children aged four or five are generally less accepting of strangers and do not like them intruding on their physical or emotional space. Children in this age group are unlikely to be comfortable if a stranger gives them a cuddle or takes them to the toilet.

Developmentally appropriate changes to boundaries occur right through to adulthood, when intimate physical experiences are limited to partners, spouses, girlfriends and boyfriends.

When teaching protective behaviours, we take account of those boundaries which are developmentally appropriate. It can also be important for a child to understand that behaviours which are not acceptable now may be acceptable later, when the child grows up and enters teenage or adult relationships. Similarly, they can learn to understand that boundaries and behaviours which were acceptable when they were younger may not be acceptable now.

Family boundaries

Ideas about family boundaries are usually transmitted from generation to generation. What was acceptable in a mother's family of origin, or in a father's, is likely to be acceptable in the child's family. However, problems sometimes arise where a mother and father come from families with different attitudes and standards. It might be interesting for you, the reader, to think about your own family and identify which boundaries and behaviours have been passed down from a previous generation and which ones are new.

Families vary, from those which are disengaged with very tight boundaries at one extreme, to those at the opposite extreme, which are very enmeshed and have open and flexible boundaries.

In a disengaged family, the family is generally seen to be an independent nuclear family, which as a group does not socialize much with outsiders. Individuals within the family may function fairly independently and there may be little communication.

By contrast, many enmeshed families live more of a community lifestyle. They extend their family to include relationships with aunts, uncles, cousins and friends, and may frequently engage in large family gatherings. Children in such families may freely and easily spend time with any of the members of their extended family. Possessions may be shared, holiday times may be spent together, and in times of need distant family members may be approached for help. Some people clearly enjoy this extended family atmosphere. However, for other people the lack of clear boundaries can be confusing and overwhelming.

When working with children on protective behaviours, it is essential to recognize the nature of the family system within which the child lives. We believe that often it is necessary to involve parents with their children in protective behaviours education. By doing this, the parents can be involved in the development of strategies for setting and maintaining sensible boundaries that provide safety and will also be acceptable in their particular family environment. Without parental cooperation, the child may be set up for failure.

Social boundaries

Social boundaries are those boundaries that are generally accepted as being socially appropriate in contemporary society. Some of the most important of these boundaries are enshrined in legislation. For example, there are laws that prohibit the expression of a variety of behaviours in public. Physical assault on one person by another is illegal. A sexual relationship between an adult and a child is illegal.

Social boundaries are most likely to be violated when family and cultural boundaries are strong, pervasive and different from socially accepted norms. Consequently, counsellors may need to help a child, and/or the child's parents, to recognize differences between social and family expectations so that sensible decisions can be made with regard to appropriate boundaries.

Cultural boundaries

Cultural boundaries are based on beliefs and values specific to a particular cultural or religious setting. People in different parts of the world have very different values and attitudes with regard to appropriate child behaviours and with regard to appropriate parenting strategies. What is permissible sexually and physically varies from culture to culture. Similarly, differences in what are considered to be appropriate boundaries are evident between people from different religions, and between people who are religious and those who are not.

Violation of cultural boundaries often has social consequences and therefore can result in significant emotional trauma. When counselling children, it is important for us to remember that we will not be effective if we ignore cultural norms. Instead, we recognize and validate cultural boundaries and address any issues that arise through the SPICC process.

Helping children to protect themselves from physical harm

Part of protective behaviours education involves helping children to develop skills to protect themselves from physical harm. Situations where physical harm could occur might involve any of the following:

- Domestic violence
- Sexual abuse
- Peer pressure
- Peer relationships.

Domestic violence

Often in families where there is violence between parents, children are not only witnesses of this violence but are also subjected to physical abuse themselves. Sometimes children find themselves in situations where they try to prevent violence from occurring between their parents. In such situations they are at risk of being harmed physically, either intentionally or accidentally. Children are also at risk of physical abuse in families where parents or siblings have poor anger-management strategies.

Children in situations such as those described may need counselling help to enable them to develop protective behaviour plans that can be used in times of danger. Clearly, it is desirable for parents to be involved in the construction of such plans so that their children are assured of their support.

Sexual abuse

Sexual abuse involves misuse of power and control, making it hard for children to protect themselves because they do not have adult physical strength. Perpetrators may threaten to harm children physically if they attempt to resist, or if they disclose abuse. When sexual abuse occurs there is a high risk of physical harm. Perpetrators often penetrate the bodies of both female and male children, causing physical injury. Some perpetrators of sexual abuse use seductive techniques, which can be confusing for a child. This confusion is exacerbated if the child is unsure about appropriate boundaries.

Hence, it is important for counsellors to educate children with regard to appropriate sexual boundaries, and to help them to develop strategies for protecting these boundaries. They can also empower children so that they are able to report instances of inappropriate behaviour.

Peer pressure

Most children want to be accepted by their peers and are therefore highly susceptible to peer pressure. This is particularly true for pre-adolescent children. Consequently, children will often respond to dares and bets in ways which require them to perform physically in situations where they have limited skills or experience. For example, if a child swings on a rope over a waterfall to prove that he is brave or courageous, he may incur serious injury. It follows that protective behaviours education includes information about how to resist inappropriate peer pressure.

Peer relationships

Social relationships among children focus heavily on being accepted, being popular, being brave, being tough, having skills and having other attributes perceived by children as 'desirable'. Children often find themselves in situations where they are challenged and need to protect themselves physically from others. They are especially vulnerable in school playgrounds where peer relationships can involve undesirable behaviours such as bullying by individuals or groups.

As part of protective behaviours education, children can learn skills and strategies to deal with the possibility of being harmed physically by peers.

Helping children to protect themselves from emotional harm

When children are young, their emotional needs are usually met by adults. However, as children grow older they become more responsible for meeting their own emotional needs; therefore need to develop skills to enable them to do this. It is also important for children to learn skills to avoid emotional trauma whenever possible and to deal with it when it does occur. For children, emotional harm frequently occurs as a result of:

- Keeping secrets
- Being victimized
- Poor communication skills and lack of assertiveness.

Keeping secrets

Sharing secrets is a strategy often used by younger children when developing 'best friend' relationships. This strategy allows children to signal to their peers that a relationship is exclusive. It is developmentally appropriate for young children to behave in this way, and such secrets generally don't cause problems for them. However, secrets between adults and children often cause marked emotional distress, especially when the secret involves the violation of social, family or cultural boundaries.

In families where violence is occurring, children often feel unable to talk about it to people outside the family. They feel compelled to keep the violent behaviour a secret, either because they are ashamed of it or because they are afraid that there may be unpleasant consequences if they tell others. A child may also feel obliged to be supportive of one parent's behaviours even if these violate appropriate boundaries.

An important component of protective behaviours education is to help children to realize that having secrets can cause problems, and to help them to feel OK about divulging secret information, when that is appropriate.

Being victimized

For a variety of reasons children often find themselves as victims. In families, they may be victimized because they are the youngest, because they are the only female or male in the family, because they are the oldest, or because certain characteristics or behaviours have been attributed to them. At school, children may be victimized because they are the fattest, the thinnest, the slowest, the clumsiest, because they wear glasses or because they have a disability. Behaviours and characteristics which are perceived negatively are often attributed to such children. Consequently, they may be stereotyped as victims and may be unable to challenge the stereotype and the recurring victimization. As a result they commonly develop maladaptive behaviours such as becoming aggressive or over-compliant. This inevitably has emotional implications for future relationships and behaviours.

Poor communication skills and lack of assertiveness

Children frequently suffer emotional trauma because they have poor communication skills and are unable to express their feelings or talk about their needs and worries. Children who are unable to discuss important issues with others may develop self-destructive beliefs which are emotionally damaging for them. They may also develop maladaptive behaviours in order to cope.

Children who have poor communication skills are unlikely to have the ability to stand up for themselves and to assert their rights. In situations involving peers or adults, this lack of assertiveness can result in feelings of helplessness and powerlessness, and in a perception of not being in control. Protective behaviours education can also include some training in communication skills, in particular with regard to assertiveness.

The use of worksheets for education in protective behaviours

Following from the previous discussion, it is important that children be able to make decisions so that outcomes for them will be positive in terms of their physical and emotional safety. They also require skills to solve problems if their physical or emotional safety is threatened, and to understand what behaviours are acceptable in society and what behaviours are not. Developing an understanding of limits, expectations and boundaries is also essential. Thus, if children are to develop protective behaviours, it is important that they learn problem-solving skills, decision-making skills and how to set appropriate boundaries.

We believe that these skills can be achieved through the use of worksheets, and have designed worksheets to cover the following three specific areas (see Table 33.1):

1 Setting appropriate boundaries
2 Behaviours for physical protection
3 Behaviours for emotional protection.

As before, the worksheets are intended to provide the stimulus for discussion of the relevant issues.

Setting appropriate boundaries

When helping a child to set appropriate boundaries, it is important for us to take account of the developmental needs of the child and to consider the child's family

TABLE 33.1 *Protective behaviours education worksheets*

Issue addressed	Worksheet number	Title	Page number
Setting	28	Ages & stages	318
appropriate	29	My place, my space	319
boundaries	30	Rainbow road	320
Behaviours for	31	My safety plan	321
physical protection	32	Biffin the bully	322
	33	The three A's	323
Behaviours for	34	Surprises & secrets	324
emotional	35	From blame to fame!	325
protection	36	Crystal ball	326

system and wider social system. Additionally, we can help the child to gain decision-making and problem-solving skills. We have taken all of these factors into account in the design of the following worksheets:

Ages & stages (Worksheet 28, p. 318)

My place, my space (Worksheet 29, p. 319)

Rainbow road (Worksheet 30, p. 320)

Ages & stages presents three vignettes of situations which children might experience and invites a child to consider and to discuss the decisions that children of various ages would need to make. Consequently, the child is encouraged to recognize that appropriate decisions, relevant to a particular situation, might be different for children of different ages. For example, in vignette number one it would be developmentally appropriate for a young child to keep the door locked and seek an adult's help, whereas a teenage child might ask the stranger what he wants, while still protecting himself from danger.

My place, my space explores the issue of privacy within the home. It invites a child to consider what are appropriate personal boundaries, for children of different ages, within a family setting.

Rainbow road is designed to help children to explore social boundaries and to consider the appropriate responses to the variety of people with whom they may come into contact. Children who have a poor understanding of appropriate social boundaries are indiscriminate about the ways in which they greet and relate to strangers or distant associates of their family. By colouring in the blocks at the top of this worksheet, using the rainbow sequence suggested, the child can visually recognize the continuum from intimate closeness to distant relationship. As the child colours in the 'road' from the START box, travelling in a spiral, the colours generally follow a rainbow sequence. However, this sequence is sometimes interrupted, highlighting the need to be alert in recognizing situations in which clear boundaries are needed or when more open boundaries are acceptable. For example, when a child visits the doctor, personal touching for specific medical purposes is acceptable, even though the doctor may not be a close family member.

Behaviours for physical protection

The three worksheets here focus on domestic violence, peer pressure and sexual abuse. The worksheets are:

My safety plan (Worksheet 31, p. 321)

Biffin the bully (Worksheet 32, p. 322)

The three A's – Alert! Avoid! & Action! (Worksheet 33, p. 323)

My safety plan is designed to help children to explore possible outcomes if they become involved in violent or physically threatening situations. It is specifically designed for use with children from violent homes, where it is often difficult for children to know whether to protect themselves or to defend the victim of the violence. The worksheet provides an opportunity for counsellors to help children to realize that the perpetrators of violence are solely responsible for the violence. The worksheet also encourages children to develop individual protection plans for their personal safety.

Biffin the bully aims to help children to label abusive behaviour. Clearly, even though abuse at any level is not OK, some abusive behaviour is not as severe as other abusive behaviour. Using this worksheet, the child is invited to plot abusive behaviours on a continuum from least serious to most serious. The child's attention can then be drawn to the fact that all of the abusive behaviours have been plotted within the international symbol that signifies 'Not Permitted'. A strong message is therefore given that *all abusive behaviour is unacceptable*, no matter how minor it may be. Although the abusive behaviours are attributed to Biffin the bully, the child is invited to consider the possibility that Biffin may change. Hence the child can be encouraged to see that it is the behaviour and not the person who is to be criticized. While using the worksheet, the child can be invited to think about and discuss bullying behaviour they might encounter at school.

The three A's – Alert! Avoid! & Action! targets the protective behaviours which a child might need to use when encountering strangers, or in situations that might be antecedents for sexual abuse. The emphasis is on encouraging the child to be alert to the possibility of danger. The worksheet provides a list of questions children can ask themselves in order to make the best decisions when encountering possible threatening situations. After considering the questions, the child is invited to find a way through a maze in which they can either avoid danger by choosing their route carefully or take action to deal with risky situations. Use of the worksheet gives the child strong permission to avoid situations that may be risky. It also invites them to think about what action they could take if they were to find themselves in a potentially dangerous situation.

Behaviours for emotional protection

When exploring behaviours to prevent emotional trauma we will focus on secrets, victimization and communication skills using the worksheets:

Surprises & secrets (Worksheet 34, p. 324)

From blame to fame! (Worksheet 35, p. 325)

Crystal ball (Worksheet 36, p. 326)

Surprises & secrets can be used to help a child to understand that surprises can be pleasurable, whereas keeping secrets can be uncomfortable. The child can then explore the idea that some secrets are not OK and can consider the consequences of keeping, or disclosing, such secrets.

From blame to fame! explores the issue of victimization. Often, children who see themselves as victims believe that they are trapped in this role and that there is no possibility of change. The worksheet promotes a more positive outlook by encouraging the child to construct assertive statements, which could result in moving the characters in the illustrations from a 'victim' position to a 'hero' position. When using the worksheet, the child is first asked to imagine what each character in the illustrations might be thinking, feeling and might like. We suggest that the counsellor could next invite the child to nominate a powerful hero (for example, Catwoman or Superman). The child can then be asked what that hero might say, using assertive statements beginning with the words, 'I think', 'I feel' and 'I would like' with reference to each illustration.

Crystal ball encourages children to verbalize their needs and to ask for things they have a right to have, rather than hoping that other people will guess or mind-read. The worksheet helps children to explore the pitfalls of guessing how others might feel, or might want. It helps children to recognize that other people, too, are unlikely to be able to guess what it is that they themselves need or want. Consequently, they can learn that in order to get their needs met, they can state them clearly and firmly.

KEY POINTS

- Protective behaviour requires an understanding of appropriate boundaries and the ability to seek assistance in gaining protection from harm.
- Because attitudes regarding boundaries vary between families it is often necessary to involve parents with their children in protective behaviours education.
- It may be necessary to help the child and/or parents recognize differences between social, cultural and family expectations so that appropriate decisions are made regarding boundaries.
- It is usually desirable for parents to be involved in the construction of the child's safety plan so that the child is supported in carrying out the plan.
- It is important for children to be empowered so that they are able to report instances of inappropriate behaviour and to divulge secret information when appropriate.

Part 6

In Conclusion

Although we have written this book as an introductory text, we hope it will be a useful resource for both new workers and experienced counsellors by providing ideas for engaging children in the counselling process and helping them to work through issues. We hope that readers will be able to join their ideas together with ours for a useful purpose.

We have a strong belief in individual difference and in the need to respect the ideas of others. We realize that our readers may have strong commitments to particular theoretical frameworks and therapeutic models. However, we are hopeful that many of the ideas we have described can be adapted to suit different ways of working. We also realize that counselling approaches need to be varied to suit specific cultures, lifestyles, beliefs and values. We have not addressed particular cultural issues in this book, but in this regard refer you to Ivey et al. (2001) and Yan and Wong (2005).

We respect the contributions made by different professions to the work of counselling children and have a strong preference for work with children to occur in multi-disciplinary teams wherever possible. Perhaps this preference has arisen because of our own personal differences. We all have had many years working as counsellors with children and families, but our backgrounds are different. Kathryn initially trained as an occupational therapist, and David and Rebecca as psychologists. In particular, Rebecca is trained as an Educational and Developmental psychologist. We believe that by working together our different backgrounds have significantly helped us to enhance the quality of the work we do with children.

We would like to reiterate that we do not believe that counselling children should be restricted to one profession or one environment. Often, the counselling needs of a child can be met in the child's own environment by those workers, of whatever profession, who have direct access to that environment. For example, we have found that workers in women's refuges are often able to address a child's immediate needs. Similarly, teachers and counsellors in schools, and nurses and medical officers in hospitals, are generally able to provide a level of immediate counselling help, which is especially useful because it addresses the child's needs within their own context. Nevertheless, it is important for workers to recognize their own limitations and to refer children to professionals with more specialized experience and skills when necessary.

We recognize that counsellors in many settings do not have the high standard of facilities that we have enjoyed in our private practice. However, these facilities are not essential. A counsellor armed with drawing paper and pens (see Chapter 25), a box of miniature animals (see Chapter 22), a box of symbols (see Chapter 23) and a few books (see Chapter 27) has all the basic tools needed for useful counselling interventions to occur in any available space. This may not be ideal, but we do not live in an ideal world and a counsellor with some portable aids can be of considerable help in enabling children to tell their story and thus to feel better.

Finally, we would like to stress the importance of training and supervision. This book is not intended to be sufficient in itself, rather it is a source of ideas. We believe that counsellors of children need to be properly trained by experienced and qualified professionals. Additionally, we believe that all counsellors of children need ongoing professional supervision to ensure the quality of their work and to address the needs of specific children. Even though we, the authors, are experienced counsellors, we still regularly discuss individual cases with another competent professional in order to get a different perspective and to keep a check on the influence of our own personal issues. Whether we like to admit it or not, our own issues will from time to time interfere with our counselling work. A good professional supervisor can identify these issues and help us address them so that they will be resolved and will not continue to interfere with our counselling work.

Finally, we wish you, the reader, all the best for your future counselling work and hope that you will get as much satisfaction from counselling children as we have.

Kathryn, David, and Rebecca

Worksheets

I can do anything . . .

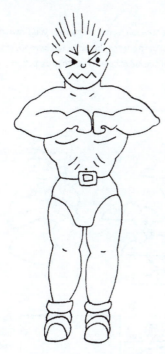

**I AM THE
GIANT KAZOO**
**I CAN MOVE BRIDGES
WITH ONE HAND**

*I am the empress
. . . . and I am
able to . . . .*

**I AM THE WISE ONE
CALLED . . . .
AND I CAN . . . .**

I am the quiet one called . . . .
and I can . . . .

*I am the brave spirit they call . . . .
and I am able to . . . .*

Worksheet 1

Where am I? . . . .

Sometimes we hide parts of ourselves and only let others see what we want them to see. We do this for many reasons. Can you think of some?

Imagine that the tree is you, and the characters around the tree can represent parts of you. Draw lines from those characters which are like you to the tree. Draw a line from the character to the roots of the tree if you hide that part of you, and a line to the branches if you like others to see that part of you.

Can you draw another part of you here? Where does it fit?

Worksheet 2

My Choice . . .

Plot your interests by selecting those activities from the categories below which appeal to you most and placing them on the chart. Do this by using a coloured felt pen to identify a particular activity (put a coloured dot beside the activity). Then put a dot of the same colour on the grid to indicate how much time you spend doing the activity during an average day, and whether you do the activity alone or with others.

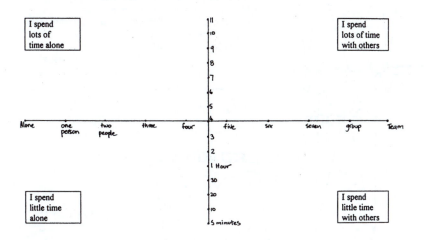

Working	Travelling	Learning	Looking after your body
Housework	Car	School	Eating, sleeping, washing
Chores	Train	Music lessons	Grooming
Shopping	Bus	Visiting counsellor	Exercising: dancing, skateboarding,
Job	Bike	Homework	gym, soccer, surfing, or other sport

Socializing	Relaxing	Being occupied alone
On the phone	Listening to music	Hobbies, e.g. models, craft,
Visiting a friend	Reading	drawing, cooking, collections,
Having a friend over	Daydreaming	jigsaws, Lego, gardening,
Talking with adults	Meditating	magic tricks, playing on the
Playing a game	Watching TV	computer
Helping someone		

You may want to add more . . . .
Look at the chart. What have you discovered about yourself?

Worksheet 3

Inside-Out

Here is a list of things which you may think about, feel emotionally, or experience in your body. Use a red pen to connect the items listed to the figure which would be most affected.

- Eat lots
- Hunch shoulders
- Bite nails
- Feel tense
- Headache
- Hold them in
- Clench teeth
- Pretend that I don't have them
- Let them out when I'm not ready
- Stress out
- Fiddle with things
- Think that people don't like me
- Should work harder
- Stomach ache
- Slouch
- Worry about tomorrow
- Look shabby
- Pretend I've got them (when I really
- Shouldn't take risks   haven't)
- Sleep a lot
- Should behave better
- Think the worst will happen

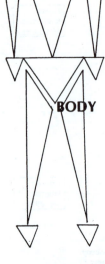

BODY

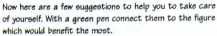

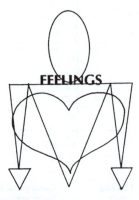

FEELINGS

THOUGHTS

Now here are a few suggestions to help you to take care of yourself. With a green pen connect them to the figure which would benefit the most.

- Ring a friend
- Relaxation
- Watch TV
- Ask for help
- Accept my mistakes
- Tell myself that I am lovable and capable
- Listen to music
- Count to ten
- Remember that I am made up of opposites
- Take a bath
- Read a book
- Bake a cake
- Blow gently 10 times (like blowing out candles)
- Talk to someone else
- Go for a walk

Worksheet 4

NEWS HEADLINES
DAILY COURIER

Today . . . .
committed the worst crime in history.
While the rest of the world slept the
small town of Pinchgut was astounded
at the news that . . . .
. . . .
. . . .
. . . .
. . . .
Many people said . . . .
. . . .
. . . .
. . . .
. . . .
However, a few said . . . .
. . . .
. . . .
. . . .

In a statement by . . . .
it was clear that . . . .
. . . .
. . . .
. . . .
The outcome will be that . . . .
. . . .
will . . . .
. . . .
. . . .
. . . .

Worksheet 5

Changing your mind is OK.

Jump the Hurdle

Changing your mind means that you discover the hurdles which stop you from exploring new and different experiences, and from making new and different choices.

WOULD YOU RATHER crawl through a long dark tunnel to get to the best fun park in the world

OR play with a friendly tiger

Who, or what, would you need to help you so that you could change your mind?

WOULD YOU RATHER
fly an aeroplane

OR drive in the Grand Prix

WOULD YOU RATHER
sit in a tub of live snails

OR walk along a thin bridge over a harmless snake pit

Worksheet 6

BALANCE YOUR LIFE

Each day we find ourselves doing things in one of the categories listed below.

- Occupying ourselves alone
- Relaxing
- Mixing with others socially
- Looking after our bodies
- Learning
- Working
- Travelling

Colour the box red for the category which best fits with what you are doing now . . . .
GREAT!! You've got the knack . . . . . NOW . . . . . . Begin the daily journey below - each time
when you come to a blank square draw in it the symbol which best represents what you
would be doing at that time.

SCHOOL DAY

START	Get out of bed				Go into class			Morning break

Arrive home			Time to go home			Lunch		Back to class

					Go to bed		

WEEKEND DAY

START	Get out of bed							Lunch

Dinner								

					Go to bed		

What would you like to change?

Worksheet 7

These are my wishes . . .

Wish 1, for today . . . .

Wish 2, for tomorrow . . . .
. . . .

And then wish 3, for the future. .
. . . .

Picture yourself ... then, now, and in the future

At each stage on the time-line write down:

1. What you have achieved or what you hope to achieve.
2. Who, or what, you need or needed to help you achieve these things.
3. Mark an X to show where you are now.

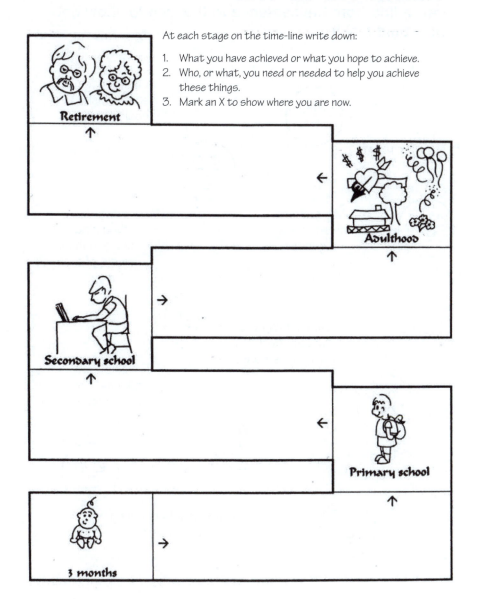

Worksheet 9

Find A Feeling

Draw a line from the sentence to the face to show how you would feel if . . .

I had a bad
secret which I
couldn't tell

My pet was
run over

My mother
talked to the
neighbour

I heard a
thumping
noise in the
middle of the
night

I wasn't allowed
to stay over at
my friend's house

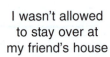

I fell off my
bike in front
of my friends

I didn't study
for my spelling test

I was caught cheating
on my test

Worksheet 10

Artemus is Anxious !

Can you help Artemus find out what makes him feel anxious?

Artemus is a bit like you . . .

Draw a line from Artemus to the things which make him feel anxious.

- Going to the doctor or dentist

- Being called to the Principal's office

- Wondering whether Mum or Dad will be in a good mood tonight

- Not understanding the rules of a game

- Having to ask questions in class

- Remembering what time you have to be home

- The spelling test tomorrow

- . . . .

Worksheet 11

Guess what?

Worksheet 12

Your Body

We can guess how people feel from the way they use
their bodies and the expressions on their faces.
How do these people feel?
Circle the body part used to express the feeling.

Worksheet 13

THE VOLCANO

What makes you angry?

I get angry when . . . .

Find the spot on the volcano which is most like you when you get angry.

EXPLODE

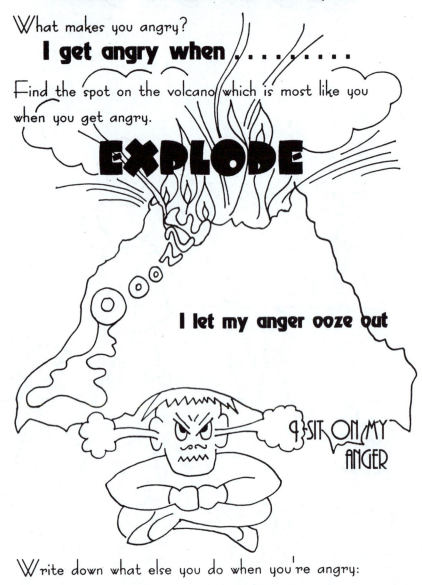

I let my anger ooze out

I SIT ON MY ANGER

Write down what else you do when you're angry:

. . . .

Worksheet 14

Fighting FEAR with Felix

Everyone feels frightened sometimes. Some things are more scary than others. Draw a red line from Felix's head to a spot on the life saver to show what you would do in each of the following scenes if you were scared.

Mum & Dad fighting

A stranger asks me directions

Fierce dogs

Telling a BAD secret

Getting into trouble

Getting lost

Missing the bus

Sports day

Being bullied

Going to the doctor's to get an injection

Having a bad dream

Getting a bad report card

TELL SOMEONE · CRY · HIDE · GET TOGETHER WITH SOMEONE ELSE · FREEZE · SCREAM · FIND AN ADULT · PRETEND I'M NOT SCARED

Feel OK

Conversation starters

Put a tick in the box next to the conversation
starters which would be OK to use on your first day
at a new school.

.... what's wrong with
the conversation starters
you haven't ticked?

?? QUESTIONS ??

Look at this picture. Ask three questions beginning with:

a) What . . . .   d) When . . . .

b) Where . . . .   e) Why . . . .

c) How . . . .   f) Who . . . .

to find out more about it.

Worksheet 17

Advice for JIM

Jim needs help. He has a brother who always gets to go with Uncle Ben. Jim's brother is often invited to spend the night with Uncle Ben, so that he can get up early and help his uncle on the farm.

Every time Jim asks to go, Uncle Ben says, 'Next time. You're a bit young yet.'

- What do you do when you feel left out?
- Put a circle around your answers.

GET ANGRY

cry

Make a FUSS, so that people pay attention

TELL SOMEONE
HOW I FEEL

Don't say anything

GERTRUDE & GROMMET GUMBO
THE GOSSIPS

The Gumbos say untrue things about people to other people
= THEY GOSSIP =
Gossiping can hurt and make you feel left out.

If people ask you questions about others you might get caught gossiping.
Here's a good rule:

IF YOU CAN'T SAY SOMETHING NICE – DON'T SAY ANYTHING AT ALL

Tick the things you could do or say if people try to gossip.
- ☐ 'Let's talk about something else.'
- ☐ 'I don't know them very well, so I can't know if that's true.'
- ☐ 'I think you're gossiping.'

Tick the things you could do if people gossip about you.
- ☐ Gossip about them (it would serve them right!).
- ☐ Talk to the 'Gumbo' gossipers, and ask them not to gossip.
- ☐ Ask someone to help you to solve your problem.

Worksheet 19

FIGHTING !! ! ! !

Fights happen when people:

TEASE	GOSSIP	TELL TALES
CHEAT	STEAL	SHOVE
BULLY	LIE	HIT
BREAK PROMISES	SHOW OFF	DON'T BELIEVE

See if you can find these words in the square below and circle them:

A	N	C	F	H	M	P	Q	U	W	A	B
B	R	E	A	K	P	R	O	M	I	S	E
Z	L	B	U	L	L	Y	A	T	S	P	Q
F	G	K	T	E	L	L	T	A	L	E	S
O	E	S	T	E	A	L	O	Q	F	R	S
G	L	C	Z	X	D	S	P	A	W	K	I
M	R	H	F	S	C	H	I	T	L	O	A
P	N	E	B	K	G	O	S	S	I	P	W
W	I	A	D	P	H	V	X	Z	E	D	J
Z	D	T	E	A	S	E	J	B	A	J	Z
K	S	H	O	W	O	F	F	H	W	B	I
X	D	O	N	T	B	E	L	I	E	V	E

When you were in a fight, what caused it? . . . .
. . . .
. . . .

Can you think of any more reasons why fights happen? . . . .
. . . .

Worksheet 20

TERRY, TYRONE AND ME

We can choose to respond to people who want to fight by asserting ourselves in a firm but non-threatening way.

Join the dots to find Terry.

What do you think would happen if Terry got into a fight?

Join the dots to find Tyrone.

What do you think would happen if Tyrone got into a fight?

Write on the dotted lines what you would do if you got into a fight.

Worksheet 21

LOOK BEFORE YOU LEAP

	True	False		True	False
Sometimes I say things and later regret it			Sometimes I make a decision without thinking		
Sometimes I do things without listening to the rules			Sometimes I go ahead without reading the instructions		
Sometimes I don't listen to both sides of the argument			Sometimes I make arrangements without listening to the details		
Sometimes I take messages and leave out most of the information					

If you answered 'true' for 5 or more of the above then you need to 'chill out'

Chilling out means going slow, not hurrying and using the
STOP – THINK – DO plan.

STOP – and discover what the problem or task is.

THINK – of three things you can do to solve the problem or task.

DO – Choose the one which is best for you.

Worksheet 22

Choices & Options

There are many ways to respond when we have trouble with our friends.

* Take a coloured pen & trace the path you would like to take if you were Sue. At each decision box, think about how you might feel when making a choice.
* In a different colour trace a path you would like to try.

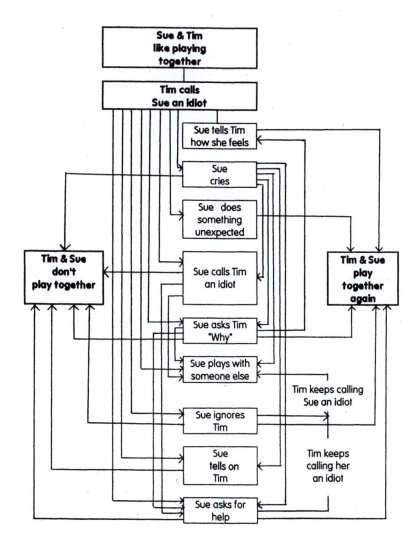

Worksheet 23

If - Then - But

Fill in the blanks! Here is an example:

If I borrowed my mum's bike without permission,
Then . . . I would get to the video shop faster,
But . . . I'd probably be grounded for the weekend.

Now fill in the missing parts of the following 'if – then - buts'.

If I cheated in my spelling test.
Then . . .
But . . .

If I skipped school tomorrow,
Then . . .
But . . .

If I tell my best friend that she hurt my feelings,
Then . . .
But . . .

If I spend all the money I earned doing jobs, on one item,
Then . . .
But . . .

If I tell this secret I have,
Then . . .
But . . .

If I stay home and study for my test,
Then . . .
But . . .

Worksheet 24

CRIME & PUNISHMENT !

Here is a list of behaviours. Some are worse than others. The really bad behaviours would probably result in severe consequences.

- Rearrange the list in order of the worst to the mildest.
- On your list, write the punishment or consequence, which you believe fits the 'crime'.

CRIME	My list	Consequence
Murder		
Back-chatting		
Hitting		
Lying		
Stealing		
Interrupting		
Disobeying		
Bullying		
Name calling		
Gossiping		
Cheating		
Keeping secrets		
Telling tales		
Changing your mind		

Saying 'No' ... made easy

Match the responses you would use to the requests!
Draw a line to join them together.

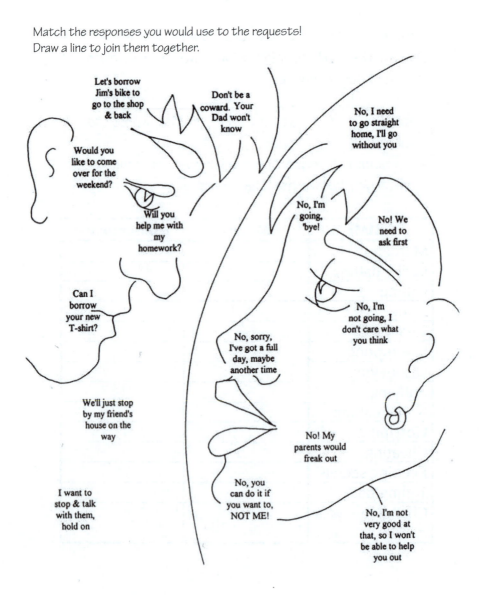

REWARD YOURSELF

We often don't realize that we can be proud of many of the things we do or say. In each of the shields below, write or draw something you feel proud of, and could tell somebody about.

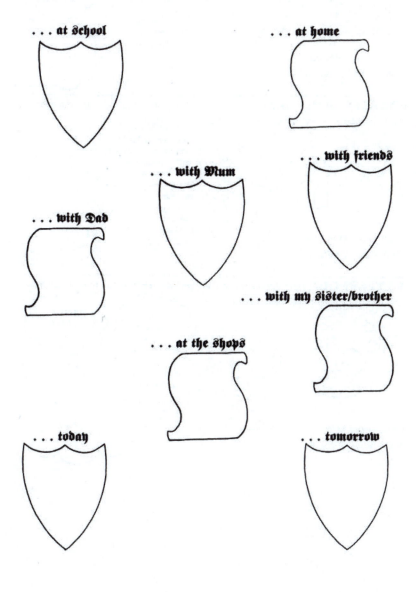

Worksheet 27

AGES & STAGES

4 YEARS OLD: Miffy is 4 years old. Help Miffy to make the right decision about what to do when someone knocks on the door.

Smile & invite the stranger inside

Open the door & go & get a grown-up

Slam the door shut & run away

What would Taffy do?
What would Vanda do?

8 YEARS OLD: Taffy is 8 years old. Help Taffy to make the right decision about how to respond to Mr Nice at Church on Sunday.

Let him put his arm around me & ruffle my hair like he always does

Avoid him all morning. I could hide behind the wall!!

What would Miffy do?
What would Vanda do?

14 YEARS OLD: Help Vanda make the right decision about how to respond to Burford, a new friend, next door.

I'll let him kiss me today

We can stay out late & talk

I'm going to ignore him completely

What would Miffy do?
What would Taffy do?

My Place, My Space

Test your respect for privacy by circling true or false in response to the following questions:

- Toby is two years old. He should be allowed to bath on his own so that he has privacy.

    True   **False**

- Tina is sixteen years old. She needs to be able to spend time alone in her room if she wants to.

    True   **False**

- Simon is nine years old. If his bedroom door is closed, members of his family should knock before going in.

    True   **False**

- Mum & Dad should always be supervised by someone when they are together.

    True   **False**

- Samantha is thirteen years old. Everyone in the family should be allowed to read her diary without asking.

    True   **False**

- Matthew is four years old. When he is playing alone in the front yard his family should leave him by himself if he tells them to go away.

    True   **False**

- Roberta is seven years old. She should always let her uncle shower with her when he is visiting.

    True   **False**

Worksheet 29

RAINBOW ROAD

The boxes below represent the different ways in which we greet, or make contact with other people. Colour the boxes in as indicated.

Touch private places (Red)	Cuddle (Orange)	Hug (Yellow)	Shake hands (Green)	Wave (Blue)	Watch (Dark Blue)	Ignore (Purple)

Sophie is your age & she is getting ready to go out. Along the way, she will meet many people. Sophie will need to decide how to greet these people. Can you help her? Follow Sophie's journey from the START box below. As you go, colour each box to match with the colours above, to show how you think Sophie should greet the people on her journey.

DR DRAKE	TAXI DRIVER	LADY AT THE BUS STOP	TICKET SELLER	MAN WALKING HIS DOG
BUS DRIVER	DAD	AUNTY JO	UNCLE BOB	MAN IN A CAR
SHOP KEEPER	MUM	START ←ME	NEIGHBOUR	
DAY CARE PERSON	TEACHER	BEST FRIEND	BOY NEXT DOOR	

My SAFETY Plan

Sometimes in families where adults fight, younger children may also get hurt. Mason lives in a family like this. Below are plans that Mason could use to look after himself. Follow the path that you think will lead to the best SAFETY PLAN for Mason, so that he can protect himself from being hurt.

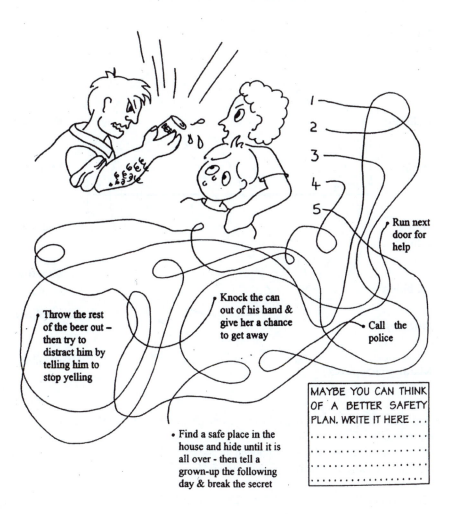

Worksheet 31

BIFFIN THE BULLY

The words outside the circle describe abusive acts, things that BIFFIN THE BULLY might do.
Write each word along the line inside the circle. Place the words on the line from left to right according to how serious you think the abuse is.

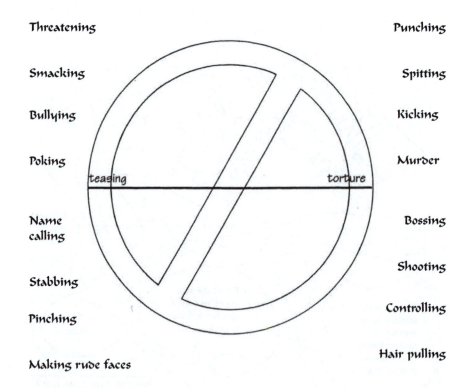

Threatening

Smacking

Bullying

Poking

teasing   torture

Name
calling

Stabbing

Pinching

Making rude faces

Punching

Spitting

Kicking

Murder

Bossing

Shooting

Controlling

Hair pulling

- Did you notice that all the words are now inside a symbol which means 'not permitted'?
- How many of these behaviours happen at the school?
- Can you add any other bullying behaviours?

- DO YOU THINK THAT 'BIFFIN THE BULLY' CAN CHANGE?

Worksheet 32

The three A's - ALERT! AVOID! & ACTION!

Keeping physically safe sometimes means knowing how to protect your body from being hurt even when everything 'seems' OK. Have you ever felt as though you know that something isn't right but you can't put your finger on it? Taking notice of that feeling is called being *ALERT*.

Find your way through the maze below. You can *AVOID* risky situations by taking a path without obstacles. Alternatively, you can deal with obstacles by making decisions and then taking *ACTION* in order to stay safe.

As you travel through the maze, ask yourself these questions:
QUESTIONS:
- Is this person someone I know?
- When I am with this person do I feel safe and not worried?
- Will I be able to get help if things get out of control?
- Does Mum or Dad or someone else I can trust know where I am and will be?

If the answer to any of these questions is 'No', then use one of the following options:
OPTIONS:
- Say, 'No, stop that!'
- Make a fuss
- Tell an adult

- Walk away
- Run to the nearest safety house
- . . . .

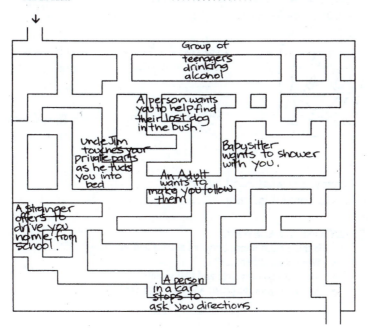

Worksheet 33

SURPRISES & SECRETS

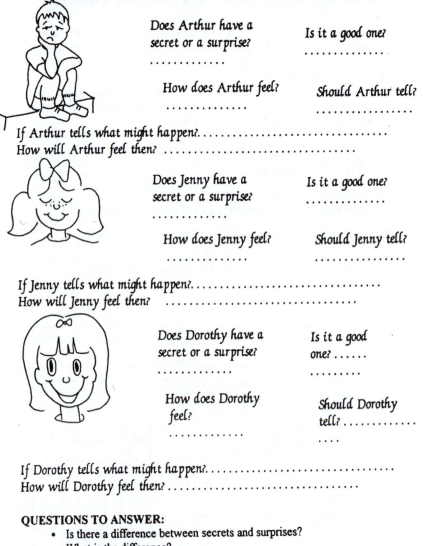

Does Arthur have a
secret or a surprise?

. . . .

Is it a good one?

. . . .

How does Arthur feel?

. . . .

Should Arthur tell?

. . . .

If Arthur tells what might happen? . . . .

How will Arthur feel then? . . . .

Does Jenny have a
secret or a surprise?

. . . .

Is it a good one?

. . . .

How does Jenny feel?

. . . .

Should Jenny tell?

. . . .

If Jenny tells what might happen? . . . .

How will Jenny feel then? . . . .

Does Dorothy have a
secret or a surprise?

. . . .

Is it a good
one? . . . . . .

. . . .

How does Dorothy
feel?

. . . .

Should Dorothy
tell? . . . .

. . . .

If Dorothy tells what might happen? . . . .

How will Dorothy feel then? . . . .

QUESTIONS TO ANSWER:

- Is there a difference between secrets and surprises?
- What is the difference?
- Are there good secrets and bad secrets?
- Are there good surprises and bad surprises?

Worksheet 34

From BLAME to FAME !

Sometimes when we feel picked on, we blame others for how we feel and behave.
If we tackle the problem ourselves, we generally feel better.

Making statements that begin with:

* I think . . . . . .
* I feel . . . .
* I would like it if . . . . .

is a good way to start.

What do you think that you would say in the examples below?

	◆ Tony thinks that Bosco expects him to fetch things for him all the time. ◆ It makes him feel used and worthless. ◆ He'd like to help Bosco sometimes but would like to say, 'No' at other times. ◆ He'd also like Bosco to say, 'Please' and 'Thankyou'.	I think . . . . . . I feel . . . . I would like it if . . . .
	♣ Jack is the youngest in the family and **always** has to clean the family's shoes. ♣ His brothers did do this when they were his age. ♣ He feels like he's missing out on doing other things, and also that this job isn't very important. ♣ He'd like to do a different job sometimes, instead of the same one over and over.	I think . . . . . . I feel . . . . . . I would like it if . . . .
	♥ Tina is the only girl in the family. ♥ She is always having to look after her younger brother when her parents are busy. ♥ Tina loves her brother, but she doesn't get much time for herself and her friends. ♥ Tina has 2 older brothers. They all get along with their baby brother really well.	I think . . . . . . I feel . . . . I would like it if . . . .

Worksheet 35

CRYSTAL BALL

- By looking into the crystal ball you might GUESS how Kristel is feeling and also guess what it is that she wants.

- What could Kristel say so that you would KNOW what she felt and wanted?

Worksheet 36

Bibliography

Adler, A. (1964) *Social Interest: A Challenge to Mankind*. New York: Capricorn.

Alford, B.A. (1995) 'Introduction to the special issue: psychotherapy integration and cognitive psychotherapy', *Journal of Cognitive Psychotherapy*, 9: 147–51.

Athanassiadou, E., Tsiantis, J., Christogiorgos, S. and Kolaitis, G. (2009) 'An evaluation of the effectiveness of psychological preparation of children for minor surgery by puppet play and brief mother counseling', *Psychotherapy and Psychosomatics*, 78: 62–3.

Australian Psychological Society (2007) *Code of Ethics*. Melbourne: Author.

Australian Psychological Society (2009) *Ethical Guidelines* (9th ed.). Melbourne: Author.

Axline, V. (1947) *Play Therapy*. Boston: Houghton Mifflin.

Baggerly, J.N. (2004) 'The effects of child-centered group play therapy on self-concept, depression, and anxiety of children who are homeless', *International Journal of Play Therapy*, 13(2): 31–51.

Baggerly, J.N. and Bratton, S. (2010) 'Building a firm foundation in play therapy research: response to Phillips (2010)', *International Journal of Play Therapy*, 19(1): 26–38.

Baggerly, J.N. and Jenkins, W.W. (2009) 'The effectiveness of child-centered play therapy on developmental and diagnostic factors in children who are homeless', *International Journal of Play Therapy*, 18(1): 45–55.

Bandler, R. (1985) *Using Your Brain for a Change: Neuro-linguistic Programming*. Moab: Real People Press.

Bandler, R. and Grinder, J. (1982) *Reframing*. Moab: Real People Press.

Bauer, G. and Kobos, J. (1995) *Brief Therapy: Short Term Psychodynamic Intervention*. New Jersey: Aronson.

Bay-Hinitz, A.K., Peterson, R.F. and Quilitch, H.R. (1994) 'Cooperative games: a way to modify aggressive and cooperative behaviours in young children', *Journal of Applied Behavior Analysis*, 27(3): 435–46.

Beck, A.T. (1963) 'Thinking and depressions: 1. Idiosyncratic content and cognitive distortions', *Archives of General Psychiatry*, 9: 324–33.

Beck, A.T. (1976) 'Cognitive therapy and the emotional disorders', *Archives of General Psychiatry*, 41: 1112–14.

Beebe, A., Gelfand, E.W. and Bender, B. (2010) 'A randomized trial to test the effectiveness of art therapy for children with asthma', *The Journal of Allergy and Clinical Immunology*, 126(2): 263–6.

Bond, T. (1992) 'Ethical issues in counselling in education', *British Journal of Guidance & Counselling*, 20(1): 51-63.

Bowlby, J. (1969) *Attachment*. New York: Basic Books.

Bowlby, J. (1988) *A Secure Base*. New York: Basic Books.

Braverman, S. (1995) 'The integration of individual and family therapy', *Contemporary Family Therapy: An International Journal*, 17: 291–305.

Brewer, S., Gleditsch, S.L., Syblik, D., Tietjens, M.E. and Vacik, H.W. (2006) 'Pediatric anxiety: child life intervention in day surgery', *Journal of Pediatric Nursing*, 21(1): 13–22.

British Association for Counselling and Psychotherapy (2010) *Ethical Framework for Good Practice in Counselling and Psychotherapy*. Lutterworth: Author.

British Association of Play Therapists (2008) *An Ethical Basis for Good Practice in Play Therapy* (3rd ed.). Weybridge: Author.

British Psychological Society (2002) *Professional Practice Guidelines: Division of Educational and Child Psychology*. Leicester: Author.

British Psychological Society (2007) *Child Protection Position Paper*. Leicester: Author.

British Psychological Society (2009) *Code of Ethics and Conduct*. Leicester: Author.

Bucci, W. (1995) 'The power of the narrative: a multiple code account', in J.W. Pennebaker (ed.), *Emotion, Disclosure, and Health*. Washington, DC: American Psychological Association.

Burroughs, M.S., Wagner, W.W. and Johnson, J.T. (1997) 'Treatment with children of divorce: a comparison of two types of therapy', *Journal of Divorce & Remarriage*, 27(3/4): 83–99.

Cade, B. (1993) *A Brief Guide to Brief Therapy*. New York: Norton.

Caselman, T.D. (2005) 'Stop and think: an impulse control program in a school setting', *School Social Work Journal*, 30 (1): 40–60.

Cattanach, A. (2003) *Introduction to Play Therapy*. New York: Brunner-Routledge.

Chantler, K. (2005) 'From disconnection to connection: "Race", gender and the politics of therapy', *British Journal of Guidance & Counselling*, 33(2): 239–56.

Chemtob, C.M., Nakashima, J.P. and Hamada, R.S. (2002) 'Psychosocial intervention for postdisaster trauma symptoms in elementary school children: a controlled community field study', *Archives of Pediatrics & Adolescent Medicine*, 156: 211–16.

Christ, G.H., Siegel, K., Mesagno, F. and Langosch, D. (1991) 'A preventative program for bereaved children: problems of implementation', *Journal of Orthopsychiatry*, 61: 168–78.

Clarkson, F. (1989) *Gestalt Counselling in Action*. London: Sage.

Colwell, C.M., Davis, K. and Schroeder, L.K. (2005) 'The effect of composition (art or music) on the self-concept of hospitalized children', *Journal of Music Therapy*, 42(1): 49–63.

Copeland, W.E., Keeler, G., Angold, A. and Costello, J. (2007) 'Traumatic events and post-traumatic stress in childhood', *Archives of General Psychiatry*, 64: 577–84.

Corsini, R.J. and Wedding, D. (eds) (2004) *Current Psychotherapies* (7th ed.). Illinois: Peacock.

Culley, S. (1991) *Integrative Counselling Skills in Action*. London: Sage.

Dale, E.M. (1990) 'The psychoanalytic psychotherapy of children with emotional and behavioural difficulties', in V.P. Varma (ed.), *The Management of Children with Emotional and Behavioural Difficulties*. London: Routledge.

Davison, G.C. (1995) *Abnormal Psychology* (6th ed.). New York: Wiley.

Dene, M. (1980) 'Paradoxes in the therapeutic relationship', *The Gestalt Journal*, 3(1): 5–7.

De Shazer, S. (1985) *Keys to Solution in Brief Therapy*. New York: Norton.

Dougherty, J. and Ray, D. (2007) 'Differential impact of play therapy on developmental levels of children', *International Journal of Play Therapy*, 16(1): 2–19.

Driessnack, M. (2005) 'Children's drawings as facilitators of communication: a meta-analysis', *Journal of Pediatric Nursing*, 20(6): 415–23.

Dryden, W. (1990) *Rational Emotive Counselling in Action*. London: Sage.

Dryden, W. (1995) *Brief Rational Emotive Behaviour Therapy*. London: Wiley.

Duncan, B.L., Hubble, M.A. and Miller, S.D. (1997) *Psychotherapy with Impossible Cases: Efficient Treatment of Therapy Veterans*. New York: Norton.

Ehly, S. and Dustin, R. (1989) *Individual and Group Counseling in Schools*. New York: Guilford.

Ellerton, M.-L. and Merriam, C. (1994) 'Preparing children and families psychologically for day surgery: an evaluation', *Journal of Advanced Nursing*, 19: 1057–62.

Ellis, A. (1962) *Reason and Emotion in Psychotherapy*. New York: LyleStuart.

Erikson, E. (1967) *Childhood and Society* (2nd ed.). London: Penguin.

Ernst, A.A., Weiss, S.J., Enright-Smith, S. and Hansen, J.P. (2008) 'Positive outcomes from an immediate and ongoing intervention for child witnesses of intimate partner violence', *American Journal of Emergency Medicine*, 26: 389–94.

Fantuzzo, J., Manz, P., Atkins, M. and Meyers, R. (2005) 'Peer-mediated treatment of socially withdrawn maltreated preschool children: cultivating natural community resources', *Journal of Clinical Child and Adolescent Psychology*, 34(2): 320–5.

Fantuzzo, J., Sutton-Smith, B., Atkins, M., Meyers, R., Stevenson, H., Coolahan, K. and Manz, P. (1996) 'Community-based resilient peer treatment of withdrawn maltreated preschool children', *Journal of Consulting and Clinical Psychology*, 64(6): 1377–86.

Fatout, M.F. (1996) *Children in Groups: A Social Work Perspective*. Westport, CT: Auburn House.

Favara-Scacco, C., Smirne, G., Schiliro, G. and Di Cataldo, A. (2001) 'Art therapy as support for children with Leukemia during painful procedures', *Medical and Pediatric Oncology*, 36: 474–80.

Felder-Puig, R., Maksys, A., Noestlinger, C., Gadner, H., Stark, H., Pfluegler, A. and Topf, R. (2003) 'Using a children's book to prepare children and parents for elective ENT surgery: results of a randomized clinical trial', *International Journal of Pediatric Otorhinolaryngology*, 67: 35–41.

Freud, A. (1928) *Introduction to the Technique of Child Analysis*. Trans. L.P. Clark. New York: Nervous and Mental Disease Publishing.

Garaigordobil, M., Maganto, C. and Etxeberria, J. (1996) 'Effects of a cooperative game program on socio-affective relations and group cooperation capacity', *European Journal of Psychological Assessment*, 12(2): 141–52.

Garza, Y. and Bratton, S. C. (2005) 'School-based child-centered play therapy with Hispanic children: outcomes and cultural considerations', *International Journal of Play Therapy*, 14(1): 51–79.

Geldard, K. and Geldard, D. (2001) *Working with Children in Groups: A Handbook for Counsellors, Educators and Community Workers*. Basingstoke: Palgrave Macmillan.

Geldard, K. and Geldard, D. (2010) *Counselling Adolescents: The Pro-active Approach* (3rd ed.). London: Sage.

Geldard, K., Yin Foo, R. and Shakespeare-Finch, J. (2009) 'How is a fruit tree like you? Using artistic metaphors to explore and develop emotional competence in children', *Australian Journal of Guidance and Counselling*, 19(1): 1–13.

Glasser, W. (1965) *Reality Therapy*. New York: Harper & Row.

Glasser, W. (2000) *Reality Therapy in Action*. New York: HarperCollins.

Gold, J.R. (1994) 'When the patient does the integrating: lessons for theory and practice', *Journal of Psychotherapy Integration*, 4: 133–58.

Goldfried, M.R. and Castonguay, L.C. (1992) 'The future of psychotherapy integration. Special Issue: The future of psychotherapy', *Psychotherapy*, 29: 4–10.

Goymour, K.-L., Stephenson, C., Goodenough, B. and Boulton, C. (2000) 'Evaluating the role of play therapy in the paediatric emergency department', *Australian Emergency Nursing Journal,* 3(2): 10–12.

Gupta, M.R., Hariton, J.R. and Kernberg, P.F. (1996) 'Diagnostic groups for schoolage children: group behaviour and DSM-IV diagnosis', in P. Kymissis and D.A. Halperin (eds), *Group Therapy with Children and Adolescents.* Washington, DC: American Psychiatric Press Inc.

Gutheil, T.G. and Gabbard, G.O. (1993) 'The concept of boundaries in clincial practice: theoretical and risk-management dimensions', *The American Journal of Psychiatry,* 150(2): 188–96.

Hall, A.S. and Lin, M.-J. (1995) 'Theory and practice of children's rights: implications for mental health counselors', *Journal of Mental Health Counseling,* 17(1): 63–80.

Hallowell, L.M., Stewart, S.E., de Amorim e Silva, C.T. and Ditchfield, M.R. (2008) 'Reviewing the process of preparing children for MRI', *Pediatric Radiology,* 38: 271–9.

Hamre, H.J., Witt, C.M., Glockmann, A., Ziegler, R., Willich, S.N. and Kiene, H. (2007) 'Anthroposophic art therapy in chronic disease: a four-year prospective cohort study', *Explore,* 3: 365–71.

Hanney, L. and Kozlowska, K. (2002) 'Healing traumatized children: creating illustrated storybooks in family therapy', *Family Process,* 41(1): 37–65.

Hatava, P., Olsson, G.L. and Lagerkranser, M. (2000) 'Preoperative psychological preparation for children undergoing ENT operations: a comparison of two methods', *Paediatric Anaesthesia,* 10: 477–86.

Heidemann, S. and Hewitt, D. (1992) *Pathways to Play.* Minnesota: Redleaf Press.

Henry, S. (1992) *Group Skills in Social Work* (2nd ed.). Pacific Grove, CA: Brooks/Cole.

Ivey, A.E., D'Andrea, M., Ivey, M.B. and Simek-Morgan, L. (2001) *Theories of Counseling and Psychotherapy: A Multi-cultural Perspective.* Needham Heights, MA: Simon & Schuster.

Jacobson, N.S. (1994) 'Behaviour therapy and psychotherapy integration. Society for the Exploration of Psychotherapy Integration (1993, New York: New York)', *Journal of Psychotherapy Integration,* 4: 105–19.

Jones, E.M. and Landreth, G. (2002) 'The efficacy of intensive individual play therapy for chronically ill children', *International Journal of Play Therapy,* 11(1): 117–40.

Jung, C. (1933) *Modern Man in Search of a Soul.* New York: Harcourt Brace.

Kaduson, H.G. and Finnerty, K. (1995) 'Self-control game interventions for Attention-Deficit Hyperactivity Disorder', *International Journal of Play Therapy,* 4(2): 15–29.

Kain, Z.N., Caramico, L.A., Mayes, L.C., Genevro, J.L., Bornstein, M.H and Hofstadter, M.B. (1998) 'Preoperative preparation programs in children: a comparative examination', *Anesthesia & Analgesia,* 87: 1249–55.

Karcher, M.J. and Shenita, S.L. (2002) 'Pair counseling: the effects of a dyadic developmental play therapy on interpersonal understanding and externalising behaviors', *International Journal of Play Therapy,* 11(1): 19–41.

Karver, M.S., Handelsman, J.B., Fields, S. and Bickman, L. (2006) 'Meta-analysis of therapeutic relationship variables in youth and family therapy: the evidence for different relationship variables in the child and adolescent treatment outcome literature', *Clinical Psychology Review,* 26: 50–65.

Klein, M. (1932) *Psychoanalysis of Children.* London: Hogarth Press.

Kohlberg, L. (1969) 'Stage and sequence: the cognitive developmental approach to socialization', in D. Groslin (ed.), *Handbook of Socialization Theory and Research.* Chicago: Rand McNally.

Koocher, G.P. and Keith-Spiegel, P. (2008) *Ethics in Psychology and the Mental Health Professions: Standards and Cases*. Oxford: Oxford University Press.

Kool, R. and Lawver, T. (2010) 'Play therapy: considerations and applications for the practitioner', *Psychiatry*, 7(10): 19–24.

Kot, S., Landreth, G. and Giordano, M. (1998) 'Intensive child-centered play therapy with child witnesses of domestic violence', *International Journal of Play Therapy*, 7(2): 17–36.

Kraft, I. (1996) 'History', in P. Kymissis and D.A. Halperin (eds), *Group Therapy with Children and Adolescents*. Washington DC: American Psychological Association.

Kymissis, P. (1996) 'Developmental approach to socialization and group formation', in P. Kymissis and D.A. Halperin (eds), *Group Therapy with Children and Adolescents*. Washington, DC: American Psychiatric Press Inc.

Lambert, M.J. (1992) 'Psychotherapy outcome research: implications for integrative and eclectic therapists', in J.C. Norcross and M.R. Goldfried (eds), *Handbook of Psychotherapy Integration*. New York: Basic Books.

Lambert, M.J. and Ogles, B M. (2004) 'The efficacy and effectiveness of psychotherapy', in M.J. Lambert (ed.), *Bergin and Garfield's Handbook of Psychotherapy and Behavior Change* (5th ed.). New York: John Wiley & Sons, Inc.

Lawrence, G. and Robinson Kurpius, S.E. (2000) 'Legal and ethical issues involved when counseling minors in nonschool settings', *Journal of Counseling & Development*, 78(2): 130–6.

Lazarus, A. and Fay, A. (1990) 'Brief psychotherapy: tautology or oxymoron?', in J. Zeig and S. Gilligan (eds), *Brief Therapy: Myths, Methods and Metaphors*. New York: Brunner/Mazel.

Leebert, H. (2006) 'Reflections on … the colour blindness of counselling', *Healthcare Counselling & Psychotherapy Journal*, 6(4): 4–5.

Legoff, D.B. and Sherman, M. (2006) 'Long-term outcome of social skills intervention based on interactive LEGO play', *Autism*, 10(4): 317–29.

Lendrum, S. (2004) 'Satisfactory endings in therapeutic relationships: Part 2', *Healthcare Counselling & Psychotherapy Journal*, 4(3): 31–5.

Li, H.C.W. (2007) 'Evaluating the effectiveness of preoperative interventions: the appropriateness of using the children's emotional manifestation scale', *Journal of Clinical Nursing*, 16: 1919–26.

Li, H.C.W. and Lopez, V. (2008) 'Effectiveness and appropriateness of therapeutic play intervention in preparing children for surgery: a randomized controlled trial study', *Journal for Specialists in Pediatric Nursing*, 13(2): 63–73.

Li, H.C.W., Lopez, V. and Lee, T.L.I. (2007a) 'Effects of preoperative therapeutic play on outcomes of school-age children undergoing day surgery', *Research in Nursing & Health*, 30: 320–32.

Li, H.C.W., Lopez, V. and Lee, T.L.I. (2007b) 'Psychoeducational preparation of children for surgery: the importance of parental involvement', *Patient Education and Counseling*, 65, 34–41.

Lowenfeld, M. (1967) *Play in Childhood*. New York: Wiley.

Lynch, M. (1994) 'Preparing children for day surgery', *Children's Health Care*, 23(2): 75–85.

Macner-Licht, B., Rajalingam, V. and Bernard-Opitz, V. (1998) 'Childhood Leukaemia: towards an integrated psychosocial intervention programme in Singapore', *Annals of the Academy of Medicine, Singapore*, 27(4): 485–90.

Macy, R.D., Macy, D.J., Gross, S.I. and Brighton, P. (2003) 'Healing in familiar settings: support for children and youth in the classroom and community', *New Directions for Youth Development*, 98: 51–79.

Madden, J.R., Mowry, P., Gao, D., McGuire Cullen, P. and Foreman, N.K. (2010) 'Creative arts therapy improves quality of life for pediatric brain tumor patients receiving out-patient chemotherapy', *Journal of Pediatric Oncology Nursing,* 27(3): 133–45.

Malekoff, A. (1997) *Groupwork with Adolescents,* New York: Guilford.

Margolis, J.O., Ginsberg, B., Dear, G.D.L., Ross, A.K., Goral, J.E. and Bailey, A.G. (1998) 'Paediatric preoperative teaching: effects at induction and postoperatively', *Paediatric Anaesthesia,* 8: 17–23.

Martin, J. (1994) *The Construction and Understanding of Psychotherapeutic Change.* New York: Teachers College Press.

McMahon, L. (1992) *The Handbook of Play Therapy.* London: Routledge.

Maslow, A.H. (1954) *Motivation and Personality.* New York: Harper.

Miller, D.E. (2004) *The Stop Think Do Program.* Longwood, FL: Xulon.

Millman, H. and Schaefer, C.E. (1977) *Therapies for Children.* San Francisco: Jossey-Bass.

Miner, M.H. (2006) 'A proposed comprehensive model for ethical decision-making (EDM)', in S. Morrissey and P. Reddy (eds), *Ethics and Professional Practice for Psychologists.* South Melbourne: Thomson Social Science Press.

Mitchell, C.W., Disque, J.G. and Robertson, P. (2002) 'When parents want to know: responding to parental demands for confidential information', *Professional School Counseling,* 6(2): 156.

Morgan, A. (2000) *What is Narrative Therapy?* Adelaide: Dulwich Centre.

Nabors, L., Ohms, M., Buchanan, N., Kirsh, K.L., Nash, T., Passik, S.D. and Brown, G. (2004) 'A pilot study of the impact of a grief camp for children', *Palliative and Supportive Care,* 2: 403–8.

Oaklander, V. (1988) *Windows to our Children.* New York: Center for Gestalt Development.

O'Connor, C. and Stagnitti, K. (2011) 'Play, behaviour, language and social skills: the comparison of a play and a non–play intervention within a specialist school setting', *Research in Developmental Disabilities,* 32: 1205–11.

Oldham, J., Key, J. and Starak, V. (1978) *Risking Being Alive.* Bundoora: Pit Publishing.

Osel, T. (1988) 'Health in the Buddhist tradition', *Journal of Contemplative Psychotherapy,* 5: 63–5.

Parry, A. and Doan, R. (1994) *Story Re-visions: Narrative Therapy in the Post-Modern World.* New York. Guilford.

Pearson, M. and Wilson, H. (2001) *Sandplay and Symbol Work: Emotional Healing and Personal Development with Children, Adolescents, and Adults.* Camberwell: ACER Press.

Petersen, L. and Adderley, A. (2002) *Stop, Think, Do: Social Skills Training for Primary Years.* Melbourne: ACER.

Phillips, R.D. (2010) 'How firm is our foundation? Current play therapy research', *International Journal of Play Therapy,* 19(1), 13–25.

Piaget, J. (1962) *Play, Dreams and Imitations.* New York: Norton.

Piaget, J. (1971) *Psychology and Epistemology: Towards a Theory of Knowledge.* Trans. A. Rosin. New York: Viking.

Pierce, R.A., Nichols, M.P. and Du Brin, M.A. (1983) *Emotional Expression in Psychotherapy.* New York: Gardner.

Pinsoff, W.M. (1994) 'An overview of Integrative Problem Centered Therapy: a synthesis of family and individual psychotherapies. Special Issue: Developments in family therapy in the USA', *Journal of Family Therapy,* 16: 103–20.

Pope, K.S. and Vasquez, M.J.T. (2007) *Ethics in Psychotherapy and Counseling: A Practical Guide*. San Francisco: Jossey-Bass.

Powell, D.H. (1995) 'Lessons learned from therapeutic failure', *Journal of Psychotherapy Integration*, 5: 175–81.

Pressdee, D., May, L., Eastman, E. and Grier, D. (1997) 'The use of play therapy in the preparation of children undergoing MR imaging', *Clinical Radiology*, 52: 945–7.

Prochaska, J.O. (1999) 'How do people change, and how can we change to help many more people?', in M. Hubble, B. Duncan and S. Miller (eds), *The Heart and Soul of Change: What Works in Therapy?* Washington, DC: American Psychological Association.

Prochaska, J. and DiClemente, C. (1982) 'Transtheoretical therapy: toward a more integrative model of change', *Psychotherapy: Theory Research and Practice*, 19: 276–88.

Prochaska, J. and DiClemente, C. (1983) 'Stages and processes of self-change of smoking: toward an integrative model of change', *Journal of Consulting and Clinical Psychology*, 51: 390–5.

Queensland Counsellors Association (2009) *Code of Ethics*. Retrieved 10 March 2012, from www.qca.asn.au/index.php?option=com_content&task=view&id=14&Itemid=32

Rachman, A.W. and Raubolt, R. (1985) 'The clinical practice of group psychotherapy with adolescent substance abusers', in T.E. Bratter and C.G. Forrest (eds), *Alcoholism and Substance Abuse: Strategies for Clinical Intervention*. New York: Free Press.

Ramzy, I. (1978) *The Piggle: An Account of the Psychoanalytic Treatment of a Little Girl by D.W. Winnicott*. London: Hogarth Press.

Ray, D.C. and Bratton, S.C. (2010) 'What the research shows about play therapy: twenty-first century update', in J.N. Baggerly, D.C. Ray and S.C. Bratton (eds), *Child-centered Play Therapy Research: The Evidence Base for Effective Practice*. Hoboken: John Wiley & Sons, Inc.

Ray, D.C., Schottelkorb, A and Tsai, M.-H. (2007) 'Play therapy with children exhibiting symptoms of Attention Deficit Hyperactivity Disorder', *International Journal of Play Therapy*, 16(2): 95–111.

Reisman, J.M. and Ribordy, S. (1993) *Principles of Psychotherapy with Children* (2nd ed.). Lexington, MA: Lexington Books.

Resnick, R. (1995) 'Gestalt therapy: principles, prisms and perspectives', *British Gestalt Journal*, 4 (1): 3–13.

Rogers, C.R. (1942) *Counseling and Psychotherapy*. Boston: Houghton-Mifflin.

Rogers, C.R. (1955) *Client-Centered Therapy*. Boston: Houghton-Mifflin.

Rogers, C.R. (1965) *Client-Centered Therapy: its Current Practice, Implications and Theory*. Boston: Houghton-Mifflin.

Rose, S.D. (1998) *Group Therapy with Troubled Youth: A Cognitive Behavioural Interactive Approach*. Thousand Oaks, CA: Sage.

Rose, S.D. and Edleson, J.L. (1987) *Working with Children and Adolescents in Groups: A Multimethod Approach*. San Francisco, CA: Jossey-Bass.

Ryce-Menuhin, J. (1992) *Jungian Sand Play: The Wonderful Therapy*. New York: Routledge, Chapman & Hall.

Scaturo, D.J. (1994) 'Integrative psychotherapy for panic disorder and agoraphobia in clinical practice', *Journal of Psychotherapy Integration*, 4: 253–72.

Schaefer, C.E. and O'Connor, K.J. (eds) (1983) *Handbook of Play Therapy*. New York: Wiley.

Schaefer, C.E. and O'Connor, K.J. (eds) (1994) *Handbook of Play Therapy – Advances and Innovations*. New York: Wiley.

Schnitzer de Neuhaus, M. (1985) 'Stage 1: Preparation', in A.M. Siepker and C.S. Kandaras (eds), *Group Therapy with Children and Adolescents: A Treatment Manual*. New York: Human Sciences Press.

Selvini-Palazzoli, M., Boscolo, L., Cecchin, G. and Prata, G. (1980) 'Hypothesizing – circularity – neutrality: three guidelines for the conductor of the session', *Family Process*, 19: 3–12.

Shechtman, Z. (1999) 'Bibliotherapy: an indirect approach to treatment of childhood aggression', *Child Psychiatry and Human Development,* 30(1): 39–53.

Shelby, J. (1994) 'Psychological intervention with children in disaster relief shelters', *The Child, Youth, and Family Services Quarterly*, 17: 14–18.

Shen, Y.-J. (2002) 'Short-term group play therapy with Chinese earthquake victims: effects on anxiety, depression, and adjustment', *International Journal of Play Therapy*, 11(1): 43–63.

Shirk, S.R. and Karver, M. (2003) 'Prediction of treatment outcome from relationship variables in child and adolescent therapy: a meta-analytic review', *Journal of Consulting and Clinical Psychology,* 71(3): 452–64.

Siepker, A.M. and Kandaras, C.S. (eds) (1985) *Group Therapy with Children and Adolescents: A Treatment Manual*. New York: Human Sciences Press.

Skinner, B.F. (1953) *Science and Human Behavior*. New York: Macmillan.

Sloves, R. and Belinger-Peterlin, K. (1986) 'The process of time limited psychotherapy with latency aged children', *Journal of the American Academy of Child Psychiatry*, 25: 847–51.

Sloves, R. and Belinger-Peterlin, K. (1994) 'Time limited play therapy', in C.E. Schaefer and K.J. O'Connor (eds), *Handbook of Play Therapy – Advances and Innovations*. New York: Wiley.

Speers, R.W. and Lansing, C. (1965) *Group Therapy in Childhood Psychoses*. Chapel Hill, NC: University of North Carolina Press.

Spitz, H.I. (1987) 'Cocaine abuse: therapeutic approaches', in H.I. Spitz and J.S. Rosecan (eds), *Cocaine Abuse: New Directions in Treatment and Research*. New York: Brunner/Mazel.

Steenbarger, B.X. (1992) 'Toward science–practice integration in brief counselling and therapy', *Counselling Psychologist*, 20: 403–50.

Swanson, A.J. (1996) 'Children in groups: indications and contexts', in P. Kymissis and D.A. Halperin (eds), *Group Therapy with Children and Adolescents*. Washington, DC: American Psychiatric Press Inc.

Tallman, K. and Bohart, A. (1999) 'The client as a common factor: clients as selfhealers', in M. Hubble, B. Duncan and S. Miller (eds), *The Heart and Soul of Change: What Works in Therapy*. Washington, DC: American Psychological Association.

Thompson, C.L. and Rudolph, L.B. (1983) *Counselling Children*. Monterey, CA: Brooks/ Cole.

Vernberg, E.M., Routh, D.K. and Koocher, G.P. (1992) 'The future of psychotherapy with children: developmental psychotherapy', *Journal of Psychotherapy*, 29: 72–80.

Walter, J. and Peller, J. (1992) *Becoming Solution Focussed in Brief Therapy*. New York: Brunner/ Mazel.

Wampold, B.E. (2001) *The Great Psychotherapy Debate: Models, Methods, and Findings*. Mahwah: Lawrence Erlbaum Associates, Publishers.

Watkins, C.E. and Watts R.E. (1995) 'Psychotherapy survey research studies: some consistent findings and integrative conclusions', *Psychotherapy in Private-Practice*, 13: 49–68.

Watson, J.C. and Rennie, D.L. (1994) 'Qualitative analysis of clients' subjective experience of significant moments during the exploration of problematic reactions', *Journal of Counselling Psychology*, 41: 500–9.

White, M. and Epston, D. (1990) *Narrative Means to Therapeutic Ends.* New York: Norton.

Yan, M.C. and Wong, Y.-L.R. (2005) 'Rethinking self-awareness in cultural competence: toward a dialogic self in cross-cultural social work', *Families in Society,* 86(2), 181–8.

Yontef, G. (1993) 'Gestalt therapy', in C.E. Watkins (ed.), *Handbook of Psychotherapy Supervision.* New York: Wiley.

Yorke, C. (1982) *Psychoanalytic Psychology of Normal Development.* London: Hogarth Press.

Zahr, L.K. (1998) 'Therapeutic play for hospitalized preschoolers in Lebanon', *Pediatric Nursing,* 23(5): 449–54.

Zeig, J. and Gilligan, S. (eds) (1990) *Brief Therapy: Myths, Methods and Metaphors.* New York: Brunner/Mazel.

Index

abuse, 11, 12, 17, 36, 60–1, 78, 95, 155, 171, 199, 228, 241, 257, 280, 284
   sexual, 11, 17, 60, 133, 183, 222, 228–9, 231, 253, 257, 279, 280, 284
action plan, 147–8, 268
active listening, 38, 106, 107–14, 115–16, 156
activity, selection, 52, 174–83
Adler, A., 30, 32, 34–35
advocacy, 92
Alford, B.A., 69
anger, 111–12, 120, 125, 141, 143, 147, 178, 209, 211, 215–16, 228–9, 252, 271, 273, 280
anxiety, 11, 30–1, 53, 56, 60, 67, 73–5, 78, 82, 84, 89, 96, 111, 125–7, 154, 170–3, 195, 228, 232, 239, 250, 254, 261–2, 270, 272
   parental, 13, 51, 97
art, 3, 32, 34, 73–5, 99, 133, 170–2, 210, 214
assertiveness, 143, 147, 165, 179, 248, 273, 281–2, 285
assessment, 43, 49–52, 56–7, 149, 151
Athanassiadou, E., 170
attachment, 32–3, 37, 150
Attention Deficit Hyperactivity Disorder, 94, 153
Australian Psychological Society, 16, 17, 18
avoidance, 61, 104, 125–6
awareness, 15, 19, 20, 39, 61–2, 69, 74–5, 85–8, 91, 104, 110, 114, 115–17, 119–21, 124, 126–30, 135–7, 157–9, 187, 195–7, 218, 220, 254, 272
Axline, V., 7, 37–9

Baggerly, J.N., 169, 172, 250
Bandler, R., 37, 38, 40
Bay-Hinitz, A.K., 173
Beck, A.T., 41
Beebe, A., 170, 171
behaviour, 4–5, 9, 10, 19, 24–5, 31, 33, 34, 36–9, 41, 42, 49, 51–4, 56, 60, 63, 69, 72, 75, 79, 82–6, 89, 91, 93, 94, 96, 98–9, 101, 103–4, 111, 114, 120, 121, 130–1, 132, 135–7, 138–48, 149–50, 153–9, 165, 169, 170, 171, 172–3, 174, 178, 179, 180–1, 186–8, 202, 203, 210, 218, 221–2, 227–31, 235, 241, 248, 251, 254, 255–6, 259–60, 261, 265, 267–76

behaviour *cont.*
   coping, 124–7
   distracting, 13
   experimenting with new, 64, 68, 70, 76, 95, 138, 147–8, 227, 244, 247–8, 251, 253, 256, 267, 277
   problems, 60–1, 75–6, 85, 88, 90–1, 95, 140, 143, 150, 152–3, 186
   rehearsing, 64, 76, 138, 147–8, 156, 252, 277
   self-management, 142, 144–7, 274–6
   unacceptable, 30, 78, 158, 209, 268, 275
Behaviour Modification, 41
Behaviour Therapy, 19, 29, 41, 42, 47, 69–70, 71, 76, 138, 145
beliefs, 8, 14, 52, 79, 80–2, 84, 90, 96–7, 108, 132–7, 158–9, 188, 193, 221, 227, 229, 231, 234, 248, 259–61, 264, 275, 277, 279, 287
   core, 41
   irrational, 42, 135
   rational, 42, 135
   self-destructive, 19, 42, 63–4, 75, 102, 123, 132, 134–7, 138, 147, 225, 255, 265, 267, 282
Belinger-Peterlin, K., 43–4
blended families, 95
bodily sensations, 39, 74, 119, 122, 215
body language, matching, 107–8, 109, 113
Bond, T., 17, 19
books, 167, 170, 172, 178, 179, 180, 227–32, 288
boundaries, 13, 19, 53, 104, 141, 179, 182, 195, 228, 249, 254, 280
   cultural, 279, 281
   developmental, 277–8
   family, 278–9, 281
   setting appropriate, 282–5
   social, 279, 283
Bowlby, J., 35, 37
Braverman, S., 69
Brewer, S., 170
brief therapy, 43–4, 129
British Association for Counselling and Psychotherapy, 16, 19, 20, 21
British Association of Play Therapists, 16
British Psychological Society, 16, 17
Bucci, W., 68
bullying, 6, 83, 221, 225, 229, 273, 281, 284